The Rainbow
Science Curriculum

FIRST EDITION

Durell C. Dobbins, Ph.D.

Bio Enterprises, Inc.
Eden Prairie, MN

Beginnings Publishing House

ISBN: 0-9666578-0-2

Direct all inquiries to Beginnings Publishing House, 11130 Kingston Pike, Suite 1-107, Knoxville, TN 37922.

Printed in the United States of America

Credits

Joel Preston, thanks for extending yourself into the unknown for the sake of loyalty and friendship. Warmest personal regards to you and your terrific family.

Thank you, Mercedes, Christina and Eric Charles, for joining forces with my family in assembling the kits.

Thank you, testers—Missy and Patsey Pennington, Brandon and Sherri Miller, Aaron Dobbins, TJ and Tim Jones/Shari Henry, Audra, Rachel and Amy Roberts and Bobbie and Gayla Wilkinson—for all of your hard work. Joseph Bingham, your support of this program has come to my attention through those who have heard you speak well of it. Thank you, my young friend, for testing it, for promoting it and for speaking well of it. Special thanks are due Brandon and Sharon Tober, and Nate and Sandy Sleck for their extra measure of hard work and for their support of this endeavor above and beyond the call of duty. You're great!

Thank you, (Dr.) Mark Bingham, my long-time friend, for your excellence in editing the text. Thank you, Melanie Bingham, for giving up your husband during those many hours of labor.

Joan Elder, thanks for your willingness to help in every way: for giving up King to this project during those long days and nights. Thanks for the meals, the edits, the moral support for Gloria and for your friendship.

Thank you, King Elder, for your loyalty, sacrifice and pursuit of quality. Your friendship and service are greatly valued, even on those many occasions when I fail to tell you.

Thank you, kids—Aaron, Ian, Kenan, Leslie and Stacey—for giving up some of the normal activities of kids to do work with your dad. I'm sure that you will someday come to know the value of hard work and the benefits of understanding both business and science, whatever your lives' occupations. Thank you for your unconditional love.

To my dearest Gloria: thank you for standing by me in yet another enterprise and for facing down some of your greatest fears in support of me. You are *so* deserving. I love you more than ever.

Thank you, Lord God, for your providence and for your patience with me.

Key to Pronunciation

Pronunciation guides appear in brackets after the words to which they apply, such as "cation [KAT-ī-on]." Long vowel sounds are represented by horizontal lines above the vowels, as in "tornado [tor-NĀ-dō]." Short vowel sounds have no special marking. The accented syllables are indicated by capital letters as seen in the previous examples.

Table of Contents

BIOLOGY—THE STUDY OF LIFE AND LIVING THINGS 136

PHYSICS—THE STUDY OF THE PRINCIPLES THAT GOVERN THE UNIVERSE

A thorough study of science might best start with the science upon which all other sciences are based. As surely as God created Adam, he placed in him a curiosity. With that curiosity he also provided him with the ability to gather knowledge and to apply it in the solving of everyday problems. In our study, we will not approach the vast creative abilities of our Creator, nor will we presume to approach his wealth of knowledge. Instead, we will seek out solutions to the practical problems that face us as people while continuing on our greater mission of pleasing Him who gave us this unspeakable blessing of fruitful curiosity.

To study physics is to attempt to know and understand the principles that God used in creating and sustaining the universe. These are the simplest (if not *easiest*) of all observations. What are space and matter, and what are their properties? What are the basic forces that operate in the universe and what are their effects on matter? The science of physics provides a viewpoint from which we are able to solve many of the problems we face. We will now begin to help you to see from that viewpoint. But be prepared—you will be introduced to things you have never seen before, nor anticipated seeing.

1: *Inertia and Flying Objects*

Where does a person begin to study the design that has gone into the universe? Well, if you're human (and I'm assuming that you are), the best way to start is to be aware and take notice of the world around you. The most famous scientists in history were particularly good at noticing and recording the things that they noticed. There were probably others who were equally good or even better at noticing, but didn't write what they noticed. We know nothing about those.

Take, for example, the scientist who is the subject of this lesson. One of the most famous scientists of all times, **Sir Isaac Newton** (1642-1727), was once on recess for a year and a half while waiting for a bout of the bubonic plague to be eliminated from his school. During this time he wrote the founding observations for the mathematics of integral calculus. What do you do in your time off?

Look about you. Notice that you are surrounded by objects. No matter where you go, or what you do, objects are everywhere. Go ahead, just try getting away from objects. You can't do it! These are the subjects of the science of physics: objects, all objects, and the things that happen to them.

Looking around, we notice right away that most objects—books, chairs, desks, pencils, pads of paper, trash cans full of crumpled paper—appear to be lazy. They don't seem to move around unless we do something to them. This is very important. Just imagine what your day would be like if all of these objects were flying about aimlessly. Life would be a continuous hazard and horribly unpredictable.

No, the universe isn't nearly as complex as it could be. There are laws—rules of nature—that all objects obey. Some of the most important laws are the simplest:

Rule 1: Objects stay where they are unless somebody throws them.
Rule 2: Once objects are thrown through empty space, they keep traveling at the same velocity and in the same direction until something stops them or changes their course.

In our universe there are laws that are obeyed by all matter. These include the observation of Sir Isaac Newton that matter tends to stay in its place unless some force causes it to move.

These two rules taken together are great simplifying rules of the universe. To demonstrate the first rule, place a pencil on the table. (If your table is lop-sided, the experiment will be a dud.) Now go away, and come back after two million years. See? The pencil is still there.

To demonstrate the second rule, roll your pencil gently across the table top. If it keeps going forever, the second rule is true. If it stops, the second rule is still true, but something has acted on the pencil to stop its rolling.

Congratulations! You've just mastered one of the great scientific observations of all time. These two rules make up **Newton's First Law of Motion**. Objects at rest remain at rest unless they are acted upon by some force. Objects in motion remain in motion at the same velocity and in the same direction unless acted upon by some force. The property of an object that makes it resist changes with regard to its motion is called **inertia**.

Imagine a disorderly universe—a place where matter does not obey this simple rule. Movement would be unpredictable, and the universe would be completely chaotic.

This is really what physics is all about—making observations that simplify a complex situation so that we can understand what we see happening and may even be able to predict what might happen.

Exercises:
1. If a perfectly round marble were placed in the middle of a perfectly flat table and left alone with no other influences on the marble, what would happen? Why?
2. In the example mentioned in the text, what forces were acting on the pencil to make it stop rolling?

2: *Jumping off Asteroids in Outer Space*

Every physicist would love to live in a complete vacuum, that is, a universe with everything sucked out of it. Experiments would be much easier to perform if there were no air or gravity to interfere with them. Of course, we would all die, and that would slow our scientific progress.

So instead, we will have to live on Earth and be content imagining what it would be like in a place where there is no gravity and there are no objects (not even air) to get in the way. But after we are done considering this odd place, we return to reality so that we can apply what we've learned to the more complex situation in which we live.

Let's start out our day in empty space by taking one step toward the grocery store. But there is no ground to push our feet against, and there is no object to pull against. There are no outside forces such as pushes from wind or gravity acting on us. Just as we learned in our last lesson, we are stranded by our inertia.

Now imagine that there is a small asteroid within reach. Using the asteroid, we point ourselves toward the grocery store, put our feet on the asteroid and kick ourselves toward the store. We find that we are suddenly flying in the right direction. Because there are no forces acting on us, we will continue to fly in the same direction and at the same velocity until…Oh, no! Smack…right into the

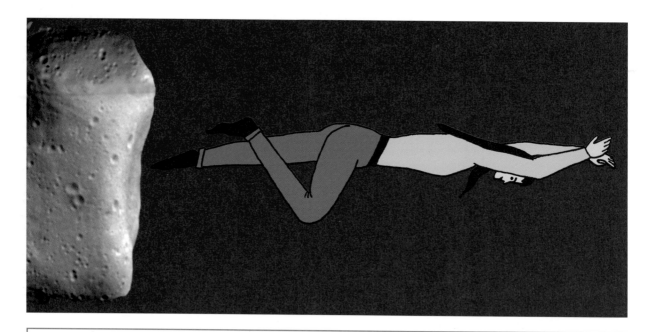

When an object is acted upon by a force, motion results. Every motion has a velocity—a rate at which the object moves. In order to reach any velocity from a standstill, the object must accelerate, or gain velocity. The greater the mass of an object, the less of an effect forces have upon it. To determine the rate of acceleration of an object under a given force, the force has to be divided by the amount of mass of the object it is acting upon. When the girl in the diagram kicks, there are equal and opposite forces acting on her and on the asteroid; but because the asteroid is the more massive, she accelerates at a much greater rate than the asteroid.

grocery store! We forgot that in space we can't stop because there is nothing to cause us to stop.

Nothing has been illustrated yet that we did not already know: First, objects at rest remain at rest until acted upon by some force. Second, objects in motion remain in motion until something stops them.

There is yet something to learn from our unfortunate trip. How fast did we travel? Do you agree that it depends upon how hard we kicked? The harder we pushed (or the stronger our leg muscles), the faster our trip would be. This is a statement of **Newton's Second Law of Motion**:

> For an object of certain mass, the greater the force applied to the object, the greater its increase in velocity over time (**acceleration**).

The opposite is also true:

> For an object of certain mass, the lesser the force applied to the object, the lesser its acceleration.

You will notice that the force of our kick lasted for only a short time. During the time in which the force was applied, we were increasing velocity, or accelerating. After we stopped applying force and we were just flying through space, we were no longer accelerating, but we continued to fly at the same velocity. So the harder we kicked, the greater our

Jet engines make a jet move, but how? They must push against something. What do jet engines push against? The air! But if they push against the air the jet still won't move unless the air pushes against the jet in return. When the engines push the air, the air pushes back with equal force in the opposite direction—the air moves and the plane moves. That's why the engines point in the direction opposite the front of the plane. This illustrates Newton's third law of motion.

acceleration during the kick, and the greater our velocity after the kick.

Do you also agree that how fast we traveled would depend upon how massive we were? The more massive something is, the harder you have to push to move it, and the more slowly it accelerates once it starts moving.

Now, what do you think happened to that asteroid—the one we kicked? As we started flying toward the store, the asteroid must have flown the opposite way. For as our feet were pushing against the asteroid, it was pushing against our feet with an equal force in the opposite direction. This is **Newton's Third Law of Motion**:

> For every action, there is an equal reaction in the opposite direction.

Does this mean that the asteroid would pick up speed as fast as we did? No. That would depend on *its* mass. And, just as we would expect, if the asteroid had 10 times more mass than we had, its acceleration would be 1/10 of ours.

In order for the boat to be thrust forward, something has to be thrust behind. But what? What does the boat push against to get its forward motion?

Exercises:
1. What two things do you have to know in order to determine the acceleration of a rocket in outer space (where gravity is absent)?
2. If you are traveling in outer space, what do you need to stop yourself?
3. Is it possible to use an object to stop yourself without putting any force on that object?
4. If you knew how much force you placed on the object that stopped you, would you know how much force was applied to you at the same time?

3: *Gravity and Gravitation*

The next time you throw an object in outer space, watch how it travels. Unless you throw it near a planet, where gravity affects it, it will travel in an absolutely straight line. Not so on Earth. Here, an object thrown in a straight line alongside the ground travels in a curved path toward the ground. Everyone knows why; it's the effect of **gravity**. But what is gravity? Although we say it's a force, nobody really knows what it is other than how it affects objects. If we observe the effects of something, even if it is something that we can't see, we can still give it a name and describe it the best way we can. Because gravity can't be seen, we can't tell what it *is*, but rather what it *does*.

Throughout time, people have observed the effect of gravity—that the Earth attracts other objects. The word *gravity* was made up to describe this effect. In fact, we later came to realize that not only the Earth, but all of the large bodies in the universe (planets, stars, asteroids, moons, etc.) display a similar **gravitation** toward other objects. The strength of an object's force of gravitation is related to its mass. The more massive the object, the stronger its **gravitational field**. It is assumed that even small bodies, like you, have gravitational fields, but you have so little mass that the effects are small.

Even though people have little mass in comparison to planets, the gravitational field of the earth still attracts them. However, the small gravitational pull of a person will have little effect on the earth.

We have said that gravity is a force, but how strong is that force? Well, we can feel its strength when we stand, jump, climb or fall. Remember that the amount of force on an object is proportional

to the object's mass. The more massive the object, the greater the force. Gravity pulls harder on a large person than on a small person, so a large person has to use more force to get up from a fall. What they say is true, "The bigger they are, the harder they fall." This is one reason why parents always send the kids upstairs to get things. It takes less force for a kid to go upstairs than it does for a parent.

It is the gravitational forces of the moon and the earth that keep them close together. But what keeps them from falling into each other? Although you may already know the answer, it won't be fully explained until Lesson 5. I don't suppose you would want to try figuring it out on your own, would you? Could you?

Exercises:

1. Jupiter is more massive than Earth. Which of these two planets has the stronger gravitational field?

2. If you could stand on Jupiter's surface under its gravitational pull, how would the way you feel differ from the way you feel on Earth?

4: *Acceleration Due to Gravity*

Galileo (1564-1642), a famous observer from old Italy, was said to have dropped two cannon balls of different sizes from the top of the Leaning Tower of Pisa to demonstrate that these balls would hit the ground at the same time. He was right. While the Earth pulls with greater force on the big mass, it takes more force to accelerate a big mass. The result is that any two objects, regardless of their mass, have the same acceleration under gravity. This is another of those great simplifying facts of the universe which cannot be explained by science. We don't know why it is; it simply is. We are glad that it is, or the universe would be far more complex. We can thank our Creator for that.

For this reason, the acceleration due to gravity is **constant**. That is, it is the same for every object. If not for friction, a feather would fall at the same rate as a brick. Any object dropped from above the earth accelerates by 9.8 meters per second for every second it travels. In the absence of friction, a baseball dropped from an airplane would be traveling at a velocity of 9.8 meters per second after the first second. For every additional second of falling, its velocity would increase by 9.8 meters per second: 19.6 meters per second after two seconds, 29.4 after three, 39.2 after four, 49.0 after five, and so on.

Exercises:

1. What would be the velocity of the baseball (mentioned in the text) after its sixth second of falling?

2. Calculate the average velocity of the entire six-second fall as follows: Because the starting velocity was 0 and the ending velocity was the answer to Exercise 1, add 0 to that answer then divide the result by 2 to get the average.

3. Calculate the total distance of the six-second fall as follows: The distance is equal to the average velocity (meters per second) times the time of the fall (seconds). Give the distance in meters.

4. Suppose the object were an anvil instead of a baseball. Assuming no friction, would the answers to these questions be different? How would the answers differ if *you* were falling?

In that famous experiment reportedly done by Galileo around AD 1600, he might have confirmed his belief that two objects of different masses would have the same rate of acceleration under gravity. That rate turns out to be 9.8 meters per second per second—that is, the velocity of any object falling under gravity increases by 9.8 meters per second for every second it moves. As a result, both of Galileo's cannon balls will hit his assistant on the ground at precisely the same instant.

5: *Play Ball!*

Now that we have introduced gravity, we can come down off the asteroids and start understanding motion in our back yards. If you throw a baseball in a straight line **parallel** to the ground, what will happen to it? It will take a **curved** path toward the ground until it hits the ground. But why is the path curved? It is because you are putting a force on the ball in one direction, and there is a second force pulling on it in another direction. Just as a single force in a single direction results in straight motion (like jumping off an asteroid in outer space or dropping a cannon ball from the Leaning Tower), so two or more forces in different directions bring about curved motion. Nearly every motion on Earth is some kind of curve. The more we understand about the forces involved in creating the motion, the better we can understand the path an object will take. Even complex motions can often be understood as curves that are the result of several forces acting on an object at the same time.

As a special case of curved motion, a ball on the end of a string, when slung around, makes a circular motion called an **orbit**. Once again there are two forces acting to create the orbit. The first force is the forward thrust of the ball. Of course, if there were no string, the ball would try to keep going in a straight line because of its inertia. The second force is the pull of the string on the ball toward your hand. The path that the ball takes under these circumstances is a circle. It "wants" to go away, but the string holds it in close. The circle is the best compromise. As we will discuss later, the planets in our solar system orbit the sun. The pull toward the center of the sun is provided by the sun's gravitational force on the planets. The planets have inertia that gives them the tendency to keep going in a straight line. Once again, the best compromise is a circular motion.

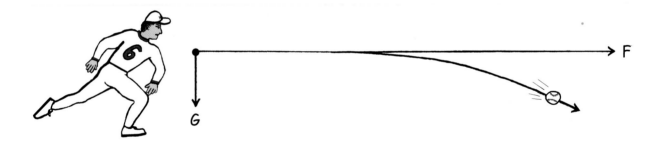

There were two separate influences on the motion of this ball—the force of the throw (followed by the ball's inertia after it left the hand of the pitcher) and the force of gravity. These influences were perpendicular (at a right angle) to one another. Notice that the path of the ball is a compromise between the directions of the two influences. It takes a lot of skill to accurately predict what direction a ball will travel when thrown in a given direction. Could an understanding of physics make you a better baseball player?

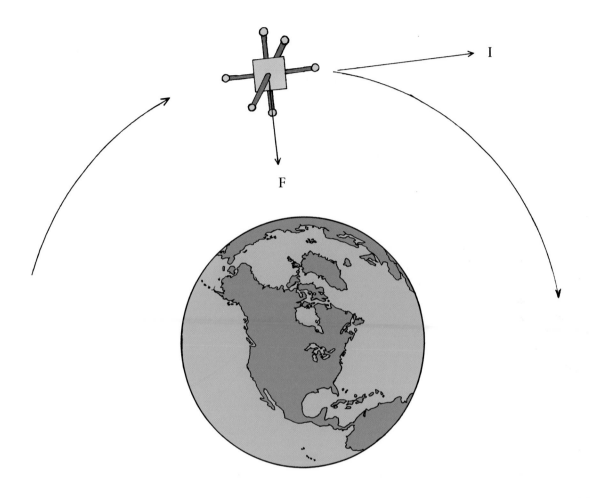

This satellite, like any other orbiting mass, continues in orbit because of two influences: gravity and inertia. As with any moving object, the motion of the satellite is the best compromise between the forces that act upon it. In this case the best compromise is an orbit.

Exercises:

1. Can you think of any other objects that naturally move in a circular pattern?
2. What is the force that holds these objects toward the center of their orbits?
3. If the Earth were to suddenly stop in its orbit, what would happen to it?

6: *Making Waves*

Another type of motion is yet more complex than a simple curve or orbit. It's called wave motion. While linear and curved motions result from simple forces acting on solid objects, wave motion results from the action of forces on **fluids**, i.e., substances that "flow." We all know that waves are associated with bodies of water. But do you know why? It's because fluids are squishy! What happens if you squish a ball of clay between two fingers? A bulge appears around your fingers. This bulge is one simple wave. You could say that a wave is a bulge that occurs when fluid is squished.

But clay is not very fluid compared with water. So when water squishes, it spreads out again, squishing the water next to it. Then that water squishes and spreads, and passes along the bulge to its neighboring water, and so on. Waves in water are a series of squishes and spreads. But there are other kinds of waves besides those in water. Air is also a fluid, and it too moves in waves.

Many objects display wave motion. For example, mechanical springs have that basic squish-and-

Even complex motions can be seen to be combinations of simpler motions. For example, there are many influences on the motion of water in the ocean, but clear patterns of simple wave motion can be seen there at a glance.

spread motion that makes them so useful. Even though they are usually made of metal, they still have a fluid-like property that allows the metal to be **compressed** and **expanded**. Vibrating strings, including strings on musical instruments, also vibrate in wave patterns.

There are other waves that cannot be seen with our eyes, but we can tell they are waves by the way they are created, the way they act, or the effect they have on other objects. Here are a few: sound, earth tremors, light, radio signals, X-rays. Sound waves, for example, are created by vibrations, like a plucked guitar string. The vibrations of the guitar string cause waves (compressions and expansions) in the air. Those wave motions in the air cause your eardrums to vibrate, and the vibrating eardrums register the "sound" with your brain.

Scientists and engineers often find it necessary to calculate wave motions, like the size of the waves in the side of a building when an earthquake strikes. **Trigonometry** is the branch of mathematics that deals with waves and other curves. We are fortunate to have had mathematicians live before us who spent their lives developing ways for us to solve problems. That way we don't have to waste time figuring out how to solve problems; we just solve them. We don't even have to be good mathematicians in order to use math to solve problems. Just think how many problems you'll be able to

This toy is a solid object, but it is unusually flexible, so its motion is like that of a fluid. This fluid-like behavior makes it an excellent tool for learning about wave motion.

solve if you do become good at math! If you like solving problems, you should look forward to learning trigonometry. It is a basic math tool that can be used to solve many common problems.

Water's chemical properties make it a good medium for transmitting motion. Next time you find yourself in a pool or lake, try talking to someone at a distance under water. Compare how loud the sounds are in and out of the water. The results may surprise you!

Exercises:

1. Have you ever felt your car get blown to the side as a big truck passes you on the freeway? What causes this to happen?

2. If a person speaks under water, will he sound the same to a listener as he would if he were speaking in air? Explain your answer.

7: *Do Something Useful!*

Have you ever been standing around doing nothing and had a parent say to you, "Do something useful"? That's because parents know that you can be useful. There are many things you know *how* to do, but you are not doing any of them. Well, in the last couple of weeks you have gained a lot of knowledge about motions: you understand what motion is, you understand that it comes about by putting force on an object, and you know what kinds of motions to expect from different kinds of objects under different kinds of forces. You know, for instance, that:

- A solid object with a single force placed on it in a single direction will accelerate in a straight line in that direction.
- A solid object that has two forces on it in different (but not opposite) directions will move in the shape of a curve.
- Objects with many forces on them in many different directions move in complex patterns
- You can get circular motion using inertia of a moving object and applying a force toward a center point.
- When force is placed on a fluid, waves result.

A seesaw is a simple lever. Notice how it reverses the direction of a motion—when one end is pushed down the other end rises. But because the fulcrum is in the middle, the force applied on one end is the same as the force applied by the other end, and the distances of travel of the two ends are the same as well.

But let's face it: unless something useful is being done, none of your new knowledge is very useful. The usefulness of forces and motions is in doing useful work. In physics, when we say **work**, we mean a force applied over a distance. In fact, we calculate the amount of work that is done by multiplying the force by the distance over which the force is applied.

If we push an object from here to there, we apply force to it. The force times the distance from here to there is equal to the amount of work done on the object. There are only so many ways of demonstrating work before we tire of pushing objects from here to there and multiplying forces times their distance. Life can be much more interesting if, instead of pushing objects, we build **machines** to do our pushing for us. As you will see, machines are useful for much more than making life more interesting. They enable us to do things that we, with our limited strength, couldn't otherwise do.

Machines can multiply the force you put into it them. Put a little force in, and you can get much more force out. Now, don't think that you can cheat nature by getting something for nothing. The amount of *work* that comes out of a machine is the same that goes into it. But by applying a small force over a long distance, we get the same amount of work as if we applied a great force over a small distance. For example, a two-year-old child could never hope to lift a 500-pound piano because the amount of force a child can supply is small. The force of gravity pulling down on such a massive object is huge. However, using a **lever**, the child can apply that same small amount of force over a great distance, and that huge mass will be lifted a small distance. This illustrates the usefulness of machines: They convert small forces into large ones by converting large motions into small ones, or vice versa.

Unlike the seesaw, a crowbar is built so that the hand of the user applies a small force over a great distance. The opposite end will travel only a short distance, but its force will be multiplied.

A lever is one type of simple machine. It is composed of a straight member, used for prying, that pivots on a **fulcrum**. One example of a lever is a crowbar. Notice how the crowbar is shaped to increase force. It has an end that swings wide for applying a small force over a large distance, and an end that barely swings. But with all of that motion at the long end, how much force do you suppose is at the short end? With our crowbar we calculated that it multiplies our force by more than a factor of six. So, if a man can push 150 pounds of force on the long end of the crowbar, he can lift an object that weighs about 1,000 pounds (half a ton) with the short end.

Never again say that you are not strong enough to lift any mass. All you need is a lever that is long enough to provide the force that is needed at its short end. If you had a lever that was long enough and strong enough, you could lift the Empire State Building right off its foundation. Now you can be *truly* useful. Anytime you see men pushing something with all of their strength, just stop and look around for a long piece of steel pipe. Then find a stone or a wood block to use as your fulcrum. You'll show them that one small physicist can be stronger than several big men.

The gears on a bicycle are machines that convert small foot movements into long wheel movements, or vice versa, depending on whether a rider is going uphill, downhill, starting out or cruising along. In lower gears it takes less effort to pedal, but you get less motion for your effort. In higher gears pedaling is really difficult, but lots of motion results.

Exercises:
1. If we wanted to lift a 500-pound block 1 inch, and we had a lever that we could push down 500 inches, how many pounds of force would we have to apply to the lever to lift the block? (Ignore friction.)
2. Can you think of a couple of different levers that are used in everyday life? For each type of lever you think of, what serves as the fulcrum?

8: *Falling Up*

One morning you came down the stairs for breakfast, and you looked particularly tired. Your mother said to you, "What's the matter, dear? You look like you hardly slept at all!"

"I didn't," you replied, "I was up all night."

"What happened?" asked your mother.

"I know this will be hard to believe," you continued, "but I was sleeping peacefully and about midnight, I fell up."

"You mean, you *got* up?" your mother asked.

"No, mom," you affirmed, "I *fell* up."

Your mother, then looking confused, asked, "You mean, you fell out of bed?"

"No mom, I mean I fell straight up— spent the rest of the night on the ceiling."

"Oh!" your mother exclaimed. "Now I understand. That happened to me once while I was in the front yard. It took your father and the whole fire department to get me out of the oak tree." (Strange family.)

The block house is an illustration of a somewhat higher level of potential energy and organization than the disorganized heap of blocks resulting from an undirected input of energy. By applying energy to the disorganized blocks it may be possible to encourage a single block to crudely land on top of another. But even the modest level of organization and structure represented by the block building in the photo could not be achieved without the guiding hand of an intelligent builder. No one would look at this building and suggest that it formed from random physical processes. It would be unnatural.

Have you ever noticed that things always go from up to down, toward the pull of gravity? When you finish an apple and throw the core out in the back yard, what happens to it after two weeks? Does it turn into a new apple? No—it turns into a rotten apple core. Can you strike a burnt match stick and get a fresh match? No—only the reverse works. These examples may not seem alike, but they are. They are situations that have gone from a higher state of organization to a lower one.

If you built a house with building blocks, and your little brother threw a shoe at it, would it be more organized or less organized after the collision? If your little brother is like ours, it would be less organized. This is one of the great laws of nature. In our universe, all things tend to become less organized over time. The more time we allow, the less organized they tend to become. Little brothers tend to speed up this process of disorganization.

The higher the level of order in a system, the less likely it is to have occurred from random processes and the more energy it will give up as it deteriorates.

It may not be obvious at first, but over time it will become more and more obvious that organization is related to the amount of energy that is stored up in a **system** (the part of the universe we are considering). Stored energy is called **potential energy**. The fresh apple has a lot of energy stored in it, as does the fresh match. There is energy stored up in a ball that is up high on a shelf, and in a charged battery. This stored (potential) energy tends to be released. This is why batteries tend to run down, balls up on shelves tend to fall, matches tend to burn once they have been struck, and apples tend to rot.

Released energy is called **kinetic energy** (energy of motion). If something occurs on its own, like a ball falling or an apple rotting, that occurrence is connected with a release of energy. If we have to make something happen with force, like putting the fallen ball back up on the shelf, we transfer potential energy to the ball so that it can fall again. Some releases of energy, like the rotting of an apple, are so complex that it is impossible for people to do the work that is necessary to restore the system to its original state. How would you like to have the job of restoring a rotten apple back to the way it was before it rotted?

Exercises:

1. Which of the following are examples of kinetic energy, and which are examples of potential energy: a skateboarder at the top of a ramp; a house made of cards; a spring in a wind-up toy that has not been turned on; a bicycle traveling downhill; a baseball flying through the air?

2. In each of the following pairs, which item represents greater organization (more potential energy): a ball that is at rest 10 feet above the ground or a ball that has fallen from 10 feet above the ground to 5 feet above the ground; a pencil standing on its tip or a pencil lying on the table; a clown on a tightrope or a clown on the ground?

9: *What's That Got to Do with Being Useful?*

Recall that work is a force applied over a distance. If a ball is lying on the ground, and we want it on the shelf, we have to do some work. In order to do the work we have to have energy, and we transfer that energy to the ball. That is, we end up with less energy of our own, while the ball ends up with more. That lousy ball gets energy at our expense! This is another one of those great universal rules. Anytime energy is stored up in one object, it is given up by another. But this rule tells us something even more amazing: the amount of energy stored up in the one object is precisely the same as the amount of energy that is given up by the other. So energy never appears or disappears, but is transferred from place to place, object to object. This has been consistently observed over hundreds of years in many different systems; it has been named the **law of conservation of energy**.

Energy does change forms, however. For example, a ball may lose energy as it falls from a shelf, but that energy is picked up by the air which is moved about by the falling ball. When the ball crashes to the floor, some of its energy is transferred to the floor. We might feel the floor vibrate from the crash. We might also hear the vibration as the air picks up the waves of motion from the floor and carries them to our ears. The ball will bounce because the floor will return part of its energy back to the ball. You see how even the simplest events are complex when we look at the transfer of energy.

You will also notice that each transfer of energy is accompanied by work (force applied over a distance). Gravity (force) pulls the ball down to the floor (distance). The air moves (distance), being pushed by the ball (force). The floor vibrates (moves—distance) under the force of the ball. The ball is pushed back (force) by the floor, and it bounces (distance). The air vibrates (wave motion over a distance) when the ball strikes the floor (force).

In the Mousetrap game, energy is transferred from object to object. At the end of the game, the trap is made to fall by energy added at the turn of a crank. However, before the trap falls that energy is transferred several times.

Exercises:

1. In answer to the question in the lesson title, describe the relationship between energy and work.

2. What are the missing words in the following sentences?
Potential _____ is transferred to an object when _____ is done on it. Work is done on an object when _____ is applied over a _____.

10: *The Price of Being Useful*

Once upon a time, a fantastic ride came to the fair. It was an elevator that gave rides for money. You put in ten cents and hopped on the elevator, and the elevator sky-rocketed you. Up, up, up you went, until you had reached 100 feet. Another 10 cents raised you another 100 feet. Then you added another dime, and another. After paying a dollar, you found yourself 1000 feet in the air. With your money spent, the magical elevator would go no higher. Instead, it began to fall. Down, down, down you fell, faster and faster until the elevator stopped with a *bump* on the ground.

"Wow!" you exclaimed, "I don't know when I've had a ride that was so much fun." In thinking back, you remembered how you had paid a whole dollar, but you didn't care because the fun was worth the money. You then told your friend about the elevator and how much fun it was, but your friend had only 50 cents. "That's okay," you said, "for fifty cents you can still go up 500 feet in the air. And what fun you will have!"

As far as we know, every lift on Earth is like that elevator. It will go up against the pull of gravity if you pay the price, and then it will come down without payment. But what price do we pay? That price is energy. Anytime there is a lift off the ground, a roll up a hill, or a push against a spring (different types of work), we have to make a payment of energy.

Suppose we wanted to lift a 1000-pound block of rock off the ground and set it on another block. The first thing we notice is that it will never happen on its own. We can sit and watch that block for years and years and years, and it will never hop up on the other one by itself. So if we've decided we want stacked blocks, what do we need in order to make that happen? First,

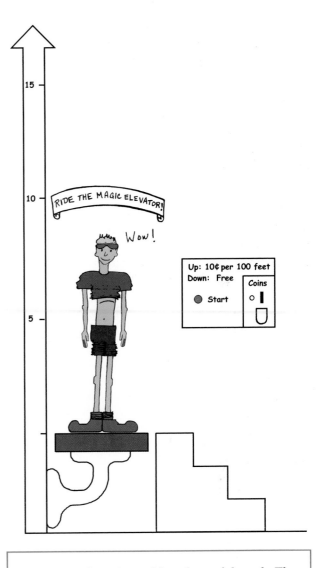

Energy is the price paid to do useful work. The more energy paid, the more work is done. When work is done on an object against a force (such as gravity), potential energy is stored in that object. That potential energy may be released, converting it to kinetic energy.

we need a machine that's designed for the task. It would have to be strong and agile enough to carry out our wishes under our direction. Second, it would have to have enough fuel to carry out the task. Third, it would require guidance, something (or someone) directing it to place one block on top of the other according to the plan.

The point is that we can't do anything without a plan, the machinery, the energy and the guidance. The energy comes from the burning of the fuel. Energy is the basis of everything that we do or that ever has been done according to some plan, because useful work cannot be done without it. It is the price we pay for doing useful work. And, like money, it isn't consumed in the process. It just changes hands and changes forms. As we will see, energy can be passed from object to object, or transferred through empty space. It can be converted from heat to light to matter and never be lost or even reduced.

We are so impressed with man-made structures like this because we know the tremendous energy that went into the construction, but the workers lacked fuel-burning machines to do the work. Where did the energy come from to pay for all of this work? From the food eaten by the workers who lifted these massive stones! (Temples of Rameses, Nubia, Egypt)

Exercises:

1. Heat energy from the burning of gasoline drives a gasoline engine. What is the source of energy for a solar calculator?

2. On the basis of the rules of nature, would you predict that a rock would ever hop up on top of another by itself?

3. Living things exist at a much higher level of organization than one rock on top of another. Would you predict that a living thing could ever organize on its own?

11: *Hide and Seek with an Oofglork*

Playing hide and seek with an oofglork is troublesome. You see, an oofglork can make himself look like many different things. When you first start playing with him he doesn't tell you this, so for a while the game is unfair. You are running about looking for a big hairy oofglork, but he has turned himself into a cloud. Now, how would you know to look for a cloud when you are trying to find an oofglork? So he gets away with it for the first few games until you catch him at his trick.

After he's been caught, he stops using the cloud disguise and starts making himself look like a rock, then like a tree, then like a patch of grass. But after you've played several games with the oofglork, you realize that he has run out of changes. He is limited to certain forms that you can recognize. Now the game may still be a little unfair, but at least you can play it.

Energy is an oofglork. At first, it may be hard to figure out where energy goes when it leaves your body or when it is transferred from object to object. But if you learn the

Water in a river flows from a higher position to a lower one under the influence of gravity. The distance between the high point and the low point represents the amount of potential energy in the water. This energy can be captured by a hydroelectric dam and converted to electrical energy.

different forms that energy can take on and if you observe carefully, you can track it all down.

One of the most common ways energy can leave one object and be transferred to another is through heat. Rub your hands together, and what do you feel? Heat is generated by the rubbing. This is the result of your own energy being converted to heat energy. Where does the heat go? It accumulates in your hands as they warm up, and is passed off to the air around your hands as they cool back down to their normal temperature. The warm air immediately next to your hands is mixed with air a little farther out, and a little farther out, and a lot farther out, so that the heat spreads itself out in all directions. This loss of heat from our hands represents a loss of ability to move our hands against each other (ability to do work) because it took some of our rubbing energy to form this heat. The more force you apply to pushing your hands together, the more energy is converted to heat.

Energy that changes the position of an object is easy to see, but there are a number of forms of energy that are easy to miss if you don't know what to look for. Heat is one, but **light** and **chemical bonds** are others. We will discuss these in more detail later. For now, let's look again at ways of storing energy. We have discussed the changes in potential energy that go along with doing work against gravity; energy can be stored by doing work against other forces as well.

A range top is an example of a resistance. Resistances convert electrical energy to heat energy.

A tungsten filament light bulb converts electrical energy to both light and heat energy. The filament of a black light bulb is easily seen.

Since no work can be done without energy, we need a source of energy to carry out the tasks that we want to accomplish from day to day. Nature has great storehouses of energy that we have learned to use for these purposes. Some examples are sunlight, petroleum fuels that can be burned to release heat, and radioactive chemicals that release nuclear energy.

Fortunately, we are not at the mercy of nature to take whatever kind of energy we are given and make use of it directly. Different tasks that we carry out require different forms of energy. When we want to bake bread, we need heat. When we want to read, we need light. Because energy is required in different forms for different uses, some of the most important processes people have discovered are those that convert energy from one form to another. The kinetic energy of water falling over a dam under the influence of gravity turns **generators** that convert it to electric energy. **Resistances**

Energy can be obtained from the nuclei of atoms as they change from a higher level of potential energy to a lower one. In later lessons we will learn how this form of energy can be released from atoms.

(the "heat coils") in our heaters and ovens convert electric energy to heat, and when electric energy is passed through a **tungsten filament** under vacuum (in a light bulb), it is converted to light energy. We will learn more about all of these important tools—how they are made and how to use them—as time goes on.

Chemical bonds are important for energy storage. We will soon learn what these bonds are and how they are formed. This is the form of energy that all living things use to fuel their activities. When we make even the simplest motions, like lifting our hands or wiggling our toes, those motions are made possible by the release of energy from chemicals.

Even matter itself has been shown to be a form of energy. The amount of energy in matter is represented by the mass of the matter. For this reason, it is often referred to as **mass energy**. An example of the conversion of mass to energy is seen in the explosion from an **atomic bomb**. In these explosions, mass energy is converted to heat, light, and the kinetic energy of the air and of solid objects that are forced outward from the explosion. Now that you know the different forms that energy can take on, you can always find it no matter where it hides.

People have long realized that the energy from falling water can be captured and put to use.

12: *Conservation of Energy*

In physics, the phrase "conservation of energy" does not refer to saving electricity by turning off the light when you leave a room. Instead, it refers to the observation that energy is "perpetual," or that it is always conserved. In other words, we don't make it or consume it. It lasts as long as the universe. But as life goes on and different tasks are done, it just changes from one form to another.

A tremendous amount of energy was readily available to us when God put man on Earth. The sun was shining far away, burning gases with such great heat that its intense, energetic light reached the Earth. Fuels were available on the Earth (as

Light energy from the sun is absorbed by plants and used to manufacture sugars, storing that captured energy in the form of chemical bonds. Cows eat grass, and the chemical bond energy from the grass is used by the cow to make its own internal chemicals.

When people eat hot dogs, they obtain the energy from the chemical bonds in the cow—the same energy that comes from the grass and, in turn, from the sun.

The energy released by kids as they play soccer comes from the hot dogs they eat, which comes from the grass that the cow eats and from the sunlight that the grass absorbs. Eating is the way people get energy for all their activities—even the simple, mundane activities like breathing and thinking.

wood) and under ground (as **fossil fuels**) that could be burned to release energy. The story goes back even further, but we know little about how the sun was formed and ignited, or how the Earth was formed and fuels were deposited because no people were here to observe. Scientists working in astronomy and geology have devoted great efforts to studying the universe and the Earth for clues that will point them to the answers to these questions.

But in our observation, the energies available to us in these forms are passed along. Here is one example of the many things that can happen to energy coming from the sun: The sunshine might fall on grasses which store this energy in chemical bonds. The plants then use this bond energy to make more plant matter. Cows feed on the plant matter. They give off heat energy to the atmosphere, but they also grow and reproduce. Humans eat steak and hamburger. The meat comes from cows, but the energy stored up in the steak's chemical bonds comes from the sun. We use that energy as fuel for our own activities: growth, reproduction, exercise, etc. Our work results in conversion of energy to body heat that escapes to the air. It is also converted to potential energy in things we lift, and to kinetic energy in soccer balls we kick. But isn't it fascinating that the energy we use and pass along to the atmosphere and the Earth started out as sunshine 93 million miles away?

Some of our own energy may leave the Earth's atmosphere as infrared light and travel through space until it strikes another planet or star or interstellar dust and warms it very slightly. How does it make you feel that you may be helping to warm a dust particle millions of miles from Earth? So the energy that was originally provided by sunlight is not lost; it is just widely scattered. The universe itself still contains the same amount of energy as it did when the sun first shone its rays on the grass.

Exercises:
1. Which of the following are examples of a source of heat energy: sunshine, a coal-fired electric power plant, a tree that can be burned as firewood?
2. Think of as many natural sources of energy as you can.

13: *Forces*

As we have seen, in order to be useful (do work) you have to apply force—a kind of *push*. Up to this point, we have considered only one natural force (gravity) against which we push to do work. Scientists have so far described four forces in nature: gravitation, electromagnetism, the strong nuclear force, and the weak nuclear force. For now, we will talk about nuclear forces as though they were only one force. We now begin to discover the importance of electromagnetic forces that will lead us to a greater understanding of our universe.

Gravitation is a basic natural force. We can define it only by what it does, which is to draw objects together with a strength of attraction that is related to their masses. We have actually introduced a second force already without describing it or considering it. That force is **electromagnetism**. Do you remember when we started talking about friction? Well, friction is the result of the electromagnetic force. But before we can understand this statement, it is necessary to describe the electromagnetic force in greater detail. And just as the large masses of the universe are the centers of gravity, we need to learn what bodies are the centers of electromagnetic force.

All of the natural forces are at work in this photograph—gravity, electromagnetism and the nuclear forces. You know gravity very well. Your understanding of the universe will improve by learning where to look for and how to recognize the others.

Someday we may learn that the four forces we know are actually related somehow in ways we do not presently understand. This would be consistent with our observation that the universe tends to be simple if we can figure out those rules that simplify it. If such rules are discovered, they will surely be among the greatest discoveries of all times.

For the next few lessons we will be learning about electromagnetism. You probably know that lightning is an extreme example of electricity, but do you know what electricity is? In just a few short lessons, you will!

Exercises:

1. A force is a kind of _____ (husp). (Unscramble the word in parentheses.)

2. The opposite of a push is a _____ (lupl).

3. A person could consider a pull to be a negative _____ (reocf) and a push to be a positive one.

4. Gravity and electromagnetism are two of the natural _____.

5. Gravity is a force of attraction. It pulls, but it does not push. The strength of the pull is related to the _____ of the attracted objects.

14: *Electric Force*

Thus far, we have been considering large objects—objects that are big enough to see, throw and push. But now, in order to investigate this second of the natural forces, we turn our attention to objects that are far too small to be viewed individually. Everything in nature is made up of tiny particles called **atoms**. These atoms are made up of even smaller particles: **protons** and **neutrons** that form the center, or **nucleus**, of the atom, and **electrons** that constantly circle that nucleus at a high velocity. Like the attraction of the Earth's gravity for other bodies, protons and electrons have a great attraction for each other, even though these particles are small. However, electrons are not attracted to other electrons. In fact, they **repel** one another. For this reason, we assign a **charge** to these particles. Someone once decided to call the electron charge "negative" and the proton charge "positive." So we all have adopted this way of referring to charges. If an object has the proton charge (as glass does) then we say its charge is positive. If it has the electron charge (as rubber does) we say its charge is negative.

These attractions and repulsions are caused by a force called the **electric force**. This is part of what we will come to know later (after we discover the relationship between electricity and magnetism) as the **electromagnetic force**. Like gravity, the force of attraction that exists between particles with opposite charges causes particles to tend to accelerate toward each other. As with gravity and other forces, we have to use energy to push or pull against the electric force in order to carry out work.

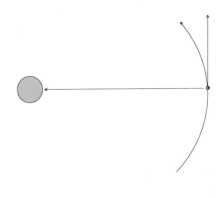

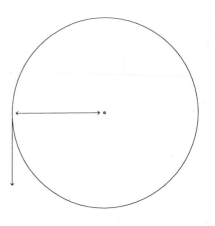

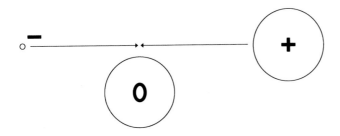

This diagram illustrates the charge attractions of the particles that make up atoms. Tiny electrons and more massive protons are attracted to one another by their opposite electrical charges. Neutrons, which have the same mass as protons, are not attracted to either electrons or protons.

A compromise between inertia and the force of gravity keeps the moon in continual orbit around the Earth (top). In the same way, electric charge attraction between an electron and its atomic nucleus compromises with the rapid motion of the electron to keep electrons in continual orbit around the nucleus of an atom (bottom). This illustrates the fact that, although forces are of different strengths and affect different types of objects, all forces have similar effects on motion.

You will remember that, with gravity, the amount of force pulling two objects toward each other depends on how massive those objects are. In the case of electric force, however, the mass of the charged objects does not determine how strongly they will be attracted toward each other. However, unlike gravity, the amount of force is not necessarily related to the mass of the charged object. Small objects can have strong electric charges, and large objects can have small or practically no electric charges. When we were considering the gravitational force between two really large objects like the Earth and the sun, we had to consider the masses of each of these great objects. But because the charges of particles are not necessarily related to their masses, we can't know the strength of the force of attraction or repulsion just by knowing the mass of the charged particles.

Another difference between charge and gravity is this: "like charges" (that is, two objects with matching charges, either both positive or both negative) repel; "unlike charges" (two objects with opposite charges, one positive and one negative) attract. This is not true of gravitation. All bodies in the universe are attracted to each other by gravitation. There is no repulsion caused by gravity, so there is no need to label masses positive and negative with reference to gravity's force. By contrast, since electric force can push objects away or pull them together, we must talk about their "charges" to describe those forces of attraction and repulsion.

The tiny particles within an atom have so very little mass—almost none. And as you know, the force of gravity between objects depends on how massive they are. Protons and electrons have so very little mass that the effects of gravity on them are of no practical importance. Within an atom, then, we can ignore gravity and concern ourselves with the electric force between charged particles.

Think of electromagnetism in the same way you think of gravity. It is a natural force of attraction. While gravity affects all masses (and is noticeable when those masses are large), electromagnetism affects charged particles, even though those particles are eensy weensy.

Exercise:

If a proton having a mass of 1 kilogram (this would be one *huge* proton!) has an electric charge of 1 **coulomb** (a real unit of charge), how much charge would a five-kilogram proton have?

15: *To Flow or Not to Flow*

Electric charges can travel rapidly from particle to particle. Because like charges repel, they tend to spread out as evenly as possible within an object. Any excess of either positive or negative charge collects and spreads itself evenly on the object's surface. Even though the charge can travel around the surface of an object, it stays on the object; that's why it is called **static** (which means "staying") electricity.

When your feet rub on a carpet, the surface of your body picks up a static charge. When you touch an object that can accept that charge, you feel a shock as the charge moves from you to the object you touch. At the moment it is released, it is no longer a static charge, but a **current**. Like a stream of water under gravity, it flows from a place of higher **potential energy** to a place of lower potential energy—the direction things always tend to go. Then, just like the ball falling under the influence of gravity, the potential energy is converted to **kinetic energy** as the charge travels to its place of lesser potential energy.

So far, we have introduced several ideas about electricity. In the last lesson, we introduced the idea of charge. We also introduced the force that pulls unlike charges together and causes like

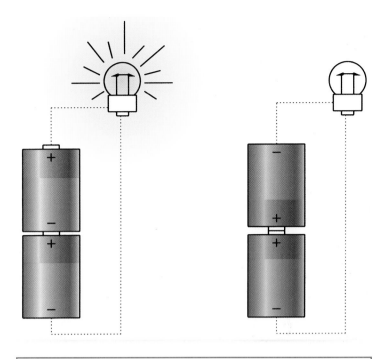

The electrical circuit diagrammed on the left is a typical flashlight circuit. Notice that electrons are flowing from the negative battery terminal to the positive terminal through the light bulb. The circuit on the right will not light the bulb because electrons will not flow from one positive terminal to another or from one negative terminal to another. In this setup, any flow of electrons in one direction will be met by an equal flow from the other.

Electrons flow through wires from a negatively charged terminal to a positively charged one. Their velocity approaches that of light. That means an electron could travel around the entire earth about eight times in one second.

charges to repel. We called this force the electric force. In this lesson we have introduced static charge and current and explained their relationship with potential energy and kinetic energy. Where will we go next? We've been there before: NOW DO SOMETHING USEFUL!

Electrical lines are the conductors that allow electrons to flow from their place of high potential energy to their place of low potential energy and thus bring electricity (electric current) into our homes.

Exercises:

1. Can you think of two sources of electricity that nearly everyone in the U.S. has in his home?

2. If you connect the positive pole of a battery with the negative pole of a battery, what will happen after a few hours? Why?

3. Is a battery that is not connected to anything a better example of a static charge or a current? Why?

4. Why doesn't a two-battery flashlight work when one of the batteries is in upside down? (See the diagram.)

16: *Electric Work*

Let's say you and your brother have opposite charges. You're positive (of course) and he's negative. Now, because opposite charges attract, you two are hard to separate—you tend to stay stuck together. But let's suppose your parents want you to sleep in separate beds. Then they have to overcome that force of attraction in order to pull you apart. In other words, they have to do work on you to separate you. The stronger your positive and negative charges, the greater will be the work done in pulling you apart.

You will remember that any time work is done, the price you pay is energy. Your parents have to use their own energy in pulling you apart; then they have to staple your jammies to the bed

Electricity comes into our homes through a series of processes. The first of these processes is the generation of electrical energy at the energy plant. This is a picture of the core of a nuclear reactor, where nuclear energy is released from radioactive metals and absorbed by water to make steam.

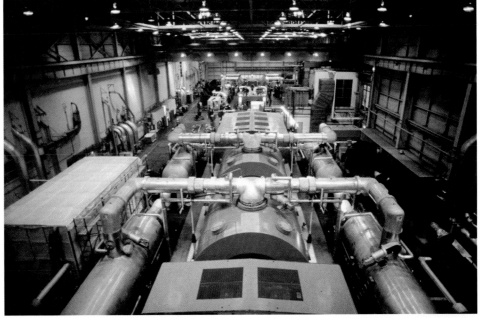

The steam that is generated by the nuclear reactor is used to turn large turbines (explained further in Red Lesson 24). The turbines operate an electrical generator. (We learned about these in Red Lesson 11.)

Electrical energy is sent from the energy plant to a transfer station like this one. At this station, the main energy source is divided into smaller currents for distribution to several areas.

to keep you from flying across the room to each other. The nice thing about this work is that electric potential energy is stored up in the two of you, so that at any time this potential energy can be released, and the two of you will go flying through the air to smack into each other halfway between the beds! This is electric kinetic energy.

It's a good thing electric potential energy differences between people don't ever get that big. Electrons move around too much. If too many electrons are accumulated in a body, giving it a strong negative charge, or if too many electrons are drawn away from a body, giving it a strong positive charge, electrons will jump from one body to another to equalize the charge with that of other bodies nearby. We have all rubbed our feet on carpet, especially on a dry day, and touched another person or a good electric **conductor** like a piece of metal. We feel a shock when our electric charge jumps to the surface of opposite charge.

Because electrons (negatively charged particles) can move around so readily within objects, materials that are good conductors for electrons can be used to carry electrons over great distances (for example, from electric energy plants into our homes). The electric company brings you not only the negatively charged conductor, but also the one bearing the positive charge. That's why electrical

You've seen these a thousand times. When the electricity comes into your home, it is distributed about your house to these. Just think of the tremendous effort that went into bringing you this electrical energy supply, so all you have to do is plug in!

outlets in your home have two holes. A great difference in electric potential energy lies between the opposite charges located at those two holes. That difference in potential energy represents a great capacity to do work.

We have defined work as the application of force over a distance. The definition is the same for moving particles against the electric force as it is for work against gravity or any other force. Because you don't actually see charged particles moving from one place to another, it's hard to appreciate that work is being done. However, the reduction in electric potential energy that accompanies this work is necessary for the operation of your toaster, TV, computer and refrigerator. You may not actually see work being done, but you can sense its effects by feeling the heat energy leaving the toaster or seeing the light energy leaving the television.

If you look at the top of the power poles near your home, you will probably find a transformer that reduces the amount of the electricity in the electrical line to a level that can be used by your household appliances.

Exercises:

1. If you pick up excess electrons by rubbing your feet on a carpet to shock a friend (Some friend you are!), would you expect the shock to be stronger or weaker if both of you pick up electrons by rubbing your feet?

2. What has to be done to separate opposite charges?

3. What is stored up when charges are separated?

17: *Magnetic Force*

Earlier we revealed four forces that are basic to our universe, and we described one of those forces as electromagnetism. Yet in recent lessons we discussed only electricity. Electromagnetism is a two-part word. As we recently demonstrated in a laboratory exercise, electricity and magnetism are connected because a magnetic field of attraction is generated by flowing electricity.

If an electric current flows through a long straight piece of wire, an electric field is generated in a circular pattern around the wire. If a second wire is placed alongside the first and an electric current flows through it in the opposite direction, what will happen? A force will attract the two wires. This is the magnetic force. Every electric current has an associated magnetic force field. Like every other force, if it is applied over a distance, it can be useful for work.

The strength of a magnetic force is directly related to the strength of the electric current that generates it. The reason why the electromagnetic forces are so useful is that they are the only forces we can precisely control. The Earth's gravity is what it is, and we just have to live and work with it. Nuclear forces are extremely powerful, but they are hard

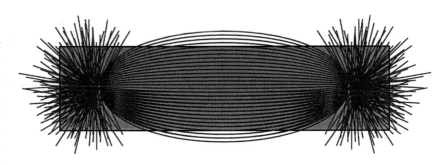

This is what the magnetic field surrounding a bar magnet might look like if we could see it. Only a few of the infinite number of the "magnetic field lines" are drawn.

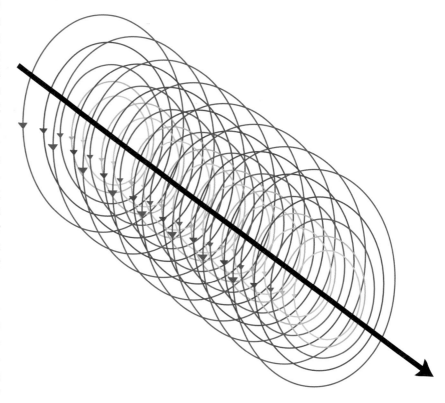

Every electrical current flowing through a conductor has a magnetic field surrounding it. The magnetic field has a direction that is related to the direction of the current in the wire. If the current were to change direction, the magnetic field lines would also change.

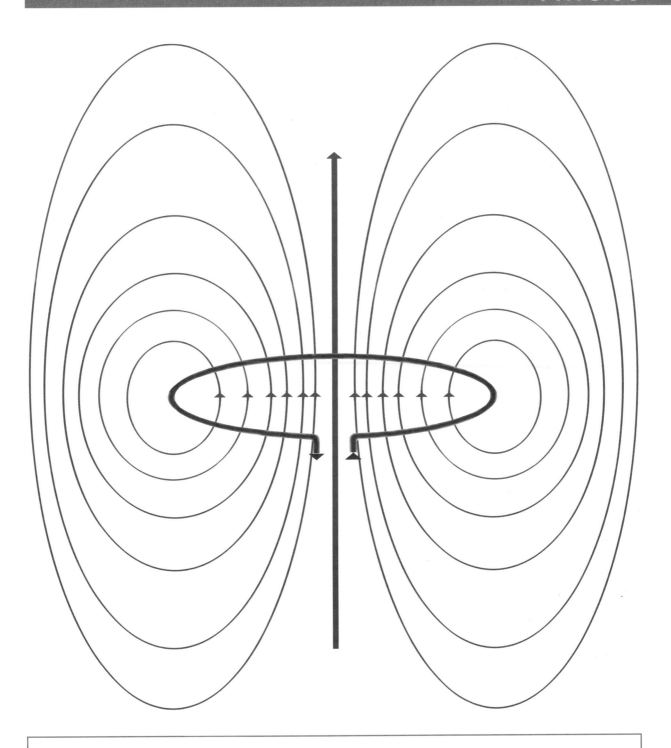

If the wire in the previous diagram were curled into a circle, this is what its magnetic field might look like. We are showing you only a thin slice of the field. You have to imagine what it would look like if the whole field were shown. You might think of the field as a big Bundt cake baked around the wire.

to get going, and they tend to go haywire because we can't control them well. Electricity and magnetism can be controlled very well indeed. We can calculate very nearly the right amount of electricity to apply to the right materials in order to get an electromagnet of a certain strength and shape. This is why we have electric refrigerators, electromagnetic televisions, and electromagnetic automatic door locks on our cars instead of nuclear refrigerators, etc. (Nuclear refrigerators? I'd hate to be around when one of those went bad!)

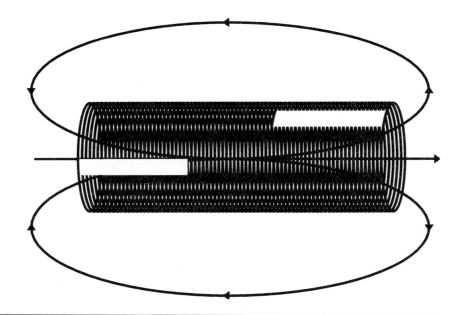

If, instead of curling a short wire into only one circle, you coiled a long wire into a row of circles, what shape would the magnetic field assume? This diagram shows it. This device is called a solenoid, and it is used in car doors to lock or unlock them depending on the direction of the electrical current through the solenoid. These devices have many uses.

Exercises:

1. Look around your house and list as many things as you can find that take advantage of electricity for operation.

2. Do the same for magnetism.

3. Do the same for gravity. (Don't look just for things that are held down by gravity, but for things that actually require gravity to do work—apply a force over some distance—like a grandfather clock with a pendulum that depends for movement on gravity to pull it down.)

4. Do the same for nuclear force.

18: *What's Left?*

As you probably guessed by the direction we were heading in the other lessons, this lesson has to introduce the other forces in nature—nuclear forces. Well, we won't get there in one little lesson, but we will begin by learning about atoms. Just as gravitation hangs out in all masses and is measurable in large masses, and just as electromagnetic force hangs out in electrons and protons, so the nuclear force hangs out in the nucleus of atoms. You won't understand how we know that until you understand how an atom is put together.

All matter in the universe is made up of atoms. But what is an atom? *Atoms are the smallest stable form of matter.* If you want to sound smart, just say that out loud in the middle of the next wedding you attend. What it means is that you can tear apart matter into pieces, then you can tear the pieces into pieces and then tear those pieces into pieces, but when you are all done, what you have left will still be made of atoms. Even when you have broken those pieces down to molecules, those molecules will be made of atoms. When you have broken apart a molecule, the pieces you will get will be atoms or groups of atoms. On the other hand, when you break apart an atom itself, the pieces will not stay as they are. They will usually combine with other particles to make atoms. This is what we mean when we say the smallest *stable* form of matter. It's the smallest form that will continue to exist the way it is. To break it down any further is to make it unstable and incapable of continuing as it is.

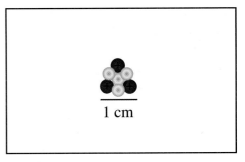

1 cm

Here is the nucleus of an overgrown atom. It is about 1 centimeter in diameter. But where are its electrons? In order to be the right distance from the nucleus, they have to be about 20 miles away.

The smaller, unstable particles making up atoms are called **protons**, **neutrons** and **electrons**. Protons have a positive charge and are located at the center of the atom along with neutrons. Neutrons are so called because they have no charge and are said to be "neutral." Electrons are negatively charged and are tiny; in fact, they are much smaller than either protons or neutrons. Electrons move about at great speed, encircling the nucleus of the atom, much like planets circling the sun in outer space. If gravitation keeps the planets circling the sun, what force keeps electrons circling the nucleus of an atom? It's the electric force—the attraction of a positive particle for a negative one. Even though an electron is much smaller than a proton, it has the same amount of (opposite) charge. For each proton in the nucleus there will be one electron circling it, so

Although protons and electrons have equivalent (but opposite) charges, they are much different in size. A proton's mass is about 2000 times the mass of a tiny electron.

the atom is charge-balanced. Its overall charge will tend to be zero. The amount of charge contained in these tiny particles is great. The strength of force between a proton and an electron is much greater for the size of the particles than is the Earth's gravity.

An example of the immense energy locked up in the nuclei of atoms is seen in this photograph of a nuclear weapons test shot. This bomb, called Romeo, was fired off the coast of California in 1954. Its released energy was equivalent to 11 million tons of dynamite.

Exercises:

1. If you could pull one single proton out of an atom, there would be one fewer proton in the atom than the number of electrons. What would that do to the charge balance within the atom?

2. What could happen to make the protons and electrons balance again?

19: *Count Your Many Protons*

We have said that all matter is made of atoms, but we know that not all matter is the same. How can we have all atoms, but different matter? The answer is that not all atoms are the same. We said that atoms are made up of protons, neutrons and electrons, and that the number of protons tends to equal the number of electrons. So the charges will balance, but how many are there of each? This is the secret: There can be any number of protons and electrons as long as the number of each is the same. Further, the number of protons tends to be about the same as the number of neutrons. The match isn't always exact, but it's always close.

Different types of atoms are simply different numbers of protons, neutrons and electrons hanging out together. If you are an atom made up of two protons, two neutrons and two electrons, you are helium. If you are six protons, six neutrons and six electrons hanging out together, you are a carbon atom. Each time another proton is added, a different **element** is formed. An

Carbon is one of the natural elements and is shown here in its pure granular form. It is quite different even from its closest neighbors in the periodic table. Nitrogen, for example, is a colorless gas. These differences in properties arise from the basic differences in the numbers of protons, neutrons and electrons among the elements.

element is a pure form of matter made of one single type of atom. If matter has more than one type of atom, it is no longer pure. There have been 109 elements discovered so far. The ones having the highest numbers of protons are not really even found in nature, but they were made by taking atoms of existing elements and adding protons or other small atoms to them. Two atoms fuse together into a larger atom. These larger atoms don't stay together well. They tend to break apart into smaller atoms again.

Exercises:
1. See if you recognize the names of these elements: hydrogen, helium, carbon, oxygen, aluminum, chlorine, iron, nickel, iodine, gold, uranium. Where have you seen these names before?
2. Do you know what each of these elements looks like?
3. Look at the table containing the list of elements, and tell whether each of the following is an element: skin, potassium, rock, silver, Formica, wood.
4. Is skin made of atoms?

The periodic table is an arrangement of elements according to their numbers of protons. Once scientists realized that elements consist of atoms having different numbers of protons, they arranged them in a table like this and began looking for the ones that had not yet been discovered.

1A	2A	3B	4B	5B	6B	7B	8B	8B	8B	1B	2B	3A	4A	5A	6A	7A	8A
H																H	He
Li	Be											B	C	N	O	F	Ne
Na	Mg											Al	Si	P	S	Cl	Ar
K	Ca	Sc	Ti	V	Cr	Mn	Fe	Co	Ni	Cu	Zn	Ga	Ge	As	Se	Br	Kr
Rb	Sr	Y	Zr	Nb	Mo	Tc	Ru	Rh	Pd	Ag	Cd	In	Sn	Sb	Te	I	Xe
Cs	Ba	La	Hf	Ta	W	Re	Os	Ir	Pt	Au	Hg	Tl	Pb	Bi	Po	At	Rn
Fr	Ra	Ac	Rf	Db	Sg	Bh	Hs	Mt									

Ce	Pr	Nd	Pm	Sm	Eu	Gd	Tb	Dy	Ho	Er	Tm	Yb	Lu
Th	Pa	U	Np	Pu	Am	Cm	Bk	Cf	Es	Fm	Md	No	Lr

20: *The Proton Repulsion Problem*

Remember when we were stapling you and your brother in your beds to keep you from flying across the room to each other? Why did we do this? It was because you had opposite charges, and opposite charges attract each other. But now let's say that you and your sister have the same charge. What will happen then? You will be repulsed! That is, there will be a force between you pushing you away from each other.

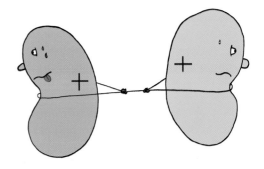

We already noted that atoms are made of protons, neutrons and electrons, and that electrons and protons attract each other. We also noted that the nucleus of an atom is made of protons and neutrons stuck together in the center of the atom. Does this bother you? Well, it should! We have protons that all have the same charge sticking together in the center of atoms. Now does it bother you? All of these protons have the same positive charge! Now does it bother you? They should be *repulsed* by each other. THEY SHOULD ALL COME SCREAMING OUT OF THERE, BUT THEY DON'T! WHY? WHY? WHY? WHY? WHY? WHY?

The nuclear force is the force of attraction that holds positively-charged protons together in the nucleus.

The answer is simple: There must be an even stronger force in the nucleus holding them together. Tah-dah: the **nuclear** [NOO-klē-er] **force**! The nuclear force is what holds the nucleus of an atom together, despite the strong electric force trying to blow it apart. Now, we have used the gravitational force to make a ball accelerate toward the Earth, and we have used the even stronger electric force to warm up a heater. Can you imagine what kind of useful work we could do if we could use the super-strong force that holds a nucleus together? We have done it, you know. It's called an atomic bomb. Another way this force has been utilized is in powering a nuclear reactor. Nuclear reactors are used for generating electricity for communities of people and for powering ships and submarines.

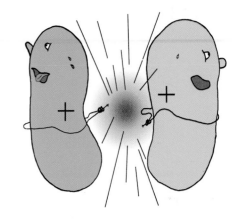

This nuclear force is the strongest of the known forces. It takes a tremendous amount of energy to break it, but, when it is broken, an enormous amount of energy is released.

Exercises:
1. What is a force?
2. Name the forces that we have studied.
3. If we have to work to operate against forces, how then can forces be useful to us?

21: *Storing Up Energy Against the Forces*

As we have seen, energy can be stored (potential) or used (kinetic). The way we store energy is by doing work against (in opposition to) some natural force. As a simple example, we can lift a mass above the Earth and store up energy "against gravity." The amount of energy stored up is related to the height of the mass above the Earth and to the strength of the Earth's gravitational field.

A second force is the electromagnetic force. We can store up electromagnetic potential energy either by storing up electric potential energy or by storing up magnetic potential energy. Electric potential energy is stored up by separating charged particles "against the electric force" that tends to pull them together. Magnetic potential energy is stored in much the same way gravitational potential energy is stored. If we pull apart opposite poles of two magnets by doing work "against the magnetic force," we will have stored up the potential for these magnets to pull each other together again. Once again, the amount of potential energy stored up is related to the distance between the magnets and to the strength of their magnetic fields.

When a mass is lifted above the earth, work is done and potential energy is stored in the mass. This potential energy may be converted to kinetic energy at any time by releasing the mass so that it falls under gravity to its original place of low potential energy.

So you can store up potential energy by working to pull apart two objects that tend to be held together by any of these natural forces of attraction. You can also store up potential energy by working to push together any two objects that tend to be pushed apart by any of these natural forces of repulsion, such as two magnetic north poles or two positive charges. In this same way, there is electromagnetic potential energy stored up in the nucleus of every atom because the nuclear force holds together protons having strong positive charges.

You would think that potential energy could be stored up against the nuclear force in the same way, but it can't. The problem is that, although the nuclear force is strong, it has no effect at all outside the nucleus. Separating particles under the nuclear force just makes two separate nuclei, each having its own nuclear forces. This separation is accompanied by a tremendous release of energy, but no energy is stored for later use. The protons will not fall back together under the nuclear force that once held them.

When opposite poles of two magnets are separated, potential energy is stored in the magnets. This potential energy may be converted to kinetic energy at any time by releasing the magnets so that they fall together under their magnetic forces of attraction. Similarly, work has to be done to separate particles having opposite electrical charges. As they are separated, potential energy is stored in the particles. This potential energy is converted to kinetic energy at any time by placing an electrical conductor between them, allowing them to fall together under their force of attraction.

While the nuclear force holds repelling protons tightly together, protons will not fall together under the nuclear force because the force has no effect outside the nucleus. However, the nucleus of an atom may be struck by another nucleus, causing the two to combine. This is called nuclear fusion. Nuclear fusion is thought to be the reaction that makes the sun shine and is the reaction used to make thermonuclear warheads.

Exercises:

1. If you have a rubber ball in one hand and an identical rubber ball in your other hand, how could you make them have different amounts of potential energy?

2. If a magnet sits on the edge of a wooden table and an identical magnet sits on the floor, does the magnet on the table have greater electromagnetic potential energy than the magnet on the floor?

22: *Artificial Forces*

Up to now, you have studied the natural forces. However, as we have seen, these are not the only forces that can be used to do work. Just consider a simple mechanical spring. It is not generally thought of as a natural object, but you can do work against it and it will certainly apply a force. We have also discussed how you apply force with your hands. You can apply force with your feet, or you can use a car, a truck, a tractor or a winch to supply force.

Force is applied by anything that supplies a push or a pull. We have noticed that anytime the natural forces are used to supply a push, work has to be done against that force in order to accu-

A mechanical spring is a useful tool. You can push against it, or pull on it, and it stores up the energy you put into it, just as if you had lifted an object against gravity. When you let go it "springs" back to its original position just like an object that falls when it is lifted and dropped in a gravitational field. However, unlike the Earth and other gravitational masses, springs are useful because they can be made to any size—you can put one anywhere it is needed.

While it may not be evident to you now, every push that is generated is somehow related to a natural force. Here you see kids pushing on a fence. To our eyes, this doesn't look like an application of electromagnetism, but it is. On a tiny scale, the molecules at the surface of the fence are being pushed by the molecules at the surface of the kids' hands. Those molecules push because of electromagnetic fields of repulsion between them.

mulate potential energy that may be released to be useful. For example, if we want a ball to fall under the force of gravity, first we have to do work on the ball by lifting it against the force of gravity. If we want to use a flow of electricity to light a bulb, we must first do work to separate charges that will allow a flow of electrons.

Such is the case with artificial pushes and pulls, too. Any time an artificial force is supplied, either energy is used to generate the force (like our energy being used to push with our hand), or energy is used to do work against some device that can then recoil to supply a push. For example, a spring can provide a push, but it has to be pushed before it will push back. So in physics, all forces are treated the same. Anytime a force is used to do work, it has to be paid for by energy, whether the force is natural or artificial.

Most of our heavy work is done using pushes and pulls generated by mechanical equipment. The energy price for this work is paid by the burning of petroleum fuel.

Exercises:
1. Which are examples of forces?
   a. the push of your finger on a doorbell
   b. the push of your feet on the ground as you jump
   c. the pull of gravity on your body as you fall
   d. inertia
   e. the attraction of particles with opposite charges
   f. the motion of two magnets away from one another
2. Which of the above are examples of *natural* forces?

23: *Mass Energy*

Scientists have long suspected, but only recently proven, that matter is a form of energy. Matter can be disassembled with an enormous release of energy that is related to its mass. However, mass is a highly stable form of energy, so it hangs around for a long time and is difficult to disassemble except under unusual circumstances. One example of such disassembly takes place when an atomic bomb explodes. This "undoing" of matter is accompanied by some of the most intense releases of energy that mankind has ever brought about.

This is what happens when matter is converted to energy. XX-12 Grable was fired on May 25, 1953 at the Nevada Test Site. A 280mm artillery gun fired the 15 kiloton nuclear shell. This was the only time a nuclear artillery shell was ever fired. (Photo courtesy of U.S. Department of Energy, Nevada Test Site).

When radioactive atoms "decay," they give up energy and tiny particles. The Geiger counter detects the products of radioactive decay and shows just how radioactive something is. It is useful for checking an area to detect radioactivity, which can be harmful.

Remember when we said that in nature, batteries tend to run down and apples tend to rot, rather than to change in the opposite direction? Nature favors situations in which potential energy is lower, not higher, like a ball on the ground instead of in the air. Well, smaller nuclei have lower potential energy than larger nuclei. Nature favors the disassembly of larger nuclei to make smaller ones. Now, we have already said that mass is a stable form of energy, but when nuclei start getting large (84 or more protons), they become unstable enough to lose small amounts of their mass. That mass comes off the nucleus as electromagnetic energy, heat energy and small energetic particles. Elements with large unstable nuclei that give off energy are called **radioactive** elements.

Because of the fantastic amount of energy available in mass, these unstable elements are useful energy sources. Unlike the more stable elements, these atoms can be caused to come undone under special conditions. When this happens, each atom's nucleus is divided into two smaller, more stable nuclei, and part of this huge storehouse of energy is released. This energy, if it can be controlled, is useful for doing work.

24: *Heat Energy*

Like the great hairy oofglork, energy can take on various forms. But if you know what to look for, you can always find it so it doesn't escape your view. For example, you may look for it as potential energy. We have just talked about several forms of potential energy in which energy can be stored up against a natural force. Energy can also be stored up against an *artificial* force such as that provided by a mechanical spring. When the spring is compressed, it stores up potential energy that is released when it decompresses. It's not hard to recognize the energy in a compressed spring. But there are a couple of ways that energy often disguises itself so that it is harder to find (unless you know where to look). These forms are heat and light.

Okay, you already know some things about heat, right? Let me ask you this: Just what is heat? Is it matter? No, because it has no mass. In fact, as we pointed out previously, heat is a form of pure energy. And if we can figure out ways to contain it, we can use it for doing useful work.

Without heat what would the world be like? Really cold! You see, even things that feel cold to us (that are less "hot" than our skin) still have heat. Even ice cubes have quite a bit of heat in them. Although we can tell roughly how much heat energy is present by how something feels to us, we can also measure heat. There are several devices for measuring heat. One of these is a simple **thermometer** (meaning "heat" + "measure"). Others include thermistors, infrared radiometers and calorimeters, designed for measuring

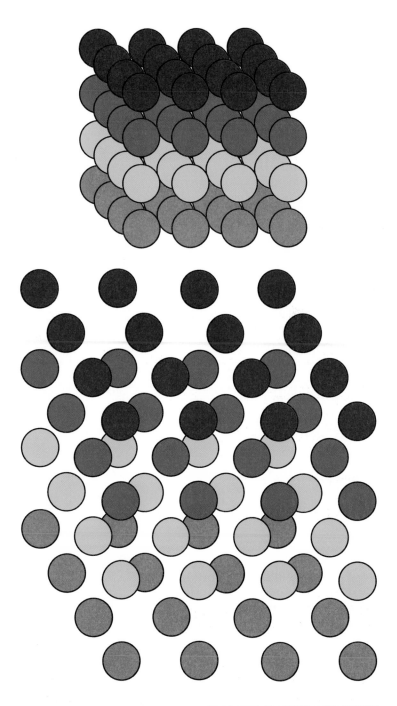

When the molecules making up matter are heated, they vibrate. This vibration causes them to spread out. The effect is for the matter to expand. Later you will learn that some substances expand more readily than others when they are warmed.

heat in different situations. For example, a turkey probe that you stick inside a cooking turkey is a simple thermistor. You wouldn't want to use a glass thermometer for that application. What if it broke?

Energy is defined by what it can do, and heat is no exception. So what effect does heat have on matter? You know by now that all matter is made up of tiny particles called atoms. The particles that make up atoms are held together by electromagnetic and nuclear forces. Atoms are held to other atoms by additional electromagnetic forces that will be discussed later. Heat causes tiny particles to move; the hotter particles become, the faster they move. In solids, the forces holding the particles together are strong. Just imagine if those tightly-packed particles all began to move. (See diagram on previous page.) They would have to spread out. So the effect of heat on solids is to cause them to **expand** (spread out). When they cool down, they **contract** (crowd together).

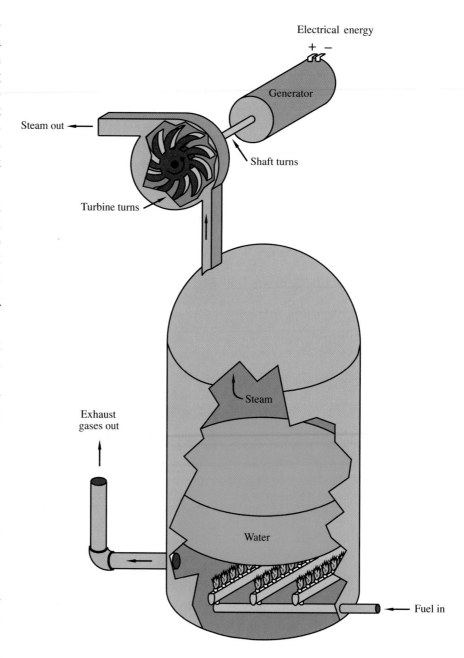

A turbine is a device that is used to turn a shaft (or rod) using energy from a moving fluid. This diagram shows how a steam generator operates. Water is heated in a boiler to make steam. Because steam takes up more space than water, it must escape from the boiler as it expands. The only route of escape is through the turbine. The steam turns the turbine, which turns the shaft, which (in this case) operates the generator. The generator converts the kinetic energy of the shaft to electrical energy.

A hot air balloon is the simplest illustration of heat being used to do work. The heat from a flame warms the air in the balloon, causing it to expand. Expanded air rises for an awesome ride!

The weaker the forces holding particles together, the more they expand in the presence of heat. In liquids, the forces holding particles together are relatively weak. This is why we can actually see fluid move around in its container as it gets hot, like water moving around in a pan when it gets close to boiling. In gases (like air) these forces are even weaker.

Because heat is a form of energy, we can use it to do work. One way is by using it to expand gases. For example, a steam engine is run by heating water to make steam. The expansion of water into steam is used to turn a **turbine** which is used either for **locomotion** or to generate electricity. (See Diagram 2).

Heat also affects the **interactions** of matter (the effects of matter on other matter). Some **chemicals** (specific types of matter) can interact with other chemicals to combine or change in some way by **chemical reactions**. Because heat has the effect of making particles more active, it also causes these reactions to take place more quickly or completely. We will have much more to say about chemical reactions at a later time.

Exercise:

Three examples of heat making our lives more pleasant are these: (1) warming our homes, (2) heating our food, and (3) heating our shower water. What form of energy is converted to heat in each of these three examples?

25: *Light Energy*

For the first part of this reading, you won't know what on Earth the lesson has to do with light, but just hang in there, and the "light" will click on.

If you remember, electric currents (moving electricity) are always associated with a magnetic field. Also, in our laboratory exercises we mentioned that an electric current can be generated from magnetism. This may be accomplished, for example, by moving a magnetic field through a coil of wire. So why can't we just have a magnetic field that generates electricity, and use the electricity to generate a magnetic field, then use that magnetic field to generate electricity, and use that electricity to generate a magnetic field, and, well…you get the point. The answer is, you can. I know it sounds like cheating nature for something to keep going and going, but in fact, it *is* nature. What we have just described is **light**—the common name for **electromagnetic radiation**. You could also call it self-perpetuating waves of electromagnetism (but why would you want to?).

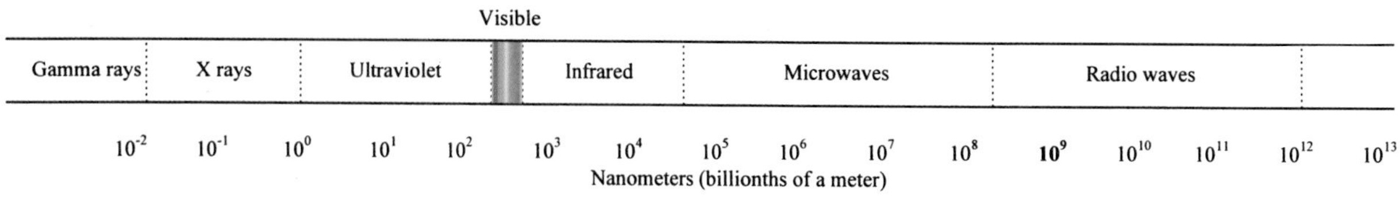

			Visible				
Gamma rays	X rays	Ultraviolet		Infrared	Microwaves	Radio waves	

10^{-2} 10^{-1} 10^{0} 10^{1} 10^{2} 10^{3} 10^{4} 10^{5} 10^{6} 10^{7} 10^{8} 10^{9} 10^{10} 10^{11} 10^{12} 10^{13}

Nanometers (billionths of a meter)

> *This diagram shows the electromagnetic spectrum beginning with the shortest (most energetic) wavelengths and ending with the longest (least energetic). As shown, wavelengths are often measured in billionths of a meter (nanometers). The lines shown separating the different groups of waves (such as microwaves and x-rays) are only imaginary and somewhat arbitrary. For example, the visible area of the spectrum might be wider or narrower depending on the sensitivity of the eyes of a particular person to those wavelengths of light.*

Light is another form of energy. Specifically, it is waves of electromagnetic energy. Like heat, light has no mass, so it is not matter. Like all other forms of energy it can be used to do many useful things. It is the price that is paid for much of the work that is done in the universe, and in our world in particular. All green plants grow by the energy of light. That energy is passed on to the animals that eat the plants, and the animals that eat the animals that eat the plants, and the people who eat the animals that eat the animals that eat the plants (and who also eat the plants). Got that?

We all know that light comes in different colors. The colors that we perceive are the result of our eyes' detecting different energies of light. Light of low energy appears red to us. Light of high energy appears violet. In between are all the different colors of the **spectrum**. If the energy of light is too low for our eyes to detect it, it is called **infrared** ("less than red"). If the energy of light is too high for our eyes to detect it, it is called **ultraviolet** ("greater than violet"). There are many more energies of light that cannot be seen than there are energies that can be seen. (See the diagram above.) Beyond the light rays that are called infrared are radio and television waves and microwaves. Beyond the light rays that are called ultraviolet are X-rays and gamma rays.

The differences in light energies can be seen by the differences in lengths of waves. When you made waves using the Slinky, those waves got shorter as you put more energy into twirling your end faster. Light waves also get shorter if the energy they carry is greater. So the energy of light can be measured by its **wavelength**. Wavelength is a unit of length; the shorter the length, the greater the energy. One common unit of light energy is nanometers (billionths of a meter). While less energetic red light has wavelengths up to about 800 nanometers, more energetic violet light has wavelengths down to about 400 nanometers.

The white light that we typically see from light bulbs is actually a mixture of many different energies of light. Different sources of light offer different energy mixtures. For instance, **fluorescent** bulbs (the long, tube-shaped lamps) give off more green light, while **incandescent** bulbs (the common, pear-shaped lamps) give off more red light. The sun gives off intense light across the entire spectrum of energies both within and outside the visible range.

Again, light is electromagnetic radiation created by the relationship between a magnetic field and an electric field continuously generating one another. Because light is not matter, it is not subject to friction which might slow it down. Unless it strikes something that might convert it to heat or some other form of energy, it can continue "forever." Light moves faster than anything else in the universe, traveling at the incredible rate of almost 200,000 miles per second (over 7 billion miles per hour).

In the near future we will see that sunlight can be spread into separate colors by water droplets in the atmosphere and by a number of devices that are useful in studying light. The rainbow is a particularly spectacular example of this.

26: *Light and Matter*

Just as we did for heat, let's describe light by the effects it has on matter. When light strikes matter, three things can happen. Suppose you got up in the middle of the night to go to the bathroom, and because you were kind of woozy, you ran into the wall. There are three things that could happen to you: (1) you could bounce off the wall, (2) you could go through the wall, or (3) you could end up as part of the wall. (I hate it when that happens.) These are the same things that can happen to light. When it runs into matter it can get "bounced off," "passed through" or "soaked up." Of course, scientists don't like to use simple words like "bounced off" so we make up our own that sound much more impressive. We say light can be **reflected** (bounced off), **transmitted** (passed through), or **absorbed** (soaked up).

First, light can be reflected. Even though light is not matter, sometimes it acts a little like matter. It can "bounce" off a particle as though it were a particle itself. However, because it has no mass, it doesn't cause the particle it hits to bounce. This tendency to bounce we call reflection. An example of reflection is the light that bounces off us to hit a mirror, then bounces off the mirror right back to us, so that we can see our own reflection.

Notice how well the water in this photograph reflects the light from the trees. Oh! Did I say light from the trees? Do trees give off light? No, the trees are reflecting the sun's light. You see, reflection is not a property that belongs only to mirrors (although mirrors do reflect light very neatly). All objects reflect some amount of light.

Second, light can be transmitted. This happens when the particles making up the matter don't absorb or reflect the light very actively. The light then gets passed through, although somewhat changed. For example, light traveling through air hits a glass of water and its direction changes slightly. When it gets to the other side of the glass of water and moves back into the air, it changes its direction slightly again. This change in direction we call **refraction**. Different substances refract light to different extents. A **refractometer** is an instrument that is used to determine the extent to which light is bent by a given substance. Using this instrument we can identify an unknown substance by how much it bends light.

Third, light can be absorbed by particles. This means that the light is converted to other forms of energy so that the particles increase in their potential or kinetic energy. For an atom, this might mean that: the electrons move faster and assume a greater distance from the nucleus, the atom vibrates faster, the atom reacts with other atoms more readily, or heat is given off from interactions between atoms. Notice that this obeys the rules of energy—that it is never used up, but only changes forms. The light energy is no longer light, but some combination of electron potential energy, particle vibration energy, chemical bond energy and heat energy.

Whether light is absorbed, reflected or transmitted depends on two things: what material it strikes, and how energetic the light is. Let's use air for an example. Do you know what happens to light when it hits air? Well, because we can see visible light through the air, a lot of light must pass right through. But also notice that air gets warm as the light passes through. This is because some of the energy is

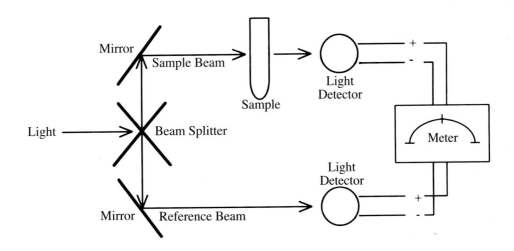

A photometer is a device that uses light absorption and transmission to determine the amount of a light-absorbing substance in a liquid. A liquid sample containing the substance is placed into the photometer. A light beam is split into two parts. One part goes through the sample and the other is used for comparison. Each of the two beams then strikes a light detector. The detector, called a phototube, converts the light energy to electrical energy. The electrical energy from each beam is measured by a meter. Since the two lights come from the same source, any difference between the two electrical signals is the result of the sample material being in the light path. If a scientist knows how much light is absorbed by the substance being measured, he can calculate how much of that substance is in the sample.

transferred to the air particles. These particles heat up and increase their motion, causing friction as the particles interact, which in turn produces more heat. So some of the light is transmitted, and some of it is absorbed to be converted to heat. Some of the light is also reflected. If we were standing on the moon, we would be able to see the Earth because the sun's light reflects off the Earth and its atmosphere.

It's a good thing the atmosphere reflects some of the sun's light or we would all roast. The sun produces enough energetic light to kill us if it were not for the protection we get from the atmosphere. The most damaging light to us is the ultraviolet light. Fortunately for us, this is the light that is reflected most effectively by the atmosphere.

The energy or color of light also affects its refraction. Higher-energy light has a greater tendency to bend than does lower-energy light. This is why the bending of light through a glass or plastic prism results in a spectrum. The colors in the spectrum are separated with the violet light having been refracted the most, then indigo, then blue, then green, then yellow, then orange, then red. On the other hand, while high-energy light tends to be refracted, low-energy light tends to be absorbed. This absorption makes matter warm up, as we described earlier. For this reason, red is a "hot" color compared with blue or violet. Heaters glow with red light and red light bulbs give off a lot of heat. It's the infrared rays of the sun that penetrate through the atmosphere to the Earth that warm it the most, while most of the ultraviolet rays that could kill us bounce off the outer atmosphere into space. We say that red is the most penetrating component of visible light, while violet is the most scattered component.

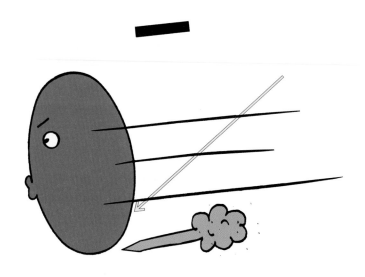

When a particle of matter, such as this electron, is struck by light, the light is absorbed by the particle and the energy is converted to other forms. One of those forms is the kinetic energy (energy of motion) of the particle.

Exercises:
1. Will ultraviolet light be bent more or less than violet?
2. How about infrared as compared with red?
3. If you wanted to get warm after being outside in the winter and all you had were three light bulbs that produced yellow, blue or red light, which would you use?

27: *Black and White*

Did you ever hear someone say, when asked whether black and white are colors, "Black is no color, and white is all of the colors"? But then he is not sure if he got that backward, so he argues with himself for a few minutes. Color can be understood without all of the fuss, but it will take a few minutes to explain.

First, ask yourself, "What is **color**?" Color is an image that our brain creates when our eyes detect light of a certain wavelength. If our eyes detect light having a wavelength of 400 nanometers (nm), our brain says "violet." When our eyes detect light having a wavelength of 750 nm, our brain says "red." Of course, light in nature is not of a single wavelength, so we generalize our names of colors to a few broad categories. The color of an army truck is quite different from the color of grass, but we call them both "green." We have even come up with names for odd colors that are not based on a single wavelength of light, like chartreuse, fuchsia, periwinkle or mauve, but most of the colors we perceive fit nicely into one of a few categories: red, orange, yellow, green, blue, or purple. There are a few other common colors, like brown, that we perceive when various wavelengths of different light are mixed.

What color do you see when your eyes are open in a dark room? The absence of light is perceived as black. This is the first important clue about color. The second is that when we see many wavelengths of light mixed together, like light from a light bulb, we call that light "white." We know this because white light can be split up into the different colors that make it up. This is what a prism does. It divides a beam of light into its colors. In a moment we will explain how a prism works, but if you don't have a prism, the most brilliant display of light-splitting can be seen by holding a compact disc (a "CD") directly under a bright light. There you can see the whole dazzling spectrum of color that comes from dividing a beam of white light.

Did you ever wonder why light goes right through a glass of water seemingly unchanged? "So? Big deal," you say. "Light can go through a glass of water. That's because water is transparent, right?" Think again. Does light go through water because the water is transparent, or is water transparent because light goes right through it? The answer lies in the discovery of what it means to be

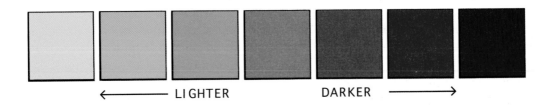

←——— LIGHTER   DARKER ———→

This diagram illustrates the range of tints (lighter colors) and hues (darker colors) that can be achieved simply by increasing the white or black level in a color. We show the effect of black and white on magenta, but the results are similar using any color.

The daytime sky is flooded with light. The stars that appear so brightly at night aren't seen at all during the day. It's the absence of light from the sun that makes the nighttime sky appear dark and that allows the dimmer light of the stars to be seen.

transparent. Atoms are mostly empty space. They have a small nucleus that is encircled by even smaller electrons with a tremendous (by comparison to their size) amount of empty space in between. If that's true, it seems like light would pass right through all matter. Why then do some substances reject (reflect) or trap (absorb) light?

One of the basic observations we can make concerning matter is how it reacts with energy, whether it be light, heat, electric or magnetic energy. How matter reacts with energy is the result of its own characteristics that distinguish it from every other form of matter. Some atomic arrangements are welcoming to light. Light gets in and is absorbed by the matter. It never comes out again, but instead is converted by its interaction with matter to other forms of energy, like heat or kinetic energy within the atoms themselves. When light strikes an object made of this type of material, it is absorbed by the object. The object does not reflect light back to our eyes, and the absence of light is what we associate with the word "black." It's the same sensation our eyes get when we are in a dark room.

28: *Color*

What about objects that appear some color other than black? They don't absorb all of the light that hits them. Some of this light bounces off and travels to our eyes, and this light gives us our idea of their color. Nearly all objects reflect some amount of light; objects that appear white to us don't absorb light of any color very effectively, so practically all of it is reflected. If light is reflected nearly perfectly off something, as with a mirror, you can see a reflection in it. Mirrors are glass plates that have highly reflective metal finely coated on one side. Light enters the glass, strikes the metal, and bounces off. The angle that the light travels from the mirror is opposite the angle at which light enters the mirror. (See the Diagram.)

If an object is hit with a beam of white light, many colors may be absorbed. These colors are collected by the atoms making up the object. But we no longer pay attention to those rays of absorbed energy. All we use to identify the object are the rays that bounce off and enter our eyes. When we look at an object that is bright red in color, we don't say, "Hey, look. There is an object that absorbs all of the colors except red." We say, "Hey, look. That object *is* bright red." We say it *is* red because red is the only color our eyes detect when we look at it. If the object appears orange, it might be because the object absorbs all but the orange light, or it could be because it absorbs all but the red and yellow light. When our eyes pick up red and yellow at the same time, they perceive that combination as orange. When we detect blue and yellow together, we perceive green, and when we detect red and blue together, we perceive purple.

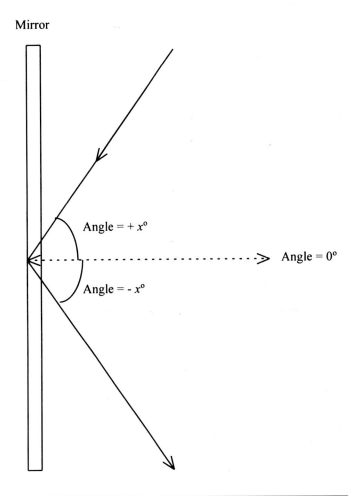

Mirror

Angle = + $x°$

Angle = 0°

Angle = - $x°$

A mirror is a piece of glass with a metal coating on one side. When light enters the mirror, it strikes the metal surface and reflects back through the glass. The dashed line in the diagram represents light going straight into a mirror. (We say that the light path is perpendicular to the plane of the mirror). If the mirror were perfect (as no real mirror can be), that light would exit on precisely the same path that it entered on. If the light entered at an angle, the exit path would have the same angle on the opposite side of the 0° line; so if the light entered at a 50° angle, it would exit at a -50° angle.

If a certain light is mostly white, but it has more yellow than any other color, we will perceive "light yellow." Pink comes from a predominantly red beam of white light; you might call it "light red."

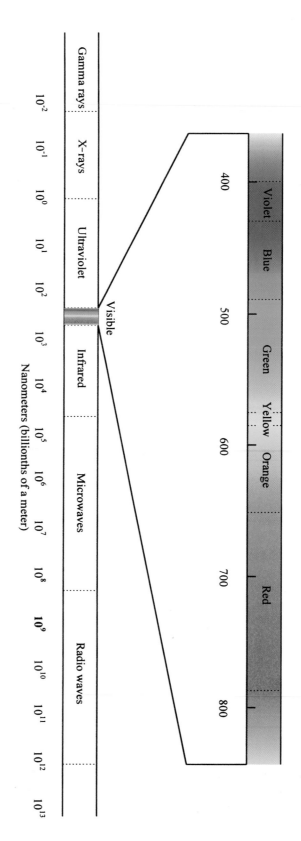

Visible light makes up only a small portion of the entire spectrum of electromagnetic radiation. It includes wavelengths from about 400 to 800 nanometers. Violet light appears at the end of the visible spectrum where the wavelengths are shorter and more energetic. Red appears at the opposite end of the visible spectrum where the wavelengths are longer and less energetic.

29: *Changing the Color of an Object*

We humans like things to be a certain color. We want our purses to match our shoes. How do we take something that is one color and make it a different color? We try to find chemicals that absorb different wavelengths of light and add them to the surface or make them part of the material we want to change. Paints, crayons, colored markers, pens and colored pencils are all devices that are made to apply colored **pigments** to the surface of something we want to see colored. Pigments are those chemicals that absorb selected colors of light. A yellow pigment, for example, is a chemical that reflects only yellow light, absorbing the others.

Pigments are trickier than light. While it may be simple to add yellow and blue light together to make the light appear green, sometimes when you add yellow and blue paint together you get some weird color. That's because pigments are chemicals, and chemicals sometimes interact in ways that we do not expect. Pigments also create the appearance of red light even though that light is contaminated with other colors of light as well. When one pigment is mixed with another, these contaminating colors may become more visible and destroy the intended color. A good experienced pigment chemist is highly valued by manufacturers of such things as paints, dyes, stains and inks.

Now, back to that glass of water we talked about in the previous lesson. We have said that light, when it strikes matter, can be absorbed or

Pigments are chemicals that absorb some wavelengths of light while reflecting others. Those reflected wavelengths are the ones that can be seen by an observer. The many pigments that exist today have been developed at great expense to give us the broadest selection and the truest colors. Today's artists have access to a greater assortment of pigmented paints than Leonardo da Vinci ever dreamed of. Back then, artists had to make their own paints from the pigments they could find in nature. That was one of the skills handed down from a master painter to his apprentice.

reflected, but as we learned in previous lessons, those are not the only two possibilities. Another option is transmission. That is, light *can* pass right through an object if it is neither reflected nor absorbed. Transparency is a characteristic held by a form of matter that neither absorbs nor reflects light. Few solids are transparent; more liquids are transparent; most gases are transparent.

There is no such thing as a perfectly transparent substance; the light is always reflected and absorbed to some minor extent. For example, water doesn't absorb much visible light at all, but if you've ever been on a lake on a sunny day, you know it reflects quite a bit. That reflected light that keeps us from seeing clearly is called **glare**. Other transparent substances include various types of glass and plastic (especially acrylic and polystyrene). Substances that allow passage of most light but distort it to some extent are referred to as **translucent**. An example of a translucent substance is polyvinyl chloride (PVC). This is the clear plastic of which most plastic bags are made. As the plastic is made thicker and thicker, the distortion of the light is greater and greater. Bags made of colored plastic (like trash can liners) have pigment added to them to make them appear white, black, green or some other color.

Glare is reflection of light off a surface. It can be distracting and even disabling (while driving, for example); but it can also be beautiful as it is here at Ocean Beach, San Francisco, California at sunset.

Exercise:

Which of the following might correctly be called a pigment?

1. the chemicals added to makeup to make it flesh-colored
2. the chemicals added to flour to make it pour more smoothly
3. the chemicals added to cereal to make it colorful
4. the chemicals added to paint to make it look like wood

30: *The Science of Light Bending*

We already mentioned prisms as tools for separating white light. Here is how a prism works. Lights of different energies are bent to different extents when going from air into water, or from any one medium into any other. Red light is bent the least, while violet light is bent the most. A glass plate bends light twice: once as it enters, and once as it exits. Because the bends are in opposite directions, the light exits in the same direction from which it enters. A **prism** also bends light twice, but because of its triangular shape, the second bend does not return it to its original direction (Diagram 1). Instead, the various colors of light are further separated the second time they are bent. Red light is bent the least, while violet light is bent the most.

Lenses are glass or plastic devices that are made for the specific purpose of bending light. The shape of the lens is specific to its purpose. Let's say we want to make an object look larger than it really is—that is, to **magnify** it. What shape of lens would be needed? We would have to take light from a small point and spread it out over a larger area. This is precisely what would happen if the object were viewed through the **biconvex** lens as shown in Diagram 2. (A convex lens is one that protrudes in the middle. Biconvex means it protrudes in two directions.) The **biconcave** lens, also shown in Diagram 3, has the opposite effect. It would make a large object appear smaller. (Concave means "caved in." The biconcave lens forms a cavity on each side. Notice the similarity between the words *concave*, *caved*, and *cavity*.)

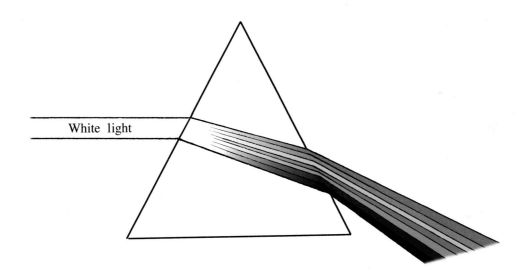

White light

Anytime light goes from one medium to another (from air to glass, for example) it makes a sharp-angled turn at the spot where it enters the new medium. The shorter the wavelength of light, the more it is bent as it passes from one medium to another. A glass prism is shaped to separate the colors of light by bending a light beam twice. Each time the beam is bent, more separation of the wavelengths takes place.

So then, light is a form of pure energy that has both magnetic and electric properties that work together, but has no mass. It may be absorbed by matter with the effect of transferring its energy to the matter, or it may be reflected or transmitted by the matter. When it is transmitted, it is bent, and thus gives us the ability to manipulate what we see by controlling the amount of refraction. It gives us our ability to see, and its wavelengths are responsible for our perception of color. If we want to change the color of matter, we coat it with pigments which interact with light to reflect only those colors we want to see. Black is our perception of the absence of light, and white is our perception of many colors of light in combination. Now you can teach those who don't understand color.

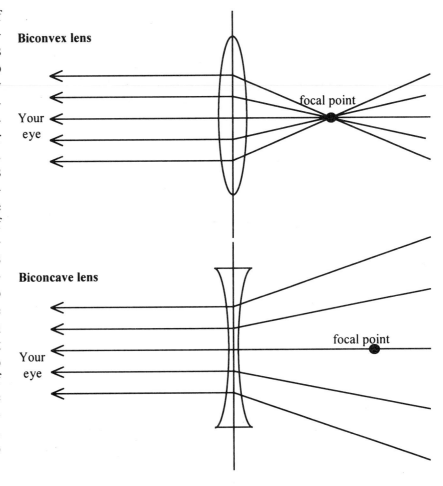

The biconvex lens shown at the top of this diagram takes light from a small area at its focal point and spreads it out. If you see that light from the opposite side of the lens, the object appears larger than it really is. Using that same lens in the opposite way, light can also be collected from a distant source and concentrated right at the focal point. Lenses may be made to bend light as needed for any given purpose.

Exercises:

1. If you had a laser that gave off a thin beam of light, but you needed a wider beam of light, what kind of device could you use to spread it out? (lens, mirror, prism)

2. If you had a beam of white light, but you were doing an experiment that required red light, what device could you use to separate out the light you need?

3. If you were decorating a room and you wanted to light the room with natural light, but there was a portion of the room that did not get direct sunlight, what kind of device could you use to cast sunlight from the bright portion of the room to the dark portion?

CHEMISTRY—A STUDY OF SUBSTANCES, THEIR PROPERTIES AND THEIR INTERACTIONS

Welcome to the Yellow section. Here we focus on the discipline of chemistry: the study of different kinds of stuff (substances) and what they do to each other (their interactions). In this section we will learn some of those fun and seemingly magical chemical reactions; but more importantly, we will learn how their "magic" works. Please begin now with the first lesson.

1: *Impress Your Friends!*

Recall that all matter is composed of **atoms**, and that atoms are composed of **protons**, **neutrons** and **electrons**. Protons and neutrons are packed tightly together in the center or **nucleus** of an atom, and electrons orbit the nucleus at high speed. The number of positively charged protons tends to be the same as the number of negatively charged electrons, keeping the charge of an atom neutral (neither positive nor negative). Protons and neutrons make up most of the mass of the atom, while electrons have some—but little—mass.

Second, recall that an **element** is made up of atoms having a certain number of protons in their nuclei. Each atom of hydrogen, for example, has one proton in its nucleus. All matter is made up of some combination of elements. If we could group atoms together by

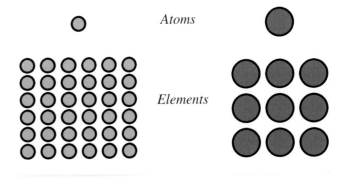

Atoms

Elements

Molecule

Compound

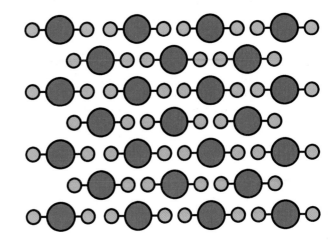

An atom is the smallest stable form of matter. Two examples of individual atoms are illustrated at the top of the diagram. An element consists of several of the same kind of atom; so the diagram shows two separate pure elements made up of the two different types of atoms. When atoms come together under their forces of attraction, they bond together to form a molecule; if there is more than one type of atom in the molecule it is called a compound. The word compound *can refer to either a single molecule or to a collection of molecules of the same type. Since there is only one type of molecule represented in the group at the bottom of the diagram, this group represents a pure compound.*

their number of protons, the result would be separate pure elements. Pure gold is a collection of atoms of gold, each having 79 protons. Because they are common or useful, some elements (like copper and mercury) have names we recognize.

No element is present in nature in its absolutely pure form. Although we can purify them from their natural forms, in nature they are found combined with other substances. So when you look around you in your world, you will find many different substances. But these are not simple elements. They are complex combinations of elements. The study of chemistry involves taking a closer look at those substances and seeing what they are made of and how they are arranged.

Atoms of different elements or of the same element can be joined together by the natural (mostly electric) forces to form **molecules**. For example, an atom of oxygen can join together with two atoms of hydrogen to make a molecule of dihydrogen oxide, which we usually call water. Molecules made up of atoms from two or more elements joined together are called chemical **compounds**. Pure water (water made up of only dihydrogen oxide molecules and no other) is a single compound.

We begin our study in the next lesson by looking at the different forms of matter.

Although the minerals found in the earth are made of elements, there are few pure elements found there. These elements are combined with other elements in ways you will grow to understand throughout the next several weeks.

Exercises:
1. Silver is the name of an element. How many types of atoms make up silver?
2. A _____ is made up of atoms held together by natural forces.
3. Two or more elements joined together make up a _____.

2: *Packaging Stuff*

So you want to understand stuff, eh? I mean, you want to understand the makeup of matter. Well, you are on your way, bright student.

Once upon a time there was a stuff packager. Her job was to package stuff. She picked the right sized box to put in just the right amount of stuff. But this wasn't just any stuff packager; she had the special ability to pack stuff in space. What I mean is, she could move stuff around in space and it would stay where she put it. That's why they paid her the big bucks. Sometimes she left out the space and packed things tightly. At other times she would put in a little space and pack things more loosely. At yet other times, she would pack things so that there was mostly empty space and very little stuff.

The "fog" that is often seen lying above a pool of water on a humid morning is water that has evaporated and cooled there. It is no longer a gas because it is not completely spread out; instead, it is tiny droplets of water that have gathered. The droplets are not massive enough to overcome friction with the air and fall to the earth under the pull of gravity, so they linger in the air until the energy from the sun becomes intense enough to evaporate them again.

Interestingly, when she packed differently, the stuff acted differently. When she packed tightly, the stuff got stiff. Stiff stuff can sometimes be useful. When she packed more loosely, she found that

A glacier is a large mass of ice that grows forward or shrinks back depending on the temperature of the surrounding air.

the stuff filled the container from the bottom up, but the stuff never got stiff. She could put her hand into the stuff and it would move out of the way for her. When she took her hand out of the container, some of the stuff would be on her hand and she would have to wipe it off. Finally, when she packed with mostly empty space, the stuff moved freely about the box. Sometimes stuff bumped together with other stuff. She had to shut the lid quickly or the stuff would bump right out of the box to spread out within the packaging room. But if she got the box closed on the stuff, it would just spread itself out within the box. If you listened carefully, you could hear that stuff bumping around in there.

What magic did this lady possess? None. You see, this lady was extremely small. The stuff she packed was particles—atoms and molecules. Particles that pack together tightly and have a love for each other make stiff solids. They are rigid, and the movement of their particles is minimal. Particles of liquids have less love for each other and move around more freely, but not as freely as particles of gases. While liquids fill a container from the bottom up, gas molecules spread out to fill any container all the way to the limits.

Compare the types of matter that we've seen. The floor is **solid**, water is **liquid**, and air is **gaseous**. That may not seem like much of an observation, but if you think about it, almost every kind of matter is either a solid, a liquid, a gas or some combination of these. There are also a few substances like gelatin and ice cream that we call **semisolids**, but for the most part everything fits nicely into one of these three categories called the **phases** of matter.

Matter sometimes undergoes a change from one of these phases to another. The way you cause matter to change phases is to put in or take away energy. For example, tightly packed solid molecules, when heated up, start moving more rapidly; this movement expands the substance and creates more distance between the molecules. If enough heat is applied, the forces binding the particles together are broken and the particles become more loosely arranged. At that point they become liquid. If you continue to add heat, they can break apart even further to become gas. To return these particles to their original state, all that is necessary is to cool them down.

When you put water in the freezer, heat leaves it and its temperature drops. When the temperature drops, the liquid changes to a solid—ice. When it warms back up to room temperature, it changes again from solid to liquid. This is not so thrilling because we've seen it since we were little kids. What is nifty is that other liquids also change to solids when they get cold (although some liquids have to get *really* cold before they turn to solids). Also, gases change to liquids. This illustrates that gases are just liquids hanging loose, and that liquids are solids hanging loose. How loose the particles of a substance are depends on the strength of the forces attracting those particles and on the amount of heat energy around them.

What happens when you boil water? **Steam** comes off the water. We say it **evaporates**, or turns to vapor. And if you boil the water long enough, there will be no water left in the pan. That's because it all turns to steam. But what is steam? It's a gas. You might say it's water gas. When steam cools, what happens? It turns back into water.

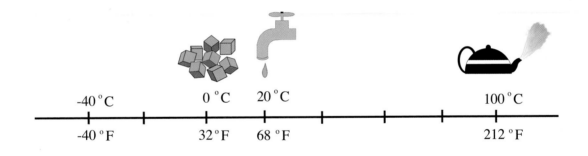

This diagram shows the relationship between the Fahrenheit and Celsius scales. Notice that there is nearly a two-degree change in Fahrenheit for each degree change in Celsius. The two scales cross at approximately -40°.

Water turns to ice when its temperature falls below 0°C. It turns to gas if the temperature rises above 100°C. But what about other liquids? Do they change from solid to liquid or from liquid to gas at the same temperatures? No. Each solid has its own unique **melting point** at which it turns to liquid, and every liquid has its own unique **boiling point** at which it turns to gas. These are just two facts of nature—observations about the way heat affects matter. At a later time, we will learn how important the melting and boiling points of different compounds are. In fact, we will learn that life as we know it would be impossible without the melting and boiling points of water being just as they are.

When a pan of water is placed on a burner, the temperature of the water starts going up. The heat passes from molecule to molecule. One molecule heats up and passes some of that heat off to its neighbors. Occasionally a molecule near the surface of the water will become so energetic with all of the heat it has received that it will yell "yowee" and break free into the air. Its neighbors will heat up in the same way until they are all bouncing around trying to get out of there. Each time a hotter molecule leaves the pan, it takes some of that heat with it. So while the heat beneath the pan heats up the water, the leaving of the overheated molecules cools it down. The temperature of the water that remains in the pan stays the same until every molecule has escaped and all the water has been boiled out. That temperature, called the boiling point, is precisely 100ºC. How did it turn out to be exactly 100ºC? Simple. Some scientist made it up.

Because of this property, the boiling of water can be used to keep a constant temperature. If a recipe tells you to simmer soup in a pot for three hours, the soup will remain at its boiling point (which will be near the boiling point of water) as long as liquid water remains in the pan and the stove provides enough heat to keep the soup boiling. When all of the water is evaporated away, there are no more particles of water

There are some scenes where all three phases of matter are present at the same time. Once again, the gaseous water cannot be seen, but where there are droplets of water in the air, they have often formed from the condensation of gaseous water.

to keep taking heat away from the pan. The temperature will rise quickly (and the stuff left in the pan will burn).

Once steam is made by heating water, the steam will go out into the cool air and its temperature will drop to below the boiling point again. Steam will cool and the tiny water droplets will combine to make liquid water again. This conversion of steam to water is called **condensation**. Condensation is the process by which rain forms in clouds, dew forms on morning grass, and fog forms in cool moist air.

A hoarfrost occurs when fog from the air crystallizes directly on the leaves of trees in the cold morning air.

Exercises:
1. Why doesn't fog form in the middle of the afternoon?
2. On which day is snow more likely—a day when the temperature is -20°C, 0°C, or 20°C?
3. If you wanted to melt a stick of butter without burning it, you could melt it at 100°C. What is a practical way of doing this?

3: *How Much Stuff Is in Stuff?*

If we're going to understand matter, we have to understand how to measure it. Let's say that I step on my bathroom scale and find that I weigh 60 kilograms. Then I step off the scale. The scale reading returns to zero because I am no longer standing on it, but how much do I now weigh? Unless something strange is going on, I still weigh 60 kilograms. Why? Because the weight of a person doesn't change just because he steps from here to there. Weight is the effect gravity has on a certain amount of stuff.

If the nucleus of an atom of an element were one centimeter in diameter, 100 grams of that substance would fill the Grand Canyon.

Now let's take our bathroom scale out into outer space and stand on it. Why does it still read zero? Because there is no gravity. Does that mean we now weigh zero? Yes, it does. But I'm still a something; that is, I haven't turned into a nothing. Why then is my weight zero? It's because there is no gravity, and weight depends on gravity. There is something about a person that doesn't depend on gravity that stays the same when he leaves the Earth. That's the amount of stuff in the person. The amount of stuff is the person's **mass**. Mass is a measure of an amount of stuff. On Earth, the mass of a body is equal to its weight. But in outer space, mass is still the same even though weight becomes meaningless.

Of course, atoms are too small to weigh on your bathroom scale, but they still have mass. And on Earth their weight is the same as their mass. So we may speak of atomic weight or atomic mass, but we're still talking about the same thing—how much stuff makes up the atom.

Different elements have different masses (or weights) for the same number of atoms. For example, the nucleus of a single hydrogen atom has but one proton and no neutrons, while a helium atom has two protons and two neutrons in its nucleus. The helium nucleus is about four times as massive as the hydrogen nucleus. Because we can't weigh them on the bathroom scale, it makes sense to have a smaller unit of measure for describing how much stuff is in an atom. We could weigh them in pounds or kilograms, but their masses would make really small numbers.

Instead, we express the masses of atoms in **atomic mass units (AMU)**. One atomic mass unit is the mass of a proton (all protons have the same mass). While the mass of hydrogen is 1 puny AMU, the mass of helium is 4 AMU. These are the two elements with the least mass. Lead, a more massive atom, has an atomic mass of 207 AMU. Through the use of a special machine called a mass spectrometer, scientists have measured the masses of the atoms of all of the elements. You could think of the mass spectrometer as a bathroom scale for atoms.

Let's try for a moment to understand just how small an atom is. Scientists often measure weights (or masses) of substances in **grams**. (One gram of a substance is approximately equal to the weight of two regular-sized paper clips.) One gram of hydrogen has approximately 602,200,000,000,000,000,000,000 atoms of hydrogen in it. So an atom must be pretty small, huh? That huge number, called Avogadro's number, is named after a physicist and chemist from days gone by. His name was Lorenzo Romano Amadeo Carlo Avogadro di Quaregua e di Cerreto, and he lived in Italy from 1776 to 1856, that is, from the time of the U.S. Declaration of Independence to near the time of the Civil War.

Your laboratory activity kit has a chart called a **periodic table of the elements** that should be posted in a location where you can look at it often. It provides the **atomic symbol** (two-letter symbol) given to each element, along with its atomic number (the number of protons in each atom) and its **atomic mass**. The atomic mass is both the mass of one atom of that element in AMU and the number of grams of that element that contains 602,200,000,000,000,000,000,000 (or 6.022×10^{23}) atoms.

For example, since helium (4 AMU) is four times heavier than hydrogen (1 AMU), Avogadro's number of helium atoms would weigh four grams instead of one. Similarly, a single carbon atom weighs 12 AMU. It is 12 times heavier than hydrogen and three times heavier than helium. That same big number of carbon atoms would weigh 12 grams.

Find the symbol Li on the periodic table. This is the symbol for lithium. Lithium can quickly be seen to have 3 protons (its atomic number is 3), and have an atomic mass of 6.941. A single atom of lithium weighs 6.941 AMU. Also, 6.941 grams of lithium contain 6.022×10^{23} atoms.

The moral of the story is this: the masses of individual atoms are measured in AMU, and visible amounts of matter are often measured in grams. But you should realize that, when you measure visible amounts of matter, you are measuring out enormous numbers of atoms!

Exercises:

1. Look on your periodic table to find out how much one atom of barium weighs in AMU?

2. How much does one atom of bromine weigh in AMU?

3. How many grams of bromine contain 602,200,000,000,000,000,000,000 atoms?

4: *Properties of Matter—Density*

Now you know that all matter has mass, and you know that all matter is made up of atoms. You won't be surprised to find out that all matter takes up space. It would be really neat if we could invent spaceless matter. All of our storage problems would be solved. You could fit an endless number of socks in your drawer. But the world just isn't that way. Everything takes up space.

The question is, do equal amounts (equal masses) of two different elements take up the same amount of space? For example, does one gram of copper take up the same amount of space as one gram of lead? The answer is "no." Every element has its own unique **density**. The more dense a substance is, the more mass is crammed into a given amount of space.

A clay brick that is used for building houses might weigh about six or seven pounds. In our laboratory, we have a brick made of lead. Although it is the same size as a clay brick and takes up the same amount of space, it weighs about ten times more than the clay brick. It weighs over 25 pounds. You see, the density of lead is much greater than the density of clay. Because density is the measure of the amount of matter (mass) taking up a certain amount of space (**volume**), you can get the density by dividing the mass by the volume:

$$density = mass / volume$$

These two bricks are approximately the same size, but the one in the bottom photo weighs many times more than the one in the top photo. Why? The matter making up the atoms of the lead brick (bottom) is packed more tightly than the matter making up the atoms of the clay brick.

If, to a lead brick, you add a second lead brick, the mass will double. Two bricks take up twice the volume of one brick, so the volume will also double. What happens to density if both the mass and the volume are multiplied by two? It stays the same. So the density of lead is the same, no matter how much lead is present. Every element has its own unique density. That is, each element takes up a certain amount of space for a certain amount of mass. Elements that are made up of a lot of matter in a small space are dense.

Let's take a moment to review the main points that have been taught in these first four chemistry lessons:

1. All matter has mass and fills space.
2. Different elements have different densities because their individual particles are more or less scrunched into the same amount of space.
3. The love that those particles have for each other, the closeness with which they are packed, and the amount of available energy will decide whether they are solids, liquids or gases.

The feather weighs less than the paper clip even though it is larger. It's because the feather has lots of empty space inside and is made of less dense elements. The matter making up the paper clip is denser.

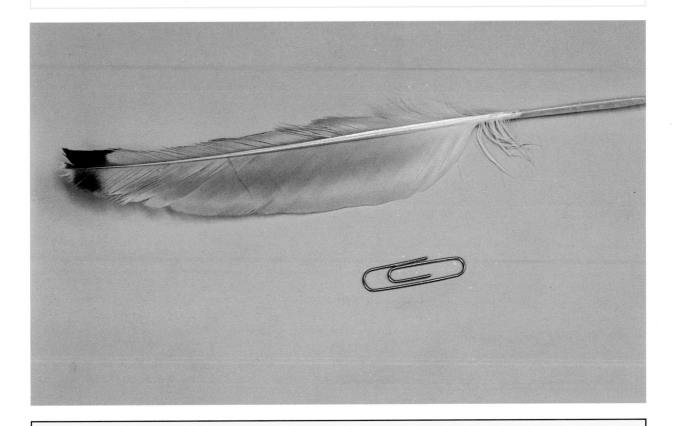

Exercises:
1. Which weighs more, a pound of feathers or a pound of bricks?
2. Which takes up more space?
3. Which is more dense?

5: *The Elemental World*

Once upon a time there was a world in which everything was a pure element. There was gold, but the gold wasn't in the shape of rings or necklaces. There was tungsten, but it wasn't in light bulb filaments or steel, just in big hunks lying around on the ground. By the way, the ground wasn't made of soil and wasn't covered with grass; it was pure silicon. Every place that wasn't a silicon mountain or a silicon plain was a silicon valley. There were heaps of carbon, piles of sulfur, and mounds of copper. Hydrogen gas just floated above everything with helium and nitrogen floating alongside.

Life was absent because life requires elements to interact in complex ways. As long as these elements just lie around in heaps, the world will be lifeless. This is a pretty boring story so far, isn't it? Well, guess what—it doesn't get any better. The point is that unless elements come together and do something, it makes for a boring story. No pizza. No soda pop. No potato chips. Just beryllium.

If everything were made of pure elements, there would be less than 100 substances, and many of those would be rare. But just think how many substances you could make if all of these elements could come together with other elements in different combinations! There are only 26 letters of the alphabet that can come together to make a enough words to fill a 5,000-page dictionary. Those words can go together in different ways to make a

These two books are among the most common laboratory tools. The one standing up, called the CRC Handbook of Chemistry and Physics, contains tables of information on the known chemical compounds. A few decades ago this was truly a "handbook." With our increasing knowledge of chemical compounds the book has grown to be much larger. The book lying down, called the Merck Index, includes short descriptions of the compounds most commonly used in laboratories.

tremendous number of sentences, and those sentences can go together to express a seemingly endless number of thoughts. In the same way, 92 natural elements can form a vast number of compounds. It is these compounds that fill the world, provide for life, and make life interesting and exciting.

Just as letters are not thrown together at random to form books, elements work together in specific ways and according to certain God-given "rules." To understand chemistry is to understand the ways elements work together. Just as words are the basic tools of a writer, compounds are the tools of a chemist. It is from compounds—combinations of elements—that things of a higher order are built, even living things. When elements come together they "**react**" with each other.

Would you like to understand why *eggs congeal when they are heated, why milk curdles when it is acidified, and why bread turns black when it is overcooked? Learn about chemistry!*

Exercises:

1. Protons, neutrons and electrons combine to form _____.

2. A substance made of atoms of a single type is called an _____.

3. When atoms of one or more elements combine, a single unit of the new substance that forms is called a _____.

6: *Chemical Bonding*

Did someone say that elements *react* with each other? What does this mean? Consider a room full of powerful magnets. Will these magnets be satisfied to stay separate? Certainly not. They will react with the other magnets by flying together. This togetherness represents a lower potential energy than separateness does. On the other hand, consider the magnet in the center of the stack in the Figure. It will have much less of a tendency to go seeking other magnets, because its "desire" for partners has been fulfilled by its companions. The same kind of attraction exists between elements. The attraction is not magnetic, however; it is electric.

For a moment, let's think back to our example of the ball held above the Earth. Like the magnet in a room full of magnets, this ball is in a condition of high potential energy. Letting the ball drop, or letting the magnet interact with other magnets, brings it to a condition of lower potential energy.

Nature likes for atoms to have certain numbers of electrons around them. Atoms having more or fewer electrons than nature prefers will be dissatisfied to stay as they are. Wherever pure elements are present, the single atoms are not in their condition of lowest potential energy. These atoms will naturally be attracted to other atoms and rearrange themselves to achieve a condition of lower potential energy. If they don't have the right number of electrons to make a low-energy package, the atoms will swipe electrons, give up electrons, or share electrons to arrive at a more stable, low-energy condition.

This rather large block of magnets is intended to illustrate a situation of low potential energy. All of the magnets in this stack are completely content with their arrangement. There is no stress among them to cause them to rearrange. This is similar to the situation with atoms that have had opportunity to react with the other atoms around them. They take on a low-energy condition that minimizes the stresses felt by particular atoms.

There are relatively few atoms that are satisfied with the number of electrons they have. (How sad.) All of those self-satisfied atoms are found in the right-hand column of the periodic table, and are known as the **noble gases**. The noble gases don't react with other elements because they are satisfied with the number of electrons they have. They have no need to share, steal or give away electrons. Another way of thinking of the noble gases is that they exist in a condition of low potential energy, so they have no tendency to fall to a lower level. Atoms of the other elements look for other atoms with whom they can swap and share.

Let's say that Knuckles Chlorine, the famous electron thief, goes about looking for electrons to steal. He comes across an electron-rich Samantha Sodium atom wearing that extra electron around her neck. Knuckles can't resist. He whizzes over to Sammy and snatches away her electron. Little does Chlorine notice that, when he takes the electron away from Sodium, she picks up an irresistible positive charge, because now she has one too many protons for her number of electrons. At the same time the thief is swiping away that electron, he is taking on the extra negative charge he stole from Sodium. All at once, Sodium and Chlorine find that they have this irresistible attraction to each other. The positive charge of Sodium attracts the negative charge of Chlorine. Now that each has satisfied the other's electron needs and they have this attraction, Sodium and Chlorine will remain together, happily ever after, as table salt (sodium chloride)!

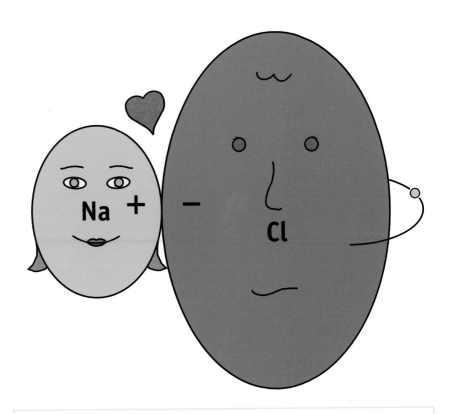

Like the other Group 1A elements, sodium has an electron that is loosely attached. Chlorine, being a group 7A element, would like to acquire ("steal") an electron. A complete atom of an element has the same number of protons as it has electrons. When elements react, one atom often loses an electron that is gained by another. Sodium loses an electron, so its charge becomes positive. Chlorine gains that electron, so its charge becomes negative. These opposite charges make sodium and chlorine attractive to each other, so they stick together or bond *to one another.*

This story illustrates the first type of **chemical bonding**, called **ionic bonding** [ī-ON-ik]. When sodium loses an electron and takes on a positive charge, it is called a **cation** [KAT-ī-on]. When chlorine gains an electron and takes on a negative charge, it is called an **anion** [AN-ī-on]. The anion and cation attract each other and remain bound together by their electric attraction. Notice that when an anion is bound to a cation, its name changes from "-ine" to "-ide." "Chlorine" becomes "chloride" when it reacts with another chemical.

CHEMISTRY

Some thieves, when they swipe away an electron, find that they are trying to steal from another thief. When two chlorine atoms try to steal from each other, neither gives up an electron; they find that it's just better to share. (Isn't that sweet?) This is the second type of bonding, called **covalent** [kō-VĀ-lent] **bonding**. Covalent bonding results when each atom donates an electron to be shared between them. So each bond represents a pair of shared electrons. This type of bond is many times stronger than an ionic bond.

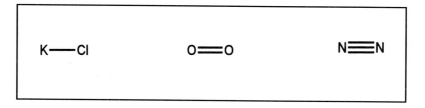

Chemical bonds can be single (as in potassium chloride), double (as in dioxygen) or triple (as in dinitrogen). The more bonds there are between two atoms the more tightly those atoms are held together and the more energy is released if the bonds are broken.

When electrons are shared, they take on a new path of motion around the two atoms. If the two sharing atoms are the same (as in the example of dichlorine) the electrons stay with each atom about the same period of time. If they are different (as when chlorine shares with sodium), one atom will tend to hold the electrons somewhat longer than the other. This will make the new molecule **polar**, having a bit of a negative charge on the end that keeps the electrons longer, and a bit of a positive charge on the end that doesn't keep the electrons as long.

Exercises:

1. Potassium fluoride is formed by an attraction between a potassium cation and a fluoride anion. Is this an example of covalent or ionic bonding?

2. What is the natural force of attraction that causes potassium and fluoride to stick together? Is it gravitation, electromagnetism or nuclear attraction?

3. An atom of oxygen bonds with two atoms of hydrogen to form dihydrogen oxide (water). In forming this bond, oxygen shares one electron with each atom of hydrogen and each hydrogen shares its one electron with the oxygen. Is this an example of covalent or ionic bonding?

4. Which would require less energy to break: the bond of a potassium fluoride molecule or the bond of a water molecule?

5. Two atoms of chlorine are identical. Would a molecule of dichlorine (two atoms of chlorine covalently bound) be polar or non-polar?

CHEMISTRY

7: *Properties of Elements*

For a long time, scientists just arranged elements in order of their number of protons. This makes a nice, neat, long, beautiful column of elements. It's much prettier, in fact, than the periodic table. But judge not according to the appearance. The periodic table has an inner beauty that the list of elements never had. The groups of elements in different columns of the periodic table *act* alike. They react similarly. By studying the periodic table you can learn what elements are likely to react with others. First, let's just take a look at th periodic table and get to know it a little better. Because elements in a given column act alike, they are given a group name and group number.

Figure 1 is a periodic table showing the names and numbers of the groups (in columns) of elements. The group 1A elements are often called the **alkali metals**. As pure elements they appear white and mushy, so they are not what we generally think of when we say metal. (We usually think of hard and shiny, don't we?) They are also extremely reactive, readily forming chemical bonds with other elements. We'll talk about this more in the next section. In fact, alkali metals are so reactive that they must be stored in oil to keep them from reacting with moisture in the air.

1A	2A	3B	4B	5B	6B	7B	8B			1B	2B	3A	4A	5A	6A	7A	8A
H																H	He
Li	Be											B	C	N	O	F	Ne
Na	Mg											Al	Si	P	S	Cl	Ar
K	Ca	Sc	Ti	V	Cr	Mn	Fe	Co	Ni	Cu	Zn	Ga	Ge	As	Se	Br	Kr
Rb	Sr	Y	Zr	Nb	Mo	Tc	Ru	Rh	Pd	Ag	Cd	In	Sn	Sb	Te	I	Xe
Cs	Ba	La	Hf	Ta	W	Re	Os	Ir	Pt	Au	Hg	Tl	Pb	Bi	Po	At	Rn
Fr	Ra	Ac	Rf	Db	Sg	Bh	Hs	Mt									

Ce	Pr	Nd	Pm	Sm	Eu	Gd	Tb	Dy	Ho	Er	Tm	Yb	Lu
Th	Pa	U	Np	Pu	Am	Cm	Bk	Cf	Es	Fm	Md	No	Lr

The periodic table of the elements shows the elements in columns called groups. *These group members tend to act alike and have group names to identify them.*

CHEMISTRY

The group 2A elements are often called the **alkaline earth metals**. They are less reactive than the alkali metals. Compounds containing these elements are abundant in the earth.

The elements in B groups are called the **transition metals**. They are so called because they form the "transition" (meaning "crossover") from the left side of the table to the right side of the table. These are the elements that look more like what we commonly call "metals." They don't react as readily as the metals in the A columns, and they are more likely to form colored compounds, so many pigments are derived from compounds of the transition metals. For example, copper forms blue and green compounds, iron forms yellow, red and orange compounds, cobalt forms red or purple compounds, and so on. These pigments are added to paints, inks, crayons, dyes and other products to give them their color.

The **post-transition elements** are in groups 3A through 7A. If the transition metals are the "crossover" elements, the post-transition elements are the "you-already-crossed-over" elements. The **halogens** (in group 7A), like the alkali metals, are highly reactive, forming compounds readily with a variety of other elements. One unique feature of this group of elements is that an atom of a halogen will react with another atom of the same kind to form a **diatomic molecule** ("two-atom") as shown below:

$$Cl + Cl \rightarrow Cl—Cl \qquad \text{(Chlorine gas is diatomic chlorine.)}$$

This is the way we write chemical reactions. We show the **reactants** (the substances that react with one another) on the left, with an arrow pointing to the **products** (the substances that result from the reaction) on the right. Cl is the symbol found in your periodic table for the element chlorine. The line between the product chlorine atoms shows that these two atoms are attached to each other by a chemical **bond**. We'll study this attachment in detail later. This diatomic chlorine may also be written as Cl_2 because the two Cl atoms are bonded together to form a molecule. It is no longer Cl and Cl, it is Cl—Cl or Cl_2.

Now back to our study of the table. Hydrogen is an oddball. It acts like a halogen by forming a diatomic molecule with another hydrogen atom. It reacts with other elements in ways similar to the halogens, too, so it is sometimes considered a halogen. However, it also has properties similar to the alkali metals. That's why hydrogen shows up twice on most periodic tables.

The series 8A elements are the **noble gases**. They are called noble because they don't react with other elements. They are called gases…well…because they are gases at natural Earth temperatures and pressures.

Note two extra rows of elements at the bottom of the table. These are labeled the **lanthanoid** and **actinoid series**. They are named this way because they act a lot like the elements from which they get their names: lanthanium (#57) and actinium (#89). Even though the elements in these two series have more and more protons as their atomic numbers increase, they all act the same. Because they all behave alike, we put them in a separate room together. After these elements are out of the way, the elements that follow them in the number series act more like we would expect. Moving these two series of elements out by themselves keeps our table looking much nicer and makes it more useful in helping us predict how the elements will act.

The lanthanoid series elements are also called the **rare earth metals** because they are rarely found in nature. These compounds have unique and useful properties, like giving the red color to our color television sets and forming compounds with "**superconducting**" capabilities that we have heard so much about lately with the invention of "superconducting supercolliders." These are tools used to study the physics of subatomic particles (the unstable particles that make up atoms).

All the metals in the actinoid series are radioactive. Only two of these, thorium and uranium, are found in significant amounts in nature. Uranium and plutonium are the two elements most often used in making nuclear weapons and in fueling nuclear reactors.

A few elements, being particularly valuable, have been the cause for excavation of ores. Gold, now slipping in value because of its abundance, caused a considerable ruckus in the 1800's in the U.S. The latest "rush" is for platinum and rarer elements.

Exercises:

Find the following elements in the periodic table, and give the group number and the group name for each:

1. potassium
2. fluorine
3. krypton
4. cadmium
5. radium

CHEMISTRY

8: *Then What Is a Metal?*

In a previous lesson we said that there are metals that don't look like what we usually think of as a metal. If a metal is not necessarily what people think it is, then what is it? Well, it's not as much a thing as it is a concept. Metals are elements that have the following properties:

1. They conduct electricity.
2. They conduct heat.
3. When polished, their surfaces reflect light.
4. They are **ductile** (stretchable) and **malleable** (shapeable).

Of course, some metals are better conductors than others, but all metals are much more conductive than non-metals. Some metals can be shaped more readily than others, but when you pound non-metals they tend to shatter rather than shape. The elements that are very **metallic** (having a lot of the characteristics of metals) are called metals; those that are non-metallic (having few or no characteristics of metals) are called **non-metals**; those that are somewhat metallic are called **metalloids**, meaning that they are "metal-like" in some ways. (Get used to hearing that "-oid" ending. It's used a

If a substance can be molded into different shapes it is said to be malleable. *If it can be stretched thin it is said to be* ductile. *Both of the items shown in the photographs are made of copper. Copper is an example of the malleability and ductility of the metals.*

lot in science. For example, something that is "ovoid"—an ovum being an egg—is "egg-like" in shape). The elements are shown in the diagram according to their type.

While you may not think there is much value in being a metalloid, these unusual elements are particularly useful because they are not really good conductors or really poor conductors of electricity. This quality gives them **semiconductor** status. You may recognize semiconductors as the stuff of transistors and computer chips.

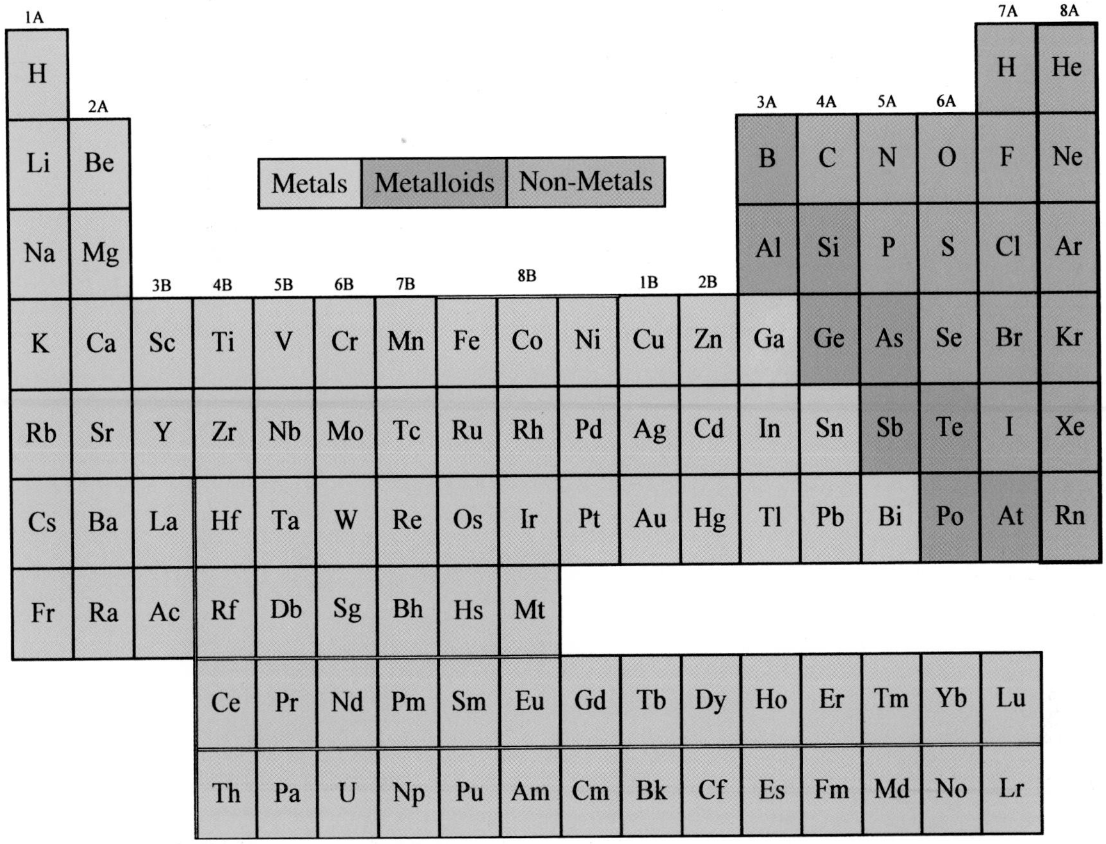

1A																7A	8A
H																H	He
	2A											3A	4A	5A	6A		
Li	Be				Metals	Metalloids	Non-Metals					B	C	N	O	F	Ne
Na	Mg	3B	4B	5B	6B	7B		8B		1B	2B	Al	Si	P	S	Cl	Ar
K	Ca	Sc	Ti	V	Cr	Mn	Fe	Co	Ni	Cu	Zn	Ga	Ge	As	Se	Br	Kr
Rb	Sr	Y	Zr	Nb	Mo	Tc	Ru	Rh	Pd	Ag	Cd	In	Sn	Sb	Te	I	Xe
Cs	Ba	La	Hf	Ta	W	Re	Os	Ir	Pt	Au	Hg	Tl	Pb	Bi	Po	At	Rn
Fr	Ra	Ac	Rf	Db	Sg	Bh	Hs	Mt									

	Ce	Pr	Nd	Pm	Sm	Eu	Gd	Tb	Dy	Ho	Er	Tm	Yb	Lu
	Th	Pa	U	Np	Pu	Am	Cm	Bk	Cf	Es	Fm	Md	No	Lr

Many of the transition metals are useful in industrial activities. For example, iron is the main element in steel, which explains why the largest steel-producing areas of the country tend to be those once rich in iron ore deposits, like northern Minnesota, Birmingham, Alabama, and Pittsburgh, Pennsylvania. Some transition metals are rare and attractive, so they are often worn as jewelry. Others are radioactive, so they are not! (Nobody wants to wear a plutonium earring!)

While many of the transition metals are necessary to life processes, others are toxic (or poisonous) to living things. In fact, some of the metals that are required at low concentrations to support life are toxic at higher concentrations. Some of the more common toxic "**heavy metals**" include copper, cadmium, silver, mercury and lead. Earlier in our industrial history, these metals were discovered to cause sickness and death in large numbers of people whose food or water supply was contaminated with them. Now, although occasional health problems arise, the food and water supplies in the U.S. are usually tested if there is suspicion of contamination with toxic substances. It is illegal to pollute our food and water sources with toxins. Company authorities who knowingly violate environmental laws can be imprisoned.

Unlike metals, non-metals cannot be pounded into shapes or stretched thin. Carbon is one example of a non-metallic element. This is what happens to carbon when you try to shape it!

Computer chips are made of semiconductor material.

9: *Molecular Weight*

We have already talked about the weight of individual atoms in atomic mass units, but now that we have seen atoms joining together into molecules, we have to talk about **molecular weight**. The molecular weight, that is, the weight of a molecule, is simply the added atomic mass units of all of the atoms that make up the molecule. Let's think for a minute about atoms as if they were large enough to see. Let's say chlorine is the size of an orange and hydrogen is the size of a grape. If we take toothpicks (but they have to be weightless toothpicks) and hook together one orange and one grape, what would be the weight of the compound we made? It would be the weight of the orange plus the weight of the grape. (DON'T include the toothpick.)

The fact that atoms are small doesn't mean that they don't have to play by nature's rules. If you add together one chlorine with one hydrogen you don't get something that weighs either more than the two or less than the two. You get something that weighs exactly the same as the two because it is the two. Get it?

Now, chlorine weighs 35 AMU and hydrogen weighs 1 AMU. How much does hydrogen chloride weigh? Thirty-six AMU plus a toothpick? You're hopeless! Only 36 AMU—no more, no less.

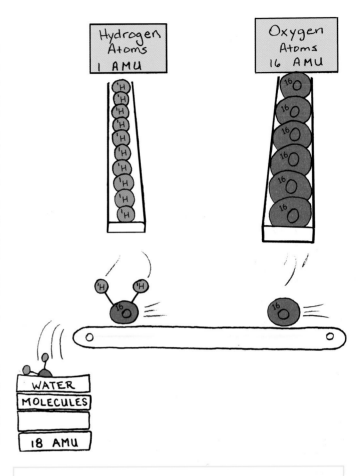

These molecules are being made by adding two hydrogen atoms, each having a mass of 1 AMU, to oxygen having a mass of 16 AMU. Together they make water. The mass of water is precisely that of the sum of the masses of the elements used to make it—18 AMU—no more, no less.

Exercises:

Use the periodic table to determine the molecular weight of each of the following in AMU:

1. KBr (called potassium bromide; has one atom of potassium and one atom of bromine)
2. H_2O (called dihydrogen oxide or water; has one oxygen atom and two atoms of hydrogen)
3. NaCl (called sodium chloride or table salt; has one atom of sodium and one atom of chlorine)
4. CH_4 (called methane; has one atom of carbon and four atoms of hydrogen)

CHEMISTRY

10: *How Can I Get a Reaction?*

There are so many elements! How can anyone predict which ones will react with which others? For a long time, early chemists did not know the answer to this question. They simply added substances together and observed what resulted. Although there is still much to learn, we now have a better understanding of reactions; we can even predict the outcome of some of them.

The group numbers of elements that will react with one another tend to add up to eight. Can I get a reaction by placing hydrogen (group 1A) with fluorine (group 7A)? Absolutely! This is how you show the reaction:

H + F → HF   One atom of hydrogen reacts with one atom of fluorine to make one molecule of hydrogen fluoride.

Will magnesium (group 2A) react with oxygen (group 6A)? Yes-sir-ee:

Mg + O → MgO   One atom of magnesium reacts with one atom of oxygen to make one molecule of magnesium oxide.

Will sodium (group 1A) react with sulfur (group 6A)? As you can see, the group numbers add up to only seven. But if you use two sodium atoms, the group numbers add up to eight. This reaction will take place as written below:

2 Na + S → Na$_2$S   Two atoms of sodium react with one atom of sulfur to make one molecule of disodium sulfide.

Na$_2$S is the way we show a single molecule made of two sodium atoms and one sulfur atom all bound together with chemical bonds.

YOU CAN'T PUT TWO SODIUM ATOMS INTO A REACTION AND GET ONLY ONE OUT! Anytime you put in two on one side, two have to come out on the other side. In this example, they both came out as part of the **product**, Na$_2$S. If we put in three sodium atoms, but only two of them react with sulfur, we will get an extra one back:

3 Na + S → Na$_2$S + Na   Three atoms of sodium in the presence of one atom of sulfur produce one molecule of disodium sulfide and one unreacted atom of sodium.

But if the group numbers have to add up to eight, what do the group 8 atoms react with? Remember, they are the noble gases; they don't react with anything:

Group 8 atoms don't react with anything $(8 + 0 = 8)$.
Group 7 atoms react with group 1 atoms $(7 + 1 = 8)$.
Group 6 atoms react with:
   one group 2 atom $(6 + 2 = 8)$, or
   two group 1 atoms $(6 + 1 + 1 = 8)$.
Group 5 atoms react with:
   one group 3 atom, or $(5 + 3 = 8)$, or
   one group 2 atom and one group 1 atom $(5 + 2 + 1 = 8)$, or
   three group 1 atoms $(5 + 1 + 1 + 1 = 8)$.

Obviously, there is more to the periodic table than meets the eye. If it allows you to predict chemical reactions, there must be some knowledge hidden there that you have not yet been told. In a couple of years you will learn about "electron orbital theory" and then it will all be clear to you. If you just can't wait, pick up a chemistry book at your local library, and take the electron orbital challenge!

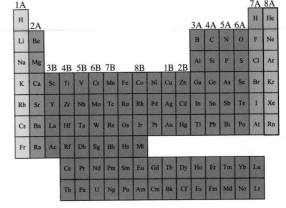

The periodic table is laid out in a way that roughly relates to the way elements react with one another. In general, the group numbers of reacting chemicals tend to add up to eight. The diagram illustrates the manner in which elements from the various groups combine.

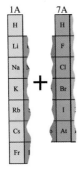   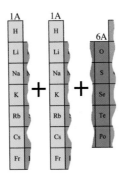   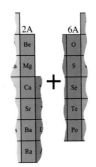   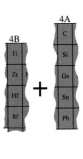

Exercises:
1. Would you predict that lithium and chlorine will react? If so, write the reaction equation.
2. Would you predict that strontium and sulfur will react? If so, write the reaction equation.

CHEMISTRY

11: *Reactions Between Compounds*

Up to now we have focused on reactions between elements, but the compounds that are formed from elements can also react with one another by swapping bonding partners. Why would they do this? Because they can reach a lower potential energy level by binding to a different partner, of course. For example:

$$NaOH + HCl \rightarrow NaCl + H_2O$$

One molecule of sodium hydroxide reacts with one molecule of hydrogen chloride (hydrochloric acid) to produce one molecule of sodium chloride (table salt) and one molecule of water.

The sodium from the sodium hydroxide swaps partners with the hydrogen in hydrogen chloride so that we get two new chemicals as products of the reaction. These products are sodium chloride (table salt) and dihydrogen oxide (water). Notice that we have taken two expensive chemical reactants and made some nearly worthless salt and water—not smart!

Look at the magnets in the photograph at the top. They look perfectly happy together. But wait! What will happen when a stronger magnet enters the picture? The loose magnet will fly to the stronger magnet, leaving the weaker one alone (bottom). This is the strongest attraction available to the loose magnet, so it takes it.

Although, on paper, this stuff looks really easy to do, *don't try any reactions of your own without proper guidance from a professional*. For instance, if you were to buy HCl and NaOH to do the reaction above, you would probably damage your lungs from breathing the hydrochloric acid vapors and burn yourself with the caustic sodium hydroxide. Then you would put your eyes out when the two chemicals violently bumped out of the beaker as you added them together. Don't worry, though; we will let you carry out some neat (but safe) reactions at home.

There are several rules to follow in writing chemical reactions. First, be sure to make the number of atoms on the right side of the equation match the number of atoms on the left side. For example, if there is one sodium atom on the left side, there must be one and only one on the right side. Second, in the names of compounds, the atoms in the lower numbered groups are usually written before their partners in higher groups. For example, H is written before I in HI, Li is written before Br in LiBr, and Mg is written before Cl in $MgCl_2$.

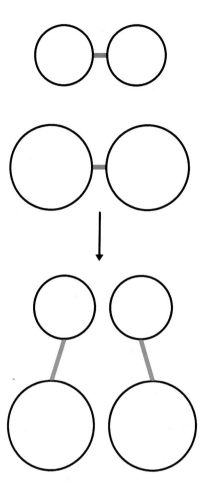

When atoms are bound together, they will be perfectly happy until another molecule comes along whose atoms offer stronger forces of attraction than they already have. The atoms in the molecules will recombine so that the attractions within the molecules represent the lowest-potential-energy arrangement of those atoms.

Exercises:
1. In the following equation, the number of chlorine atoms is different on the left side than on the right side:
$$CaS + MgCl_2 \rightarrow CaCl + MgS$$
Where would you add a "2" on the right side of the equation to get the chlorine atoms to "balance"? Pick the correct answer from the responses below:

    a. $CaS + MgCl_2 \rightarrow CaCl^2 + MgS$
    b. $CaS + MgCl_2 \rightarrow Ca2Cl + MgS$
    c. $CaS + MgCl_2 \rightarrow 2CaCl + MgS$
    d. $CaS + MgCl_2 \rightarrow CaCl_2 + MgS$

2. Please complete the following reaction equations:

$$LiF + KBr \rightarrow$$
$$MgBr_2 + CaO \rightarrow$$

12: *Atomic Gangs*

Atoms sometimes hang out in groups with other atoms with which they are comfortable. These groupings of atoms like each other so much that they begin to act as though they were a new element. They behave differently when they are together than they do when they are alone. As implied by their name, these **polyatomic ions** are groups of several atoms that carry an electric charge. They need special attention because they are such a common part of chemistry. Most of the substances people recognize contain these special groups of atoms. The following table lists several and gives their charges.

TABLE: POLYATOMIC IONS AND THEIR CHARGES			
1+	**1-**	**2-**	**3-**
ammonium (NH_4^+)	bicarbonate (HCO_3^-)	carbonate (CO_3^{2-})	phosphate (PO_4^{3-})
	chlorate (ClO_3^-)	chromate (CrO_4^{2-})	
	cyanate (OCN^-)	sulfate (SO_4^{2-})	
	hypochlorite ($HOCl^-$)		
	iodate (IO_3^-)		
	nitrate (NO_3^-)		
	nitrite (NO_2^-)		
	perchlorate (ClO_4^-)		
	permanganate (MnO_4^-)		
	sulfite (SO_3^-)		

By the charges of these groups, you can tell what ions from the table of elements they will form bonds with. For example, a single ammonium (1+) group will react with a single chloride (1-) ion (as might come from dissolving sodium chloride in water) to form ammonium chloride. Ammonium will react with any of the polyatomic ions in the 1- column of the table above as well. Two ammonium groups will also react with a single ion from the 2- column. For example:

$$2\ NH_4^+ + SO_4^{2-} \rightarrow (NH_4)_2SO_4$$

Two ammonium groups (each having a single positive charge) will combine with a single sulfate group (having a double negative charge) to form diammonium sulfate.

See? The two ammonium ions together have just the right amount of positive charge to match the negative charge of the one sulfate ion, so they are attracted to one another. Notice how we show two ammonium ions that are part of the same molecule in $(NH_4)_2SO_4$. To write $N_2H_8SO_4$ would not accurately represent the way these ions exist in nature, although the number of atoms would be correct. The atoms in polyatomic ions actually remain in their groups, even though they are bonded to another ion. (See the diagram.)

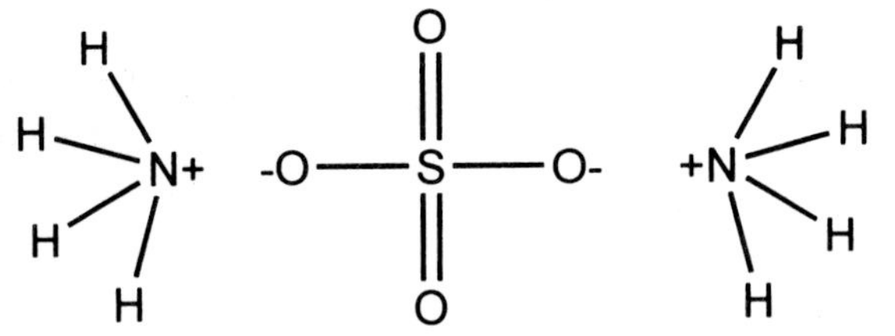

These polyatomic ions are shown the way they normally exist: ammonium ($NH_4{}^+$) and sulfate ($SO_4{}^{2-}$). Because of their opposite charges, these ions would be drawn together to form $(NH_4)_2SO_4$.

Exercises:

1. How many ammonium groups would it take to balance the charge of a single carbonate group?

2. Write the chemical formula for ammonium carbonate.

3. Where does the "2" go in the following equation if it is to be properly written?

    a. $2 H^+ + SO_4{}^{2-} \rightarrow H^2SO_4$

    b. $2 H^+ + SO_4{}^{2-} \rightarrow H_2SO_4$

    c. $2 H^+ + SO_4{}^{2-} \rightarrow 2 HSO_4$

    d. $2 H^+ + SO_4{}^{2-} \rightarrow H(SO_4)_2$

4. Complete the following reaction equation:

    $3 Na^+ + PO_4{}^{3-} \rightarrow$

13: *Why Do We Care about Chemical Reactions Anyway?*

Everyone knows that you can't make anything new or improve on anything unless you understand how things are put together. Almost everything in the world is made of compounds. If you understand compounds, then you understand the building blocks of the universe. Why do we care? If you have something in your water that tastes funny, whom do you ask about it—an accountant? No, you ask a chemist! If you want a new kind of glue that doesn't stick the potato chip bag together so tightly, whom do you ask—a plumber? No, you ask a chemist. Chemists know what chemicals to add together to change the properties of glue. So whom do you call if your refrigerator stops working? A refrigeration guy. Ah, but if you want to know *how* Freon 12 makes your refrigerator cool down, ask a chemist. Better yet, learn the chemistry yourself, and you can tell the refrigeration guy.

These are all examples of chemical reactions. They are the tools of medical technicians who do blood chemistry, chemical synthesists who make computer chips, biochemists who understand the chemical basis of plant growth, petroleum chemists who formulate textiles for carpets, couches and clothing, and geochemists who study the hot gases belched out by volcanoes when they erupt. The breakdown of food in your digestive tract, the transmission of signals to your brain when you cut your finger, and the high fever when you get sick are all the results of chemical reactions. Some of these reactions are so complex that it has taken entire careers to work out just a small part of a reaction sequence. To the wise, knowledge is valuable, and in chemistry there is much to be known. (But beware! To the foolish, knowledge is a snare.)

Can't somebody make an adhesive that's just the right strength for a potato chip bag?

Exercise:

As soon as you get out of bed in the morning, you take a deep breath of air. That's chemistry! Next you put on your clothes made of cotton, polyester, rayon and other fibers. Add three activities to this list of things you do that involve chemistry.

14: *Carbon Chemistry*

As we have said, carbon chemistry forms the chemical basis of life. How so? Because carbon *loves* to share its electrons. Carbon atoms bond readily with other carbon atoms, and since each atom has four electrons that like to bond with other chemicals, each carbon can bond with up to four other atoms that are seeking an electron or seeking to provide an electron, including other carbon atoms. Because carbon can bond with carbon and still have room to bond with three others, it can make long and branching chains. Carbon can also make double bonds and triple bonds for added bond strength.

Diagram 1	Diagram 2	Diagram 3

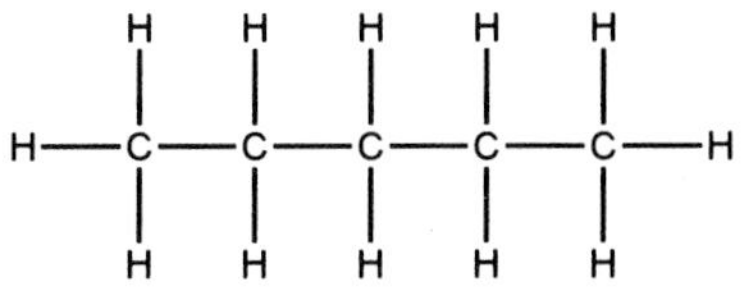

An alkane is a straight, single-bonded carbon chain completely surrounded by hydrogen atoms.

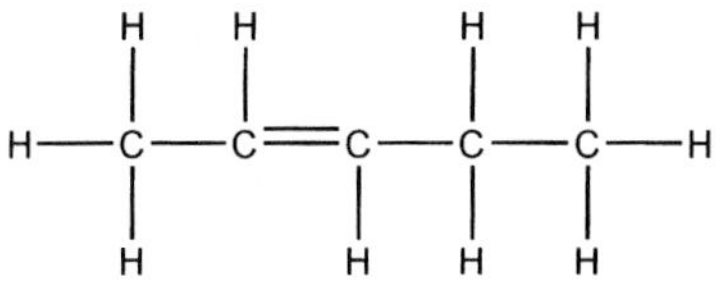

An alkene has at least one double bond in its structure.

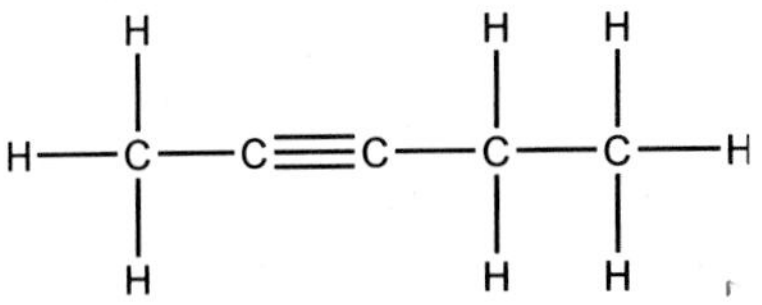

An alkyne has at least one triple bond in its structure.

Diagram 4

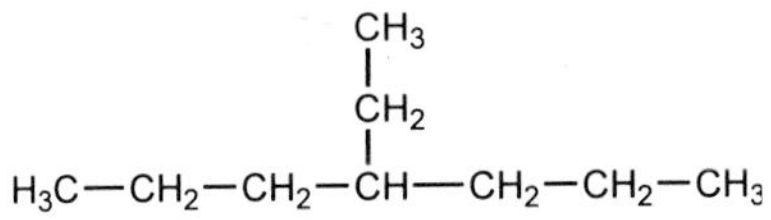

Diagram 5

A branched aliphatic molecule is a molecule having at least one carbon atom that is bonded to either three or four other carbon atoms making the chain look as though it has a branch growing from it.

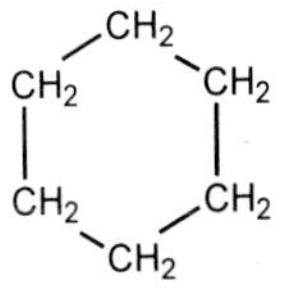

A cycloaliphatic molecule takes on the shape of a circle.

For now, it's not important that you remember the names of these molecules (unless you really want to sound smart). But notice the different forms that carbon compounds can assume depending on how the carbon atoms are arranged and bound together. This unique property of carbon (without which life would be impossible) makes carbon chemistry fascinatingly complex.

CHEMISTRY

The molecules that make up living things are the largest, most complex molecules. They are not only complex in their structure, but also in the things that they do (their **function**). This lesson introduces us to a large branch of chemistry called **organic chemistry** [or-GAN-ik], or carbon chemistry.

In this lesson you will see diagrams of lots of different kinds of molecules made from carbon and hydrogen. Don't try to learn all their names right now. Just try to enjoy the different shapes that molecules can take on when carbon does its thing.

The simplest form of organic molecules, called **aliphatic hydrocarbons** [al-i-FAT-ik], are made up of straight carbon chains of different lengths. If all of these carbons are connected by single bonds, the molecule is called an **alkane**. (See Diagram 1.) Because their chains make a straight line, they are called **linear alkanes**. They are named according to the number of carbons in their chains. These compounds are commonly found in petroleum deposits. If there is at least one double bond in their structure, molecules are called **alkenes**. (See Diagram 2.) If there is at least one triple bond in their structure, they are called **alkynes**. (See Diagram 3.)

But not all organic molecules involve straight chains of carbon atoms. Next in complexity are the **branched aliphatic** compounds. (See Diagram 4.) These are chains that branch off. Notice that we have simplified the drawing by not putting in all of those carbon-hydrogen bonds. We simply show the hydrogen atoms next to the carbon atoms to which they are bonded. Next come the **cycloaliphatic** molecules (see Diagram 5) that make loops by connecting the end of the chain with the beginning of the chain. Notice that the bonds which are not connected to other carbon atoms are connected to hydrogen atoms. Since hydrogen atoms have only one electron to share, connection to a hydrogen atom stops the carbon chain from growing any farther in that direction. These compounds that are made up of only hydrogen and carbon are generally referred to as hydrocarbons. (Big deal.)

15: *Fueling Reactions*

Hydrocarbons make good fuels because they react easily with oxygen in the air to release energy. Here is an example of a simple fueling reaction:

$$C_7H_{16} + 11\ O_2 \rightarrow 7\ CO_2 + 8\ H_2O$$

In this case, a single molecule of heptane reacts with oxygen to form carbon dioxide and water. This is the most common reaction in the burning of gasoline to fuel an automobile.

Petroleum oil (crude oil) which is pumped from the earth is made up of thousands of different hydrocarbons. After being pumped, the oil is shipped to a **petroleum refinery**. At the refinery, the oil is emptied into the bottom of a tall tower. The oil is warmed until the smaller molecules begin to boil away. As they evaporate, they are condensed by cooling and then collected in a tank. When all of those light compounds have been collected, the temperature of the oil is raised again, and the larger compounds with higher boiling points are collected. In this way the boiling points of the different compounds are used to separate them into groups called **fractions**. In general, the larger the hydrocarbon molecules, the higher their boiling point, so compounds can be roughly separated according to size by such gradual heating to higher and higher temperatures. This process for separating petro-

This is a petroleum refinery where crude oil is separated into different fuel fractions by distillation (or "cracking"). Notice the tall structures in the picture. These are cracking towers. Do you think you would recognize one of these if you saw it along the highway? Do you have one in a city near your home? Why not call and ask for a guided tour?

CHEMISTRY

leum is called fractional distillation or "cracking." The tall tower that is used to break up the oil into its fractions is called a cracking tower. If you learn to recognize a cracking tower you will know a petroleum refinery when you see one.

The different fractions of petroleum are used for different purposes. The light compounds (up to about four carbon atoms per molecule) are used as fuel gases. **Gasoline** is made up of compounds from 5 to 10 carbon atoms which boil out of petroleum at temperatures from about 40 to 200°C. **Kerosene** is the fraction that boils from about 200 to 300°C. It has carbon chain lengths mostly in the 11 to 18 range and is used for jet fuel and heating fuel in kerosene heaters. Between approximately 300 and 400°C, **diesel fuel** and light lubricating oils boil off. Their chains are generally 15 to 25 carbons long. Heavier oils, like **motor oil**, come off at above 400°C. When the cracking process is complete, there remains an ugly black scum at the bottom of the cracking tank that cannot be readily boiled off. This scum is called **asphalt**, and we pave our roads with it!

There are many other petroleum compounds that we use in day-to-day life. **Paraffin** wax is made up of purified long-chain hydrocarbons, and **petroleum jelly** (petrolatum) is a mixture of liquid and solid hydrocarbons.

The lighter a petroleum fuel is, the more reactive it tends to be. That's why gas leaks are dangerous and gasoline is so explosive. Don't come near gasoline with a flame or a spark. The vapors around gasoline are even more explosive than the gasoline itself. Methane is CH_4—the simplest of all hydrocarbons. It is the main compound in **natural gas**, which is used to fuel furnaces, ovens, water heaters and clothes dryers. Although methane has no odor, smelly compounds are added to methane so that leaks are easy to detect.

When fuels don't burn completely, we say that the reaction is **inefficient**. It may be that the fuel is not exposed to oxygen very well and the flame is smothered. It may be that the type of fuel being burned is not burned completely. These inefficient fuels can cause a number of problems besides just the loss of heat that might have come from them. Instead of generating only CO_2 and H_2O, these reactions also produce a small amount of carbon monoxide, or CO. "Monoxide" means "one oxygen"; the carbon monoxide molecule combines a carbon atom with only "one oxygen." Nearly all fueling reactions produce some CO, but automobiles now have **catalytic converters** that help the automobile convert this compound to CO_2. The danger of CO is that it binds tightly to our blood and does not allow oxygen to get in. If we're exposed to enough CO, it will suffocate us, even in the presence of plenty of oxygen. Anyone who burns fuel in his home—whether it's fuel oil (including kerosene), natural gas, liquid petroleum (also called LP gas, consisting mostly of ethane and propane), or wood—would be wise to buy a carbon monoxide detector.

Exercises:

1. Gasoline is fed to a car as a liquid and is burned (reacted with oxygen) in the carburetor. How does it leave the car?

2. Sometimes people who sleep in a small enclosed room with a kerosene heater suffocate. Why?

3. One of the products of these fueling reactions is water. Why do you suppose you can see the exhaust on a car better on a cold day than on a warm day?

16: *People Chemistry*

People and animals use fuel, but not petroleum fuel. ("I'd like to order a nice cold glass of unleaded with two straws…to go, please!") The two main types of fuel molecules used by people and animals are **sugars** and **fats**. ("I'd like to order a nice cold glass of sugar and fat—otherwise known as a milkshake—with two straws—with two straws…to go, please!") Once again, these molecules are reacted with oxygen to form carbon dioxide and water. The energy that comes from these reactions can be used for growth and other activities. Just as with other fueling reactions, sugars and fats react with oxygen to generate heat. This heat allows our bodies to stay warm on the inside, even in cold weather. Because these reactions require oxygen, every animal has some way of getting oxygen to the places throughout its body where the reactions take place. As you know, all fueling reactions produce a lot of carbon dioxide, so animals also have a way of getting rid of the carbon dioxide.

At your age, it's important that you get the reactants you need for growth. These come in the form of food and good nutrition. You may grow, but you will not be put together right if you do not get these chemicals. In our country many people get too much of the wrong things. Energy molecules (sugars and fats) go in faster than they can be used, so the body stores them for later use. If they are never used, the body's storage centers (fat cells) get bigger and bigger. You then have to stop taking in so much of these fueling molecules in order for your body to use up the ones it has stored. If you don't eat right and don't exercise, you won't be put together right. Not being built right can take years off your life and make your later life difficult.

In places where food is scarce, people can be starved. People who live with much less food can survive a few weeks of starvation when food becomes scarce. In fact, those people can be quite healthy. But if a person goes for weeks on end without food, he runs a great risk of doing irreversible damage to his body. When people starve, they use up all of their fuel molecules, and the body starts consuming itself, beginning with the less vital parts and ending up with the most vital ones.

The kind of starvation that occurs in countries where food is scarce is not to be confused with the type of starvation that people in this country put

The fuel on the left is gasoline. Gasoline is automobile fuel. Don't drink it or you will die. The fuel on the right is a milkshake. A milkshake is people fuel. Drink it.

themselves through if they have an eating disorder. Some people, most often young women, eat too much, then don't eat anything at all. This trains the body to accumulate fat during the time when food is available, and makes it difficult to lose weight without starving. People who have this problem should be under a physician's care. Many young women lose their lives to it.

Hunger is complex because it responds to many influences. It is a basic tool for knowing when to eat, but it can also lead you to eat too much if food is readily available. If a person is overweight, he should be on a program set by his nutrition specialist to lose weight. You should not think that you need to eat whenever you get hungry. Hunger pains come in cycles that are determined by eating patterns. If you eat too often or too much, you will also get hungry too often and eat too much. The only way to break this cycle is through self-discipline.

In the Bible, fasting was used as a way of demonstrating that a person had power over his own will, especially if he was preparing for an important event. If he could deprive himself of food, then he could say "No!" to his body and would be well prepared for some kind of trial or test. There are people who fast for a certain period of time for religious reasons to exercise self-control. This is fine for adults. But fasting is not a good method for losing weight. Once a person starts eating again, his body will put away as much as it can into the fat reserves to store it for the next time food is unavailable.

This flask has a layer of diesel fuel floating on water. But what's that slimy stuff in the middle? That's a bacterial mat. The bacteria grew there using the diesel fuel for food. Why can't we use diesel fuel for food? Because we don't have the enzymes needed to break it down, and because our stomachs are not lined with the right kind of slime to protect

Exercises:
1. Older Chinese people tend to be short, while younger ones tend to be tall. What do you suppose has happened in China in the last 40 years?
2. Should teenagers often go for days without eating?
3. Should teenagers restrict themselves in eating?

17: *More People Chemistry*

The following is a simplified equation of what happens to the food we take in:

$$\text{Fuel Molecules} + \text{Oxygen} \rightarrow \text{Carbon Dioxide} + \text{Energy} + \text{Body Mass} + \text{Waste}$$

When we eat, the body consumes the fuel molecules from food; if we don't eat, the body will consume stored fat and starch. If we want to lose weight, we eat less and exercise. That forces the body to take some of that extra body mass and use it as fuel. It gets converted to carbon dioxide and water, and it leaves the body.

This gal is notorious for overeating and storing up the extra fuel as fat. She might not be this way if she would stay busier.

One of the needed reactants is oxygen. **Aerobic** ("in oxygen") exercise emphasizes the need for oxygen to burn fat. This is, in fact, an important part of the energy equation. If we don't get enough oxygen when we exercise, we won't burn fat as efficiently. However, our body has natural ways of seeing that we don't get too much or too little oxygen.

How much exercise a person gets determines how fast those stored molecules are used. When you need more energy to do work, fat cells give up some of their excess fuel to produce energy. Because fat is a good fuel, a little goes a long way. When a person has a lot of extra fat, getting rid of it takes a lot of patience and self-discipline. It's important for people to understand this basic chemistry lesson. Don't think you can cheat the system. Please exercise good self-discipline now in order to live a longer, happier life. Work with your parents, and, once a year, with your doctor or nutrition specialist to determine good nutrition and weight goals *for you*. (Those goals are different for different people.) Exercise regularly, and develop godly character to be the best you can be in every respect.

As you see in the equation, one of the products of the body's fueling reaction is energy. Since energy is not used by any machine with 100% efficiency, heat is always one form of energy that is released from this reaction. That's good for us because this heat allows our bodies to maintain a constant temperature. If you get too cold, your body begins to shiver in order to generate heat. Shivering is just an unnecessary motion in your muscles which burns fuel and produces heat. If you are cold, the best way to warm up is to keep moving. Lots of clothes hold body heat in, but if you are still, your body will not produce much heat to hold in.

Exercises:

1. If you could stop eating but could continue to burn energy and produce waste at a normal rate, what would happen to your body weight?

2. If you eat at the same rate and continue to produce the same amount of waste, but you increase the amount of exercise you get (so that you require more energy), what will happen to your body mass?

3. Why do you get hot when you get plenty of good exercise?

18: *The Molecules of Life—Nucleic Acids*

A fascinating and rapidly growing area of science is the chemistry of living things called **biochemistry** ("life" + "chemistry"). Compared to the simple chemistry we have studied to this point, biochemistry is complex because the molecules of living things tend to be extremely large and complex. The chemistry of living things is unique. While chemicals seem to be just lying out there in great chemical deposits in the earth, having no particular function of their own, molecules in living systems have a specific function—a specific *reason* for existing, if you will.

These so-called **biomolecules** generally fall into one of a few classes. First, **nucleic** [noo-KLĒ-ik] **acids** are the information carriers of

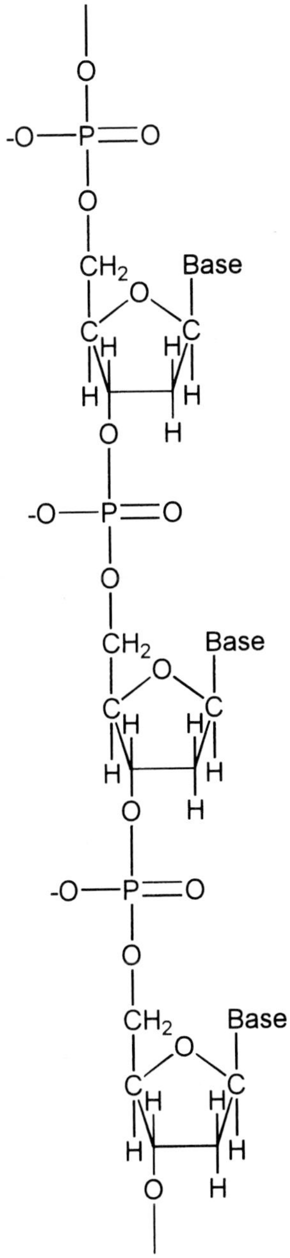

Adenine

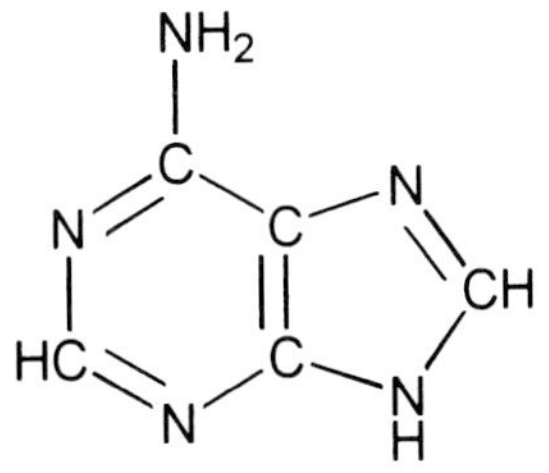

Guanine

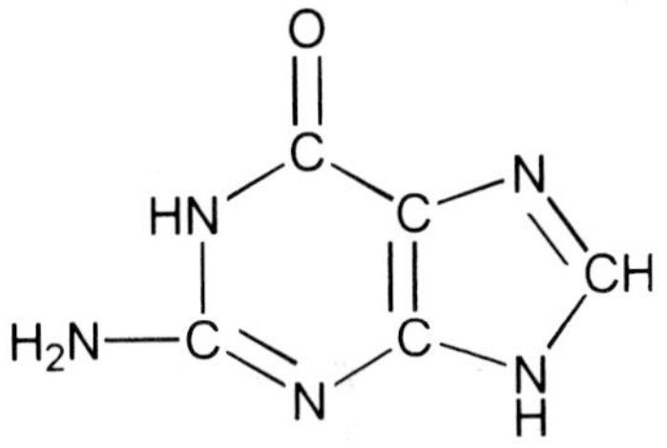

Thymine

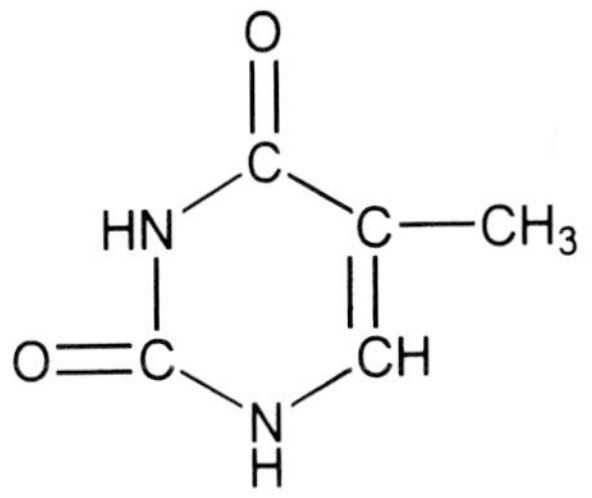

Cytosine

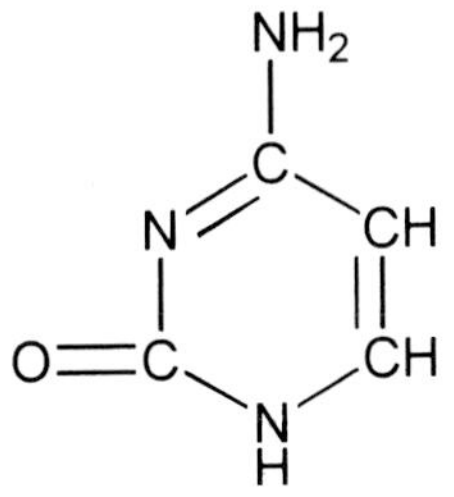

On the left is the nucleic acid backbone made of deoxyribose sugars linked together with phosphate (PO₄) groups. Everywhere the word "base" appears on the molecule, one of the four nucleotide bases (shown on the right) is substituted. The sequence of nucleotide bases forms the genetic code that directs all of the cell's activities.

living things. They are made of a sequence of smaller molecules linked together to form a long chain. This sequence carries information in the form of a code that the body can decode and use.

There are two major types of nucleic acids. **Deoxyribose** [dē-OX-ē-RĪ-bōs] **nucleic acid (DNA)** carries a code which specifies every physical aspect of a living thing, including a range of heights and weights, eye, hair and skin color, and approximate length of life. We call this the **genetic code**. Not only humans, but all animals, plants, and even bacteria have their own codes which specify their every characteristic passed to them from their parents.

The Diagram on the previous page shows the structure of a short piece of a DNA chain made of deoxyribose sugar molecules linked together by phosphate (PO_4) groups. Where the word "Base" is seen on the main chain, one of the four **bases** ("fundamental molecules") on the right-hand side of the Diagram would be found. It is the exact order of those bases on the chain which makes up the code. Bases attract other bases, so two strands of DNA attract each other. When they do, the bases pair off into **base pairs**. In base pairs, adenine is always attracted to thymine, and cytosine is always attracted to guanine, so you can be sure that if you know the sequence of bases on one strand of DNA, you can figure out the sequence of bases on its partner. Everywhere there is an adenine molecule on one strand, you will find a thymine molecule on its partner, and so on.

Scientists are now not only coming to a greater understanding of this chemistry, but are beginning to learn to modify the genetic code to some extent as well. Using a combination of chemistry and biology called **molecular biology**, they have begun to treat and to prevent certain diseases carried in this code. The discipline of molecular biology is also referred to as "**genetic engineering**."

The second type of nucleic acid is **ribose nucleic acid (RNA)**. RNA is used by living things to copy the DNA code and translate it for the building of the tiny machines that carry out all of the body functions. We will learn more about these little machines, called **proteins**, in the next lesson. In future lessons, we will also learn more about the importance of nucleic acid molecules to life, as we learn exactly what functions they perform within living things.

Exercises:

1. What molecules are linked together to form nucleic acids?
2. What do nucleic acids do?

19: *The Molecules of Life—Proteins*

Along with nucleic acids that we learned about in the last lesson, a second important group of biomolecules is called **proteins**. Just as nucleic acids are chains of bases, proteins are chains of **amino acids**. Unlike nucleic acids, which are long sequences of the four bases, proteins are made from an alphabet of over 20 amino acids. This makes them complex in structure and gives them a wide range of chemical capabilities. A short segment of a protein (called a **peptide**) is shown in the Diagram on the following page. This peptide contains only 10 amino acids. A typical protein might have several hundred to a few thousand amino acids and have a molecular weight of several tens of thousands to over a million atomic mass units.

These immensely complex structures give proteins a wide range of chemical properties, so they are useful for a wide range of functions. Proteins can be divided into two major classes. One of these is the class called **structural proteins**. These are chemicals which may be used to build bodies in the same way bricks are used to build buildings. These large, strong molecules are cemented together to make structures such as hair and fingernails. They are found throughout the body in places where strength and support, in addition to flexibility, are needed. One example of a structural protein which is found in abundance in the human body is **collagen** [KOL-luh-jen]. This protein gives the stretchy support to many of the body's internal structures.

The second class of proteins is the **enzymes** [EN-zimz]. These are the tiny machines which we mentioned in the last lesson. They are used for building and tearing down structures inside the body. Enzymes actually take individual nucleic acids and link them together like Tinker Toys to make DNA and RNA. Enzymes have so many functions in the body that it would take a book larger than this one to describe all of the ones we know, and there are many more that we don't know.

A specialized group of enzymes is the **oxidative enzymes**. These carry out the fueling reactions about which we've said so much. Remember when we said that sugars do not burn very nicely? Well, enzymes break apart the bonds in sugars one by one and efficiently capture the energy which is released. That energy is used for fueling all of the body's activities.

As we have said, one of the most striking things about biomolecules is that, compared to other molecules in the world, they are extremely large and complex. For example, while the molecular weight of water is 18 atomic mass units, the molecular weight of a typical protein may be 80,000 atomic mass units. A really large protein may weigh millions of atomic mass units. If these were just random mixtures of chemicals, they would not function at all. But proteins are far from random; they are minute but complex machines, designed with amazing precision. In fact, each tiny amino acid unit is vital to the function of every kind of protein. Changing only one of the thousands in the chain can render the protein useless.

One of the great problems of evolutionary theory is that these complex proteins must be formed precisely in order to work. DNA is required to make them this way, but proteins are required to assemble DNA precisely. How could these two molecules have come about by random assembly of chemicals if each is required before the other can be formed? Evolutionists have been unable to offer satisfying answers to this question.

Exercises:
1. What molecules are linked together to form proteins?
2. What do proteins do?

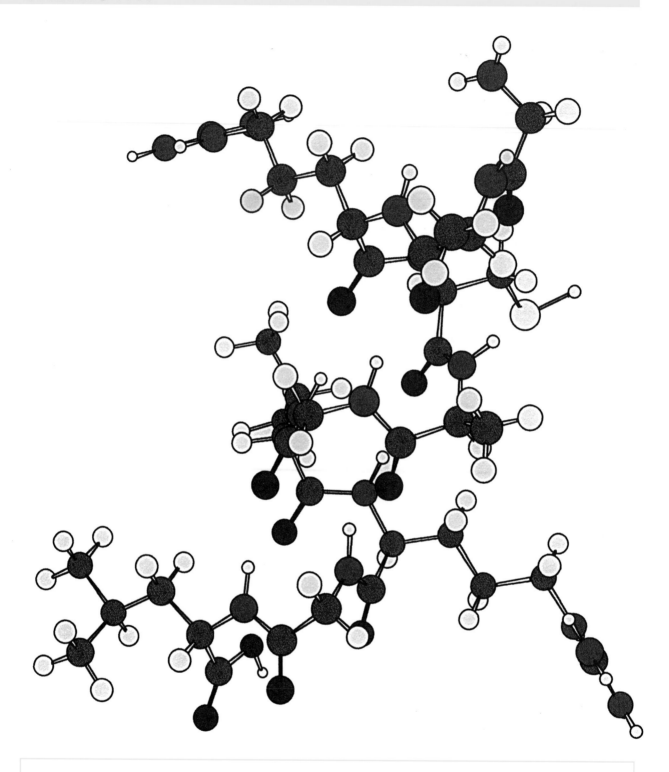

This is the structure of a peptide (portion of a protein molecule) just 10 amino acid molecules long. Just imagine how complex a whole protein would be if it had 3,000 amino acid molecules making up its structure.

20: *The Molecules of Life—Polysaccharides*

A third group of biomolecules is the **polysaccharides** [pol-i-SAK-kuh-rīdz] ("many" + "sugars"). These chains of **sugar** molecules are used for two purposes: storage and structure.

Since cells use sugars for food, polysaccharides make good compact storage materials to provide fuel during times when food is hard to come by. Plants store a polysaccharide called **starch** as an energy reserve. Animals store **glycogen** [GLĪ-kō-jen], which is similar to starch.

Both glycogen and starch are made up of **glucose** molecules. Glucose is the simple sugar molecule used by most living organisms as a source of energy. Its structure can be seen in Diagram 1. When we speak of sugar, we are not talking about the stuff in our sugar bowls. That's one particular sugar called **sucrose**. Sucrose is not nearly as use-

This is one simple glucose molecule. But glucose molecules may be linked together in different ways to form various polysaccharides including starch, glycogen or cellulose.

This is the structure of a short piece of a cellulose chain.

ful to a living plant or animal as is glucose. We like sucrose because it is sweet, but most sugars are not sweet—only the disaccharides ("two" + "sugars") are. For example, two glucose molecules hooked together (a disaccharide of glucose) form a molecule called **maltose** or malt sugar, which is sweet. Glucose itself has a somewhat bitter taste.

While animals tend to use proteins for building purposes, plants tend to use polysaccharides. Since, as we will learn, plants make sugars as their main product, building their structures from polysaccharides requires less effort of them than building from proteins would require.

Plants have the ability to produce a polysaccharide called **cellulose** for structural purposes. The wood in trees and other woody plants is made up of cellulose. Like starch and glycogen, cellulose is also a chain of glucose molecules. These molecules are just linked differently than in starch and glycogen. The larger diagram on the previous page shows the structure of a short chain of cellulose. A complete cellulose chain typically has a molecular weight of about one million atomic mass units.

Molecules like the cellulose chain on the previous page give wood its stiffness and hardness and allow trees to tower high into the air while withstanding winds against their leaves and branches. These molecules also contain considerable energy in their chemical bonds which is released from cellulose when wood is burned.

Exercises:

1. What molecules are linked together to form polysaccharides?

2. What do polysaccharides do?

21: *The Molecules of Life—Lipids and Others*

A fourth group of biomolecules is the **lipids** (fats). Many creatures store fats as energy reserves because fats contain so much energy. Different living things store different forms of these molecules. A lipid chemist can look at the chemical makeup of lipids and tell what kind of living thing they came from. Lipids are smaller molecules than the others we mentioned. However, like the other groups, they are composed of linkages of smaller units. The units are called **fatty acids**, and they often occur in groups of two or (in the case of the **glycolipid** shown in the diagram) three. A glycolipid is simply one common type of lipid. There are several others with which we won't concern ourselves at the moment.

The immense organization of the molecules of life, when compared with that of the molecules of non-life, screams out that these are not chance occurrences. They are the handiwork of an intelligence far superior to our own. Each of these countless chemicals was designed with great skill by a Being who not only knew the chemistry of each unit, but also understood, before the construction, what would be the chemistry of the great and complex finished product.

Even the simplest of living things has thousands of different chemicals that participate in its activities. The chemicals about which you have learned—nucleic acids, proteins, polysaccharides, and lipids—are among these; their large molecules are present in abundance and are most important to understanding what we have come to call "life." But you must not be led to believe that scientists are close to understanding all there is to know about it. There is much more to learn, and there still will be when we are no longer alive.

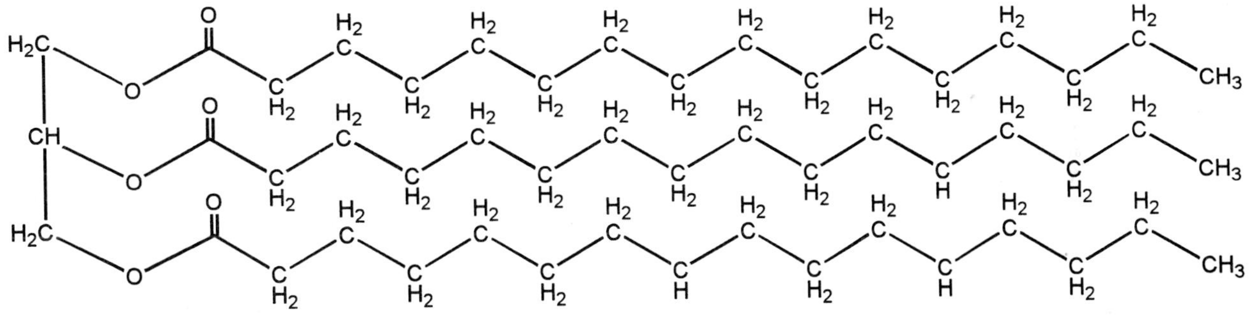

Lipids are linkages of fatty acids. This is an example of a glycolipid. Notice the three fatty acid chains lined up side by side. These molecules store a tremendous amount of energy in animal tissues that may be used by the body if food is scarce.

Exercises:
1. What molecules are linked together to form fats?
2. What do fats do?

22: *Solutions*

What happens to solids when they are placed in contact with liquids? Remember when we first started placing elements in contact with each other? We learned that elements don't exist in their form of lowest potential energy, so they combine with other elements to make a lower-energy package. In the same way, molecules interact with each other to form low energy packages. For example, when solids come in contact with liquids, they are no more satisfied with staying separated than a ball is satisfied with staying still on the middle of a hill. Just as the ball will roll down the hill, the molecules making up the solids and liquids will rearrange to make a lower potential energy arrangement.

When a liquid and solid are together, the lowest potential energy is found when the solid molecules are spread out among the liquid molecules. This condition is known as a **solution**. If we dissolve a small amount of one chemical in a large amount of another, we refer to the small amount as a **solute** and the large amount as the **solvent**.

When we think of solutions, we normally think of a solid **dissolved** (spread out within) in a liquid, but a gas can also dissolve in a liquid, one liquid can dissolve in another, and one gas can dissolve in another. In a true solution, molecules of one substance will spread out randomly among those of another. Because of this random spreading, you can take a sample from anywhere in the solution, and its makeup of molecules will be practically identical to a sample taken from anywhere else in the solution.

Most chemical reactions take place in solutions of liquids or gases. Why? Well, if you put two solid hunks on the

Notice the arrangement of the sodium chloride molecules among the water molecules. They seem to be scattered about in random fashion. This is typical of a solution. But notice how those sodium chloride molecules are bunched together at the bottom of the container. This is an area where solid sodium chloride has yet to be dispersed in the solution. At the surface of the solid, molecules are busily distributing themselves in liquid. The lowest energy state for the solution is the one in which the molecules of sodium chloride are most spread out within the water. Heat energy among these molecules will keep them bumping randomly about looking for a lower energy state to fall into.

table next to each other, what happens? Not much. But if you take those two hunks of solid and drop them in a beaker of water so that they dissolve, the molecules of the two substances come into close contact with each other as they spread out within the liquid. Now they can interact because they are in contact. Solutions of different liquids and gases are good places to carry out chemical reactions because chemicals in solution are in such complete contact with each other. Solutions of gases in gases are especially good for carrying out reactions because gas molecules are so active. This activity makes reactions fast and complete.

Although it is proper to think of a lake as a large body of water, it may be even more appropriate to think of it as a giant solution since it may contain high concentrations of dissolved minerals.

Exercises:
1. A _____ (snoutoil) results when a _____ (leosut) is _____ (oilsvedds) in a _____ (tonselv).
2. Solutions are:
   a. tiny clumps of one chemical spread out within another.
   b. individual molecules of one chemical randomly spread out within another.
   c. mixtures of two chemicals.
   d. tiny drops of snoutoil.

23: *Solubility*

Some substances don't get along in solution. Their molecules exert little force to attract each other; they may even repel each other. In those cases you won't get much of a solution. There will always be *some* interaction, but there may not be much. A common expression for predicting how well substances will dissolve in one another is "Likes dissolve likes." This means that a polar solute will dissolve in a polar solvent and a non-polar solute will dissolve in a non-polar solvent. The property of a solute that tells us whether or not it will dissolve in a certain solvent is called its **solubility** in that solvent.

One example of this principle is seen in oil and vinegar salad dressing. Oil, a hydrocarbon, is low in polarity. Vinegar is mostly water, which is highly polar. Oil and water are not very **soluble** in one another. That's why you always have to shake the dressing and then hurry to pour it before it separates again. Because you are a really smart chemist, maybe you think you can make oil and vinegar go together so that they won't come apart. What could you do? Why not add a third liquid which has an attraction for both the oil and the vinegar. This liquid would probably be more polar than oil, but less polar than water, so that it could dissolve in either vinegar or water. Acetone would be a good choice, except for one thing: if people ate it, they would

If a solid has its choice of solvents, as in this case where a layer of oil is floating on a layer of water, it will go to the solvent that it likes the most. This dye is polar, so it prefers the water to the oil. If it were non-polar the oil would be colored and the water layer would be unchanged. "Likes dissolve likes."

die. Ethanol might be the next best choice, but you would have to be careful how much you used or people would get intoxicated from the salad dressing. Ethanol is the alcohol in alcoholic drinks! It's tough to be a smart chemist.

If you are trying to dissolve something (like a stain in your new clothes) but can't do it with water, perhaps you should try a less polar solvent. Some of the common solvents (in order of decreasing polarity) are these: water, methanol, ethanol, acetone, benzene, naphtha. Acetone is a solvent of mid-range polarity. For this reason acetone can be used to dissolve all kinds of chemicals, whether they are polar or non-polar. It's often a good first choice if you don't know what else to use. But be careful; it's such a good solvent that it might just take the color out of the item you are trying to clean! Acetone is the active ingredient in nail polish remover, but it can be purchased at a hardware store for a few dollars per gallon.

Air is a solution of several gases. What might happen to us if oxygen didn't get along with the other gases in solution?

Exercises:

1. Recall the structure of the methane molecule that we made in Yellow Lab 4. Is methane polar or non-polar?

2. Will the solubility of methane in water be high or low?

3. From the end of Yellow Text Lesson 6, recall the way sodium and chlorine share electrons. Is sodium chloride polar or non-polar?

4. Will the solubility of sodium chloride in water be high or low?

CHEMISTRY

24: *Suspensions*

So you've given up on dissolving oil and vinegar together without killing people, but you are still convinced you are a smart chemist. So what do you do? Like every other good chemist in the world, you pick up the bottle of salad dressing and shake it really hard, then fret to remove the cap and pour the dressing before it separates again. But unlike the untrained non-chemists, you know the word for what you just did. You created a **suspension**. A suspension is one substance within another that is not dissolved. This is the same thing that happens when you put sand in water and shake hard. It's not amusing. The sand stays up in suspension for a second, then falls back to the bottom of the flask because of gravity.

How might you get sand to stay in suspension longer? You could use syrup instead of water. Because syrup is "thicker" than water, or as a good chemist would say, more **viscous** than water, the grains would be suspended for a long time. The reason is that syrup places more friction on the particles, making it more difficult for them to fall under gravity. Do you agree that by crushing the solid particles and making them less massive you could make the effects of friction greater? You could make a *really* stable suspension by placing powder in syrup.

It's usually pretty easy to tell the difference between solutions and suspensions. In most cases suspensions have a cloudy appearance while solutions are clear (even though they may display color). Which is which in the photo?

Although sand doesn't make an attractive suspension in water, there are some more interesting suspensions. For example, blood is a suspension of blood cells (among other things) in water. It is also a solution of minerals, chemical food compounds and chemical waste compounds. In fact, blood has to be one of the most complex liquid solutions/ suspensions in existence. Each chemical and living blood cell in there has its own purpose, and there are at least many thousands of chemicals present at a given time.

The easiest way to tell the difference between a solution and a suspension is that the particles in suspensions make them appear cloudy, while solutions are clear and free of particles, even if they are colored.

Two lessons ago we spoke of a lake as a solution, but many lakes also have considerable suspended matter as well. This green lake gets its color from algae growing suspended in the water.

Exercises:
1. Decide which of the following are solutions and which are suspensions:

    a. a teaspoon of sugar in a cup of warm water

    b. a teaspoon of flour in a cup of water

    c. ground black pepper in water

    d. air (a combination of mostly nitrogen, oxygen, argon and carbon dioxide)

    e. air in water

25: *The Pain of Suspensions*

Suspensions are important in chemistry if for no other reason than that they can be a major pain in the neck. Before being used in even the simplest chemical procedures, suspensions have to be filtered so that the solids are separated from the liquids. Suppose you want to measure how much of a toxic chemical is present in drinking water, so you pump a sample of water from underground. When it comes to the surface, you can see that the water is cloudy, so there must be particles in there. Because these solid particles will mess up your analysis, you have to get them out. A simple way to do this is to let the suspension stand for a long time. You will eventually see solid particles separate from the liquid by gravity as they settle to the bottom of the container. But if this process takes too long, it can be hurried along with a filter or a centrifuge.

A **filter** is a sheet of material (often paper) with tiny holes in it. Particles that are smaller than the holes will pass through, but larger particles will stay on top of the filter. Many types of filters and filtration devices will be seen in every laboratory. A coarse filter may be a wire screen or basket-type strainer. Some fine filters are made with holes so tiny that they can even separate large molecules from small ones.

In Lesson 24 it was explained that gravity pulls more massive particles through a liquid, but that the smaller particles fall through the liquid less rapidly because of friction. Can you think of a way to

Some filters are capable of removing the tiniest solids from a suspension. Notice how clear the liquid has become after passing through the "membrane filter" (left). That's because all of the suspended solids have been removed by the filter (above).

The centrifuge on the left is made to remove bacteria from suspension. The one on the right is made more for physical rather than biological applications. It holds larger volumes but doesn't spin as fast.

increase the amount of force on those small particles? A **centrifuge** is another useful tool for removing particulate matter from suspension. A centrifuge slings a suspension around a central axis, like the cup of water that you once whirled on the end of a string. If whirled with enough force, even the smallest particles will begin to move away from the central axis by their inertia. (See Red Lab 3 if you don't remember how this works). Centrifuges are used to take all kinds of small particles—blood cells, bacteria, and even large molecules—out of suspension by applying a centripetal force that may be up to thousands of times greater than gravity.

Exercises:
1. Muddy water is a suspension of soil particles. If all you had to drink was muddy water, how could you clean it up so it wouldn't be quite so disgusting?
2. There are several filtration devices that people have in their kitchens. Can you think of any?

CHEMISTRY

26: *Water as a Protector of Life*

Remember when we said that water is an amazing substance? Well, it still is, but now I have more reasons to share with you. Have you ever noticed that when scientists look for life on other planets, they look for planets that have water on them? There is a reason for that. It's because, without water, you can't have what scientists call "life." Did I hear you ask, "What does water do?" Water covers about 70% of the Earth's surface. Because it can absorb a lot of heat, this helps keep the temperature of the Earth from changing drastically. When water evaporates, it goes from liquid to gas. As it does, it takes heat with it, so that the unevaporated water remains cooler. If there were no water to evaporate when the sun's rays hit the Earth, the temperature of the Earth would go berserk, and we would all cook.

It is also significant that water behaves unusually when it is cooled. Most substances contract when they cool, so their density increases. Water, on the other hand, increases in density only until it gets to 3.98°C. This is its temperature of maximum density. As the temperature of water drops further, it begins to expand again. For this reason, ice is less dense than water, and because of its lower density, it floats. This unusual tendency of ice to float on water protects the entire population of a lake from freezing during the coldest winter months. If ice sank, all of the water would drop to the freezing point, and the whole lake would freeze solid from bottom to top. Fish would not be able to live through the freezing and thawing cycles. Just think: The great Designer had all of these details in mind right from the beginning!

These two beakers were placed in the sunshine about five minutes before the photo was taken. Notice that the thermometer in the empty glass shows a higher temperature than the one in the water. This illustrates the ability of water to protect the Earth from the heat of the sun. If the Earth were not largely covered with water, the sun would drive the Earth's surface temperature too high for us.

Exercises:
1. Why does it help us to sweat when we're hot?
2. The density of ice is 0.9998 g/cm^3. The density of water at 3.98°C is 1.0000 g/cm^3. The density of ethyl alcohol is 0.92 g/cm^3. Does ice float on ethyl alcohol?

27: *Saved by Water*

Water is also important to life because it serves as a solvent for nearly all the materials that living things need. Living things need to be bathed in food and minerals and to have a liquid to carry away waste materials. Water is always the carrier for these substances. Tiny creatures in lakes, streams and oceans may get the things that they need directly from water itself, but more complex animals have their own body fluids that are mostly made out of—you guessed it—water.

Blood and tissue fluid (called **lymph**) are made mostly of water. The water carries suspended blood cells, lymph cells, dissolved minerals and nutritional substances, and bathes our cells constantly. Our hearts keep the blood moving through our bodies to take dissolved oxygen to the cells. This oxygen is used to "burn" organic fuel molecules, like simple sugars; that "burning" of fuel provides us with energy from the chemical bonds in the sugars and produces carbon dioxide and water. The waste product, carbon dioxide, is removed by dissolving back into this complex water solution. So you see, water is the medium for many of the chemical reactions that take place in living things.

Water washes life-supporting minerals from the mountains where they become accessible to plants and animals living in the accumulated water in lakes, streams and oceans.

CHEMISTRY

Water is also the basis for life in our oceans. It evaporates from the Earth by heat energy from the sun and, as water vapor, enters the atmosphere where it forms clouds. When the clouds give up their water as rain and snow, it falls on land where it dissolves minerals. These minerals are carried to lakes and streams and into the world's oceans, where they provide nutrients to tiny living things in the water. These living things serve as food for larger living things, which are then eaten by even larger living things, and so on. Without the necessary properties of water which make it capable of dissolving these nutrient materials, life in the oceans would be impossible.

This single critical molecule, with its spectacular properties, is one of the basic evidences to many scientists that life does not exist because of chance happenings, but exists as part of the plan of a great Designer.

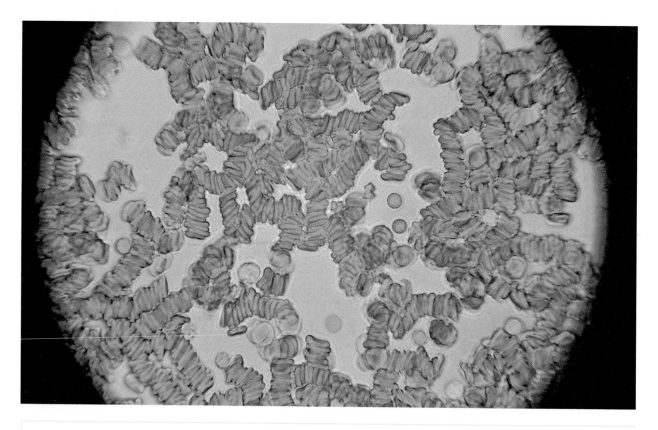

If you look at blood under a microscope it is plain to see that it is a most complex suspension containing a great many red blood cells and many white blood cells.

Exercises:

1. Give your best description of what the Earth would be like without water.

2. Speculate on the value or worth of the universe without water. Begin your answer with "I speculate that…"

28: *Acids and Bases*

Water has many unique properties. One of the most interesting properties of water is that it ionizes. That is, it splits up to make a cation and an anion:

$$H_2O \rightarrow H^+ + OH^-$$

In water, at any given time, there is a certain concentration of these ions present. Their concentrations aren't high, and they don't stay around for long because they have such a strong attraction to each other. These two ions have a great effect on the chemistry of water. The H^+ is **acid**. It looks for a negative charge that it can neutralize, and neutralizes it quickly. The OH^- anion is **base**. It is equally reactive, but, of course, it looks for anything positively charged. Because acids and bases are extremely reactive these two ions can attack compounds that would otherwise seem fairly stable.

This cellulose sponge had concentrated sulfuric acid dripped onto it. Strong acids and bases are highly reactive because of their extreme imbalance of the H+ and OH- ions that combine to form water.

CHEMISTRY

There are other ways to get H^+ ions in solution besides splitting up water molecules. For instance, HCl ionizes in water to H^+ and Cl^- ions. Because Cl^- has no effect on the acidity of water, the H^+ makes the water strongly acidic. In the same way, NaOH ionizes in water to Na^+ and OH^- ions. The OH^- ions make the water basic.

If you put water that has extra H^+ ions together with water having extra OH^- ions, what do you think happens? Let's write an equation (ignoring the water in which the reaction takes place). First, we'll ionize sodium hydroxide to get some free OH^- ions:

$$NaOH \rightarrow Na^+ + OH^-$$

Then we'll ionize hydrochloric acid:

$$HCl \rightarrow H^+ + Cl^-$$

Then we'll put the two together. The ions will recombine with their favorite partners to make combinations with the lowest potential energy:

$$Na^+ + OH^- + H^+ + Cl^- \rightarrow NaCl + H_2O$$

Each free H^+ ion bonds with an OH^- ion to form a new water molecule; then we are left with sodium (Na^+) and chloride (Cl^-) to pair off because of their electric charge attraction. The compounds that form because of a reaction between an acid and a base are called **salts**. Of course, sodium chloride, as you have learned, is table salt—the kind that grows on pretzels.

Although we have provided a single example of an acid-base reaction, there are many acids and bases, and so there are many reactions that can take place between them. In the example we selected, we made sodium chloride—simple table salt; but every such reaction forms a different salt.

Exercises:

For each of the following pairs of acids and bases, show the recombination to make a water and a salt. The first one is done for you. (Don't forget to balance your equations. I have balanced my part.)

1. $KOH + HF \rightarrow K^+ + OH^- + H^+ + F^- \rightarrow KF + H_2O$
2. $Ba(OH)_2 + H_2SO_4 \rightarrow Ba^{2+} + 2\,OH^- + 2\,H^+ + SO_4^{2-} \rightarrow$
3. $Ca(OH)_2 + 2\,HCl \rightarrow Ca^{2+} + 2\,OH^- + 2\,H^+ + 2\,Cl^- \rightarrow$

29: *Don't Say pHooey!*

The acidity (acid strength) or basicity (base strength) of water solutions can be measured in several ways: with a pH meter, with pH paper or with indicator dyes which change color depending on the pH of the solution they are in. (See the photos.) The measurements are expressed as the **pH** (pronounced as the letters "p" and "h"; don't say the "f" sound) of the water. The pH is related to the concentration of H^+ ions in water. If their concentration is high, the water is acidic, and the pH value is low. If their concentration is low, the water is basic, and the pH value will be high. If the water is neither acidic nor basic, it is said to be **neutral**, and the pH is equal to 7. Most waters have a pH between 1 and 14, 1 being extremely acidic, and 14 being extremely basic. Most natural waters (lakes, streams, oceans, etc.) are close to neutral.

The strongest acids are those that readily separate into ions when dissolved in water, making the H^+ concentration high. The acids that best fit this description are hydrochloric (HCl), hydrobromic (HBr), hydroiodic (HI), nitric (HNO_3), perchloric ($HClO_4$), and sulfuric (H_2SO_4). Notice that the hydrogen atom is written at the beginning of each of these chemical formulae. These up-front hydrogen atoms are the ones that break off to form H^+ ions in solution and give these substances their acidic character.

In the same way, the strongest bases are those that ionize to give up an OH^- ion in solution. These will be hydroxides of the group 1A and 2A metals. The most commonly used bases are sodium hydroxide (NaOH), potassium hydroxide (KOH), magnesium hydroxide ($Mg(OH)_2$) and calcium hydroxide ($Ca(OH)_2$). Also commonly used is ammonium hydroxide (NH_4OH), the chemical form of ammonia which is often used in cleaning.

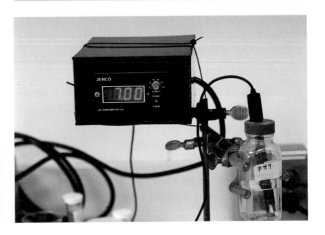

There are many systems for measuring the hydrogen ion concentration (pH) of water. They include indicator dyes (top), pH papers (middle) and pH indicator probes (bottom).

One especially good use of strong base is in the treatment of cocoa to form hydroxylated cocoa. This is the special dark chocolate that goes into "hydrox" cookies. Your assignment for this lesson is to compare the taste of hydrox cookies with that of cookies having regular non-hydroxylated chocolate in them and to decide which tastes better. You may have to eat several of each before you can decide! (**Please don't think that this means you can eat strong base. Few things in the world are more deadly.** In fact, one of the toxins which is most commonly found in homes and which kills many young children every year is the crystalline drain cleaner stored in many people's cupboards. It is typically made of sodium hydroxide.)

Hydroxylated chocolate is chocolate treated with alkali (or strong base). It is used in making hydrox cookies and other dark chocolate confections.

Exercises:

1. Show ionization reactions for the following substances, and tell whether each is an acid or a base.
   a. $Ba(OH)_2$
   b. HNO_3
   c. H_2SO_4
   d. H_3PO_4
   e. CsOH

2. Each of the following is a reaction between an acid and a base. Please show the ionization and recombination, then underline the salt that results from the recombination.
   a. KOH + HCl →
   b. $NaOH + H_2SO_4$ →

3. Hydrogen is listed among the group 1A metals, so hydrogen hydroxide (HOH) is a hydroxide of a group 1A metal. Why is it not a strong base?

30: *Thermo-dy-whatchamacall-your-namics*

The word **thermodynamic** comes from two Greek words: *therme*, which means heat (as in **thermo**meter), and *dunamos*, which (in this case) relates to change. Dynamic is the opposite of static. If something is static, it doesn't change, but if it's dynamic, there is never a dull moment; it's always changing. Thermodynamics, then, is the study of "heat change."

Let me explain: We have already said, time and time again, that systems always tend toward their state of lowest potential energy. People stick to the ground because it is the low-potential-energy place to be when gravity is pulling on them. You would have to do work to pull them up in the air. If you let go, they would go right back to their low-potential place. That is, they would crash.

Similarly, chemical reactions take place because the products are low-potential-energy combinations of atoms. Just as masses held above the Earth give up potential energy when they are dropped, chemicals also give up potential energy when they undergo change to a condition of lower potential energy. When chemicals undergo a change like

From where Stacey is sitting there is only one way to go—down! Chemical reactions take place only if the products are at a lower energy level than the reactants. To the chemicals, that's down.

this, their kinetic energy is released in the form of heat. So then, if we measure the heat change that takes place during a reaction, we will learn how much potential energy was given up during that reaction.

You can look at an object and tell how much potential energy is stored up in it by its distance from the earth. Unfortunately, we can't do that with chemicals. Instead, we measure the heat chang-

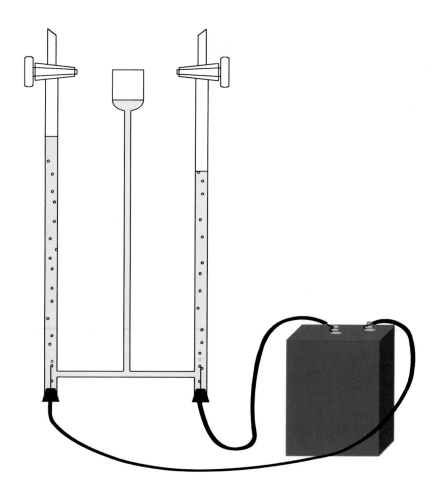

When oxygen and hydrogen are placed together they tend to react to form water. Of course, this reaction can be made to proceed in the opposite direction. That is, water can be split into hydrogen and oxygen, but this requires an input of energy. The apparatus shown in this diagram is designed to split water into its components by adding electrical energy.

es which take place during reactions. By these heat changes we can tell how much potential energy is being released when chemicals react. Thermodynamics is the study of the heat changes—energy changes—during chemical reactions. By this study we can predict whether or not a reaction will take place without having to add energy.

There are many reactions that just happen on their own when two chemicals are brought into contact with each other. These reactions are like the person falling to the ground. They are going from their high potential to their low potential, and they just happen naturally because of the forces that pull those particular atoms together. We call them **spontaneous** reactions.

If we want to force those chemicals to end up in a different arrangement than the one of lowest potential energy, we have to add energy because work is needed to keep these favored compounds apart. Energy can easily be added to the system by applying heat, light or electricity. By doing this, we can drive reactions to get results that we wouldn't otherwise get. Of course, the more energy we have to apply, the more expensive it will be to make those products.

Exercises:

1. Which of the following are spontaneous?
    a. falling to the ground after stepping out of a flying airplane
    b. two north poles of magnets coming together
    c. charging a battery
    d. $KCl + H_2O + electricity \rightarrow KOH + HCl$
    e. $KOH + HCl \rightarrow KCl + H_2O + heat$

2. Reactions happen spontaneously when they act in the direction of forces. If they have to go against forces, they will require energy, so they are non-spontaneous. In each of the non-spontaneous actions below, tell what force is being acted against (gravitational, electromagnetic, or nuclear).
    a. a ball being thrown upward
    b. pulling apart two magnets that are stuck together
    c. charging a battery
    d. $KCl + H_2O + electricity \rightarrow KOH + HCl$

31: *Heat-Producing and Heat-Robbing Reactions*

There are a few reactions that spontaneously make a product of higher potential energy than was in their reactants. There is no magic in these reactions. They get the energy they need from their surroundings. We don't need to put in energy because there is plenty available from the heat in the air, perhaps, or the light from the sun. One common example of such a reaction is the melting of ice. This is a change in the arrangement of water molecules that requires heat input. If the heat isn't available from the surroundings (as is true in the freezer), the ice won't melt. But as soon as the energy is available (when the ice is taken out of the freezer), the ice melts, and the heat required to melt the ice is stolen from the air around the ice.

These energy-stealing reactions are called **endothermic** reactions. There's that Greek word *therme* again, only this time it's coupled with *endon* which means "within." If a reaction takes up heat, it is an endothermic reaction; if it gives off heat, it is an **exothermic** (*exo-* meaning "outside") reaction. (Who'da thunk you'd learn about the Greek language in your science studies? If you stay in the sciences, you'll learn a lot about the Greek language.)

So then, thermodynamics is really a study of whether or not reactions will take place with the amount of energy available. Using our knowledge of physics, we can determine whether or not there is enough potential energy in a spring to do a certain amount of work. Now with thermodynamics we can figure out whether there is enough energy available in a reaction system to make a chemical reaction happen. So suppose you wanted to take water and break it apart to form hydrogen and oxygen:

$$2\ H_2O \rightarrow 2\ H_2 + O_2$$

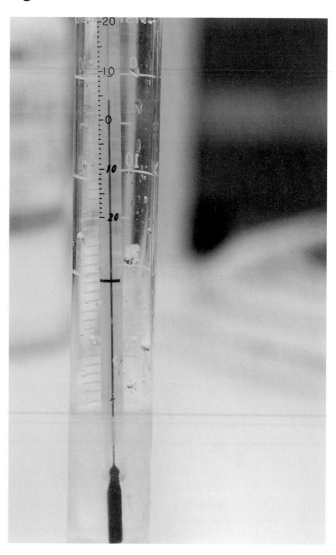

Ammonium nitrate requires energy to dissolve in water—so it takes it. The temperature of this solution while the ammonium nitrate is dissolving is about the same as the temperature of your refrigerator. The dissolution of ammonium nitrate is endothermic.

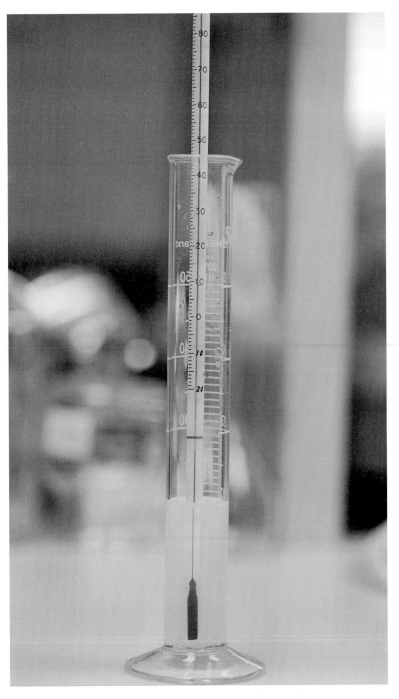

How much energy would it take? Thermodynamics is the study of the potential energy level represented by reactants (water in this case) compared to the potential energy level represented by products (hydrogen and oxygen).

If water is at a higher energy level than the products of the reaction, it will naturally break apart into its products. If it is at a lower energy level, it will naturally form whenever hydrogen and oxygen are placed together. Which do you think will happen? That is, which direction do you think is the correct direction for this reaction to proceed without any input of energy? The answer is that hydrogen and oxygen, when placed together, react quickly and spontaneously to form water and lots of heat. Once formed, you can't break water molecules apart without applying lots of energy. Were that not true, all of the water in the world would eventually convert to oxygen and hydrogen, and we'd be waterless.

Sodium hydroxide, on the other hand, gives up energy when it dissolves in water. The temperature of this solution while sodium hydroxide is dissolving approaches the boiling point of pure water. The dissolution of sodium hydroxide, then, is exothermic.

Exercises:
1. The atmosphere has lots of oxygen in it. Why do you suppose it doesn't have much free hydrogen gas?
2. What would happen to us *if there were* a lot of free hydrogen gas?

32: *Kinetics*

If you were to look up the word **kinetic** in the dictionary, you would find that it has a variety of meanings, most of them having to do with motion. If you remember our physics lessons, kinetic energy is energy of motion. While thermodynamics is the study of *whether or not* a chemical reaction will take place with the amount of energy in its surroundings, kinetics is a study of *how fast* a reaction will take place. For example, sucrose (table sugar) reacts with oxygen in the air to form carbon dioxide and water. This reaction is spontaneous, and proceeds without any input of energy:

$$C_{14}H_{22}O_{11} + 14\ O_2 \rightarrow 14\ CO_2 + 11\ H_2O$$

Why then does it sit for years on your table in the sugar bowl and in your cupboard without obvious change? It's because the reaction is slow. In fact, if left alone, a bowl of sugar would take thousands of years to react with oxygen. However, if it is placed in a furnace (a super-hot oven) at 550°C, it will first melt (change from solid to liquid); then it will begin reacting quickly with oxygen. As it converts to water (which, when hot, vaporizes as steam) and carbon dioxide gas, pure sucrose will vanish from our view. The heat makes this reaction proceed so quickly that we can actually watch it happen.

If a chemical reacts, but reacts slowly, we say that it is **kinetically stable**. That is, because it reacts so slowly, it appears as if it were not even reacting. Other chemicals just don't react in any amount of time under their usual circumstances. They tend to hang around forever. We say these are **thermodynamically stable**. Remember, thermodynamics is the study of the energy state of the chemical. If it's already in a low en-

A muffle furnace is a laboratory device used for reaching and holding high temperatures (perhaps 2000°C). This kind of energy input can drive reactions that would otherwise fail either because they are not favored at room temperature or because they occur too slowly at room temperature.

ergy state, there is no reason for it to seek a lower one. The noble gases are all great examples of thermodynamically stable chemicals. These elements don't readily react with any other substance:

$$He + He \rightarrow He + He$$
$$He + O_2 \rightarrow He + O_2$$
$$He + Li \rightarrow He + Li$$

Life is pretty boring for helium. Just be glad you weren't born as a noble gas.

Sugar before baking

Graphite before baking

Sugar after baking

Graphite after baking

Here are two examples of reactions that are slow at room temperature. Carbon in either of these forms (sucrose or graphite) will react with oxygen from the atmosphere, but the reactions are extremely slow. It would take thousands of years for these reactions to be completed at room temperature. But notice how both the sugar and the graphite are converted completely to carbon dioxide in less than an hour at 900°C in the muffle furnace. These crucibles were placed in the furnace and then removed without any cleaning or other treatment of any kind. Only traces of contaminating metals remain from the original substances. These are two examples of kinetically stable substances. They react with oxygen, but the reaction is slow under normal circumstances.

BIOLOGY—THE STUDY OF LIFE AND LIVING THINGS

Just about every textbook on the subject of biology—the study of living things—will be found to begin with a lesson on how life originated from non-living things. Well, we were not there to witness the origin of life, nor do we have adequate scientific evidence to demonstrate how life arose. There are theories on the origins of life, some weaving together a large amount of scientific evidence while others are nearly unfounded. Of course, the theory most widely held among scientists on the origin of life is the theory that all living organisms **evolved** from one simple, single-celled **organism** that was successful in multiplying. The theory goes on to suggest that all of the different organisms present today are the result of changes within groups of organisms that arose from this common **ancestor**.

This theory, which we will call the **general theory of evolution**, is so widely accepted in scientific circles that a person can hardly be a scientist without understanding it. That doesn't mean that a person has to *believe* it is all true in order to be a scientist. I personally know many scientists who do not adhere to this theory. These scientists are prominent in their disciplines: one is the dean of a school of science education, one is the chief cardiac surgeon at a major research hospital, one is a leader of a research institute, another is a chief researcher in a medical genetics lab, yet another is the president of a high-tech company. Their lack of belief in this most popular theory does not in any way prevent them from excelling in their disciplines, making new discoveries, publishing articles in respected research journals, or contributing to the advancement of knowledge. On the contrary, sometimes it takes a person who is thinking differently from others to see things that others do not see. It is this diversity of thought that causes the truth to be preserved. If everybody thought the same things and were wrong on the same things, the truth would be forever lost.

In this text we will attempt to teach the general theory of evolution because a good education in the sciences requires it. We present it as a **theory**—a working model into which scientific data are fitted—but which we ourselves do not accept. As new observations are made, models will be altered, radically changed or altogether discarded. After many years of study and observation in my discipline as a microbiologist, I hold that the general theory of evolution is in serious error and is entirely inadequate for explaining a great volume of scientific evidence. I also hold that the universe was created by a Supreme Being possessing design and creative capabilities far beyond our comprehension.

The belief in a Supreme Being is not as uncommon among scientists as students are often led to believe. In a recent study, 40% of scientists were found to believe in a Creator. Science is full of challenges, including challenges to the Faith. In time, you can accept and answer those challenges without allowing them to erode your confidence in what you have learned from God. Now please begin Lesson 1.

1: *So What's Life?*

Perhaps the first, most important question to be answered in the study of life is the nature of the subject itself: What is **life**? The Bible and science define life differently. The Bible says, upon the creation of Adam, that God "breathed into his nostrils the breath of life, and man became a living spirit." Note that it says, not a living *body*, but a living *spirit*. A spirit has no physical dimensions, which places it outside the realm of science. Science defines life not by what it does not know or understand, but by what it does know and understand. We can't see a living spirit, but we can see a living body and know what it does. So science defines life as those characteristics held in common by living *bodies*.

At this point we agree to play a "game." We will look strictly at "scientific" life, or life in the physical sense. Let us not forget that we are but playing the game. Sometimes I like to play the game, and sometimes I do not. In this book we will play the game so that you will understand the "scientific" viewpoint, but we will point out differences of viewpoints where we feel it is helpful.

No matter how we define it, life is represented by a marvel of different forms—each highly organized.

So life, by scientific definition, is the set of characteristics shared by living bodies:

1. They are made up of one or more cells. (We will learn more about these in the next lesson.)
2. Their cells contain deoxyribose nucleic acid (DNA). (We learned something about this in our study of chemistry. We will learn more as time goes on.)
3. They consume food and produce wastes.
4. At some point in their lives they may reproduce—give forth new living beings like themselves.
5. They tend to be self-maintaining. That is, they use energy and raw materials to build themselves, to grow and to repair damage done to them.

There are many forms that fall within this definition of life. These forms, to be defined later in our study, include **archaea**, **bacteria**, **fungi**, **plants** and **animals**. By most scientists, **humans** are included among the animals. This is because humans are regarded by many scientists to have evolved from animals, or because humans fit a scientific definition of what it means to be an animal. In this text, even if we talk about humans as though they were animals, we recognize the supreme position over the animals which was given to man by God. We also recognize that, although similar to the animals in many ways, man is different from the animals in that he is created in the image of his Creator.

When we define life according to the scientific definition, problems arise in figuring out what is alive and what is not. There is not a clear distinction between the living and the non-living. Some "non-living" things act an awful lot like living things. Examples of these include **prions** and **viruses.** These curiosities take on some of the characteristics of life at different times, but they are not generally regarded as "living." Way down the road we will learn how to handle these oddballs. For now, we will attempt to learn about different forms of life according to the way they are commonly grouped by biologists.

Perhaps the most basic of all life characteristics is **reproduction**—the ability of living things to form other living things. Some living things produce **asexually** ("not" + "sexually"). That is, one single organism can form a small package of living material that can break off, shoot out, or otherwise leave the parent to become a separate living thing of the same kind. A second type of reproduction is called **sexual** reproduction. This requires two organisms of the same kind. One of these organisms, referred to as the **male**, passes a package of DNA to a **female** of its own kind. This genetic material combines with a similar package from the female to begin the formation of a new individual. Whether sexual or asexual, the ability to reproduce is enough by itself to separate all living things from the non-living.

Exercises:

1. Which of the following would the field of science directly address? (Give the letters of all correct answers.)
   a. the Biblical definition of death
   b. signs that a living organism has ceased to live
   c. life after death
   d. everyday habits of early people
2. New bacteria (daughter cells) are formed from their parent cells by pinching off directly from the body of the parent. Is this an example of reproduction?

2: *Organization in Living Things*

Organization at every level—that's the way to describe our universe. I once had an old professor at the university who said, "Our universe is much more organized than it need be. I think you should thank whoever you believe is responsible." He's right. Our universe is highly ordered.

We have already talked about the orderliness of matter, orderliness which is caused by the basic forces. We've talked about the organization of particles into atoms, atoms into elements, and elements into molecules. But the organization doesn't stop there. Living things represent a higher level of orderliness. In the living, molecules can be large and have organization which allows them to do something special. They can be built for a specific job or even have special "active sites" that carry out specific tasks. They can contain codes for storing, decoding and using information. They can even be used to communicate information to other living bodies and to decide the features of their offspring.

These highly organized molecules are further organized into **cells**. Just as atoms are the basic units of matter, cells are the basic units of life. All of the characteristics of life are displayed only when molecules are arranged and work together as cells. As we introduce cells, we introduce life. But our study of organization is not finished. Only the simplest living things live only as cells. These cells can be further organized to make different kinds of living things.

A living thing which exists free from other living things is called an **organism**. An organism can be a person, a dog, a tree, a fish, a worm, a mushroom or an insect. It can also be something much simpler like a single-celled organism: a yeast cell, a paramecium, or the smallest of all organisms, a bacterium. A human skin cell may be alive and show all of the signs of life, but it is not an organism by itself because it does not live free from other skin cells, or from blood, or nerves, or any other cells that make up the human.

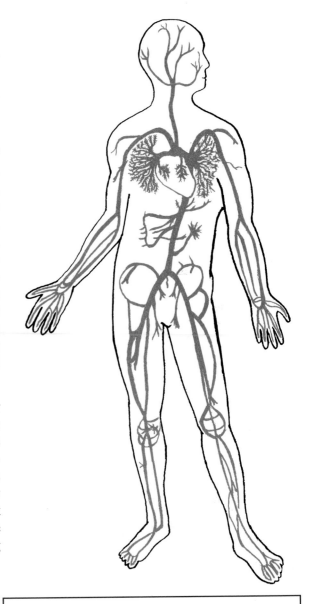

Every free-living organism is made up of intricate systems that organize one of the body's major functions. An example is the human circulatory system which serves to deliver nutrients and oxygen to every part of the body. Every system is made up of organs, just as the circulatory system is made up of a heart, aorta, arteries, arterioles, capillaries, venules, veins and vena cava. Each organ has a job to do that contributes to the purpose of the entire system of which it is a part.

Organisms can be organized at any number of levels. Some are single cells that live alone. Others are collections of similar cells. The most complex organisms have many different kinds of cells. They have groups of similar cells organized into **tissues**; different kinds of tissues come together to form **organs**. These organs are "body parts," each having its own specific purpose. Examples are a hand, a stomach, a liver or a heart. But if a body were made up of a random assembly of parts, it would be an ugly monster! These parts are further organized into the functioning **systems** that make up the organism.

Each tissue is made up of a unique type of cells that are well-suited to the function that tissue performs—the inner lining cells offer a smooth protective surface, the cells of connective tissue offer strength, the muscle cells offer motion, and the nerve cells offer the ability to communicate.

Every organ is made up of tissues—groups of similar cells. An example is the human artery which has an inner lining tissue, connective tissue, nervous tissue and muscle tissue. Without any one of these tissues, the artery would not function as an artery.

Every cell is what it is and does what it does because of the arrangement of molecules that make it up. The most orderly of those molecules is DNA which directs the construction of the cell itself.

To illustrate the organization represented by these complex organisms, consider the human circulatory system. This is the system that carries food and oxygen to all of your body's cells and takes waste away from those cells. The human circulatory system is made up of several organs: a heart, arteries of different sizes that carry blood away from the heart, capillaries that take blood to the individual cells, and veins of different sizes that return the blood to the heart. The heart, arteries, blood, capillaries and veins are the organs of the circulatory system.

Each of those organs is made up of various tissues. For example, the arteries have an inner lining called "epithelial tissue," a middle layer of connective tissue, some muscle tissue, some nerve tissue, and an outer coat of connective tissue. The tissues are made up of cells, and the cells are made up of molecules, many of which are highly organized themselves. Each molecule is made of atoms, and the atoms are made of subatomic particles (protons, neutrons and electrons).

Notice how highly organized this one system is. It is just one of many systems that make up the human body. Later on we will study these systems in greater detail. Even if you already have a sense of amazement at the human body, your amazement will grow as you learn more of the details of how it works.

At each level of organization, every component part obeys the laws of physics. Organisms with such a high level of organization as we have just described are referred to as "**higher organisms**," as compared to simpler "**lower organisms**" like those made up of a single cell.

The amount of organization found in even lower organisms is astounding. Just imagine the amount of potential energy represented by such complex organization. Given that we live in a universe where things tend toward lower potential energies, it takes a tremendous amount of energy to produce and maintain that high level of organization. When an organism dies, it decomposes rapidly back to more stable forms of matter. Life as we have defined it is a brief and unlikely lift to an exquisitely high level of potential energy. I think you should thank the One responsible.

Exercises:

Unscramble the words to fill in the following blanks. These sentences describe living organisms at each level of organization beginning at subatomic particles and ending at organisms.

1. Atoms are more organized than _____ (bautmiocs sieaptcrl) and are the units that make up the different _____ (tmeeenls).

2. _____ (locumeels) are made up of the atoms of a number of elements bound together. In biological systems they may be large and complex even to the point of containing encoded information that is passed on from generation to generation.

3. A _____ (lecl) is the basic functioning unit of all living things. It is a complex orderly arrangement of molecules constantly carrying out chemical reactions that allow it to function as a living organism. In "lower animals" a single one of these units may constitute an entire organism. In "higher animals" several or even billions come together to make up _____ (isssuet), which in turn make up _____ (soargn), which work together in _____ (sssymet), which make up an entire _____ (gorniams).

3: *It's a What-cha-ma-callit*

The science of naming organisms is called **taxonomy**. Every organism is described based on its features and placed in its proper category with other similar organisms. The classification starts with broad groups and becomes more and more specific right down to particular organisms, the names of which are based on the Latin language.

The broadest category is called a **kingdom**. There is a lot of controversy surrounding the number of kingdoms that should be recognized and even about which kingdom certain large groups of organisms belong in. Evolutionists attempt to fit organisms into a pattern of changes from a presumed common ancestor. More conservative scientists simply group them based on what is known about them. For our studies, we will refer to five kingdoms by their English names: Eubacteria, Archaea, Plants, Fungi and Animals.

Kingdoms are further subdivided into **phyla** (plural for phylum). Phyla are divided into **classes**, classes into **orders**, orders into **families** and families into **genera** (plural for genus). The group of organisms that are considered taxonomically identical to other organisms in their group is the **species**. The book of Genesis says that animals reproduce after their own kind. You could refer to a species of animals as one "kind" of animal. This Biblical definition works as well as any other that scientists have been able to come up with.

As an example of a classification, take the organism *Homo sapiens*. This organism is in the Kingdom Animalia (animal kingdom), the phylum Chordata, the class Mammalia, the order Primates, the family Hominidae, the genus *Homo*; it represents the species *sapiens*. Notice how the genus and species names are always italicized or underlined. Whether you realize it or not, you have just been classified. *Homo sapiens* is the **binomial** ("two" + "name") designation for humans. This two-name system of classification was begun in the mid 1700's by a Swedish man named Carolus Linnaeus. In addition to being an undisputed top-notch botanist, this man was an early champion of the idea of classifying animals according to a scheme laid down by God at the time of creation.

There is a series of methods used by taxonomists (people who name organisms for a living) for this purpose. The "rules" have accumulated over a long period of time into the complex science of **systematics**. Systematics was developed mostly around the variations in body parts, like the differences in lengths of forearm bones, or the number of scales from snout to tail, or the breadth and thickness of skull bones. Nearly every known organism has been measured in all possible ways and compared with every other organism thought to resemble it. Taxonomists rank these features in an order of importance and use them to decide which animals are "most alike" in an evolutionary sense.

Lately, biochemists have developed more modern ways to decide—on an evolutionary basis—how alike or different organisms are. Oddly enough for the evolutionist, many of the old methods and the new methods don't match up very well. It is unclear to them which of the techniques is in error, or whether the fossil record is right and the evolutionary model just doesn't work in putting the whole picture together. Instead of missing links, we have missing chains with only a few supposed links to suggest that there might at one time have been a chain.

Exercises:
1. Can two animals in the same genus also be in the same species?
2. Can two animals in different orders possibly be in the same phylum?
3. Can two plants in different classes be in the same family?

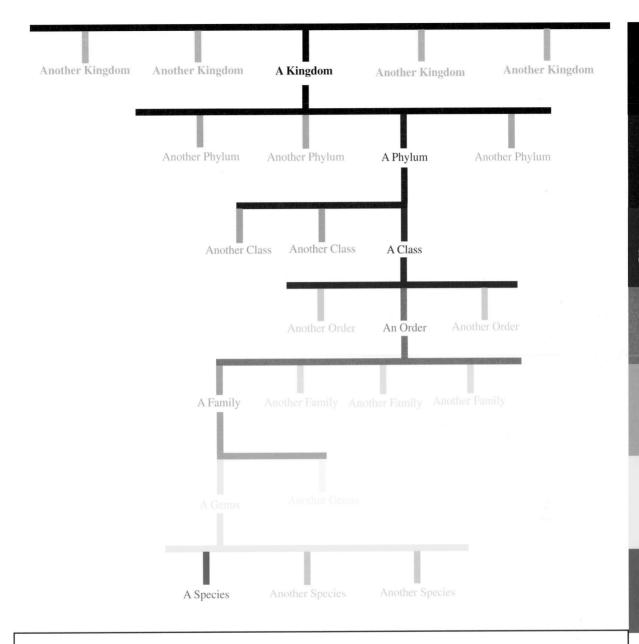

Kingdom · Phylum · Class · Order · Family · Genus · Species

Another Kingdom · Another Kingdom · **A Kingdom** · Another Kingdom · Another Kingdom

Another Phylum · Another Phylum · **A Phylum** · Another Phylum

Another Class · Another Class · **A Class**

Another Order · **An Order** · Another Order

A Family · Another Family · Another Family · Another Family

A Genus · Another Genus

A Species · Another Species · Another Species

Taxonomic trees that look like this one will be used throughout the remainder of the Blue Section to help you keep track of where we are in the taxonomic system of living organisms. The first level of the table represents the kingdoms; the second level represents the phyla. We will try to show you examples of the most important phyla of living organisms and, in many cases, show you examples from the different classes of animals in a phylum. Once we get to the vertebrate animals, we will go even further down the tree. To see the order in any collection of objects, it helps to sort those objects into groups based on their similarities and differences. The taxonomic tree is a method of classifying organisms into groups based on their similarities and differences. As the groups get smaller, their organisms get more and more alike. At the species level they reproduce to make organisms that are still in the same species. You might say that they reproduce "after their own kind."

4: *Cells*

At every level of organization, life offers us much to learn. We will begin by learning what life is like at the level of a single cell, since the cell is the basic unit of life. As we examine the way cells operate, we will see how important chemistry is in making cells work. First, we'll describe the parts of a cell. Just as parts of a person are called organs, the parts of a cell are called **organelles**, meaning "tiny organs." These cell parts are the subjects of the following paragraphs.

A cell has a clear boundary that separates it from the outside world. That boundary is actually a structure called the **cell membrane**. This membrane is like a sac holding in the contents of the cell. But designed into this membrane is the ability to let certain molecules pass through. Foods (not like chicken and roast beef, but food molecules like simple sugars and amino acids) and other needed substances can come in, and waste molecules can go out. The cell membrane also stands guard against many things that would harm the cell.

Inside a cell you will find a most important and large molecule or group of molecules that make up the **genome** [JĒ-nōm]. The genome is made of deoxyribose nucleic acid—that's right, our old friend **DNA**. The genome contains information vital to everything a living cell does. It tells the cell what the cell needs, how much it needs, and when. It directs the cell in making the things it lacks or importing the things it can't make. This is all communicated through complex chemical signals. Scientists have discovered, traced and recorded a great number of these signals, and yet only a small fraction of the existing signals are known. Maybe you would like to spend a part of your life trying to understand our chemistry!

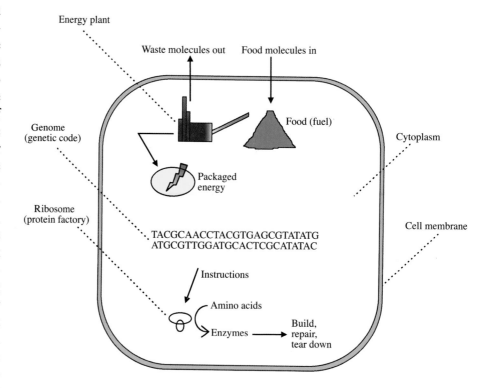

If you were to draw a picture of a cell without being told what kind of cell to draw, this is about the best you could do. All cells have a membrane that separates the cell's insides from the outside world. They all have genetic material (DNA) to guide their activities, RNA to decode the information in the DNA and ribosomes to make proteins. They also have other features, but these are the main ones that separate them from groups of chemicals found in non-living matter.

The genome also directs a cell's growth. When a cell grows to a certain size, it has to divide in two in order to continue to live. If each half of the dividing cell is to have its own genome with all the same information, the genome has to be copied. The genome itself directs this copying process, called **replication**.

In order for the information stored in the genome to be useful, a cell must be able to uncode it and put it to work. One especially useful group of proteins—**enzymes**—are responsible for carrying out most of the directions given by the genome. Enzymes are molecules that can make chemical reactions go faster. Does the genome call for more glucose? No problem. It will direct the production of enzymes that degrade starch to glucose in just a few minutes. When the enzymes are made, they will crank out plenty of glucose in seconds. When the genome detects plenty of glucose, other enzymes will be made to chop up the starch-degrading enzymes and recycle their pieces for making other proteins.

Enzymes are just one example of the many kinds of proteins used for lots of different purposes within living cells. One important purpose is building. Proteins are used as raw materials to add to the structure. They may be added to other materials to provide strength or flexibility, or used to make one type of material adhere to another.

Obviously, since each cell depends so much on proteins, it must have some kind of protein-making device. That device is called a **ribosome** [RĪ-buh-sōm]. The ribosome accepts messages from the genome and produces proteins according to its instructions.

Wow! This cell seems to be a busy place, and we have only begun! Does it bother you that we have all of this activity going on, and we haven't yet decided how we are going to PAY for all of it? After all, we learned in physics that you can't do anything useful without paying the energy price! Where does the cell get all of its energy? It comes from chemical bonds. High-potential-energy chemicals are broken apart to make lower-potential-energy products. Of course, as you know, anytime a chemical goes from a high-potential-energy state to a low-potential-energy state, energy is released. Enzymes can make this release quick and efficient. The released energy is stored in special energy-saving molecules so that the cell can use it to pay for its activities. If a cell divides, it needs energy. If it makes proteins, it needs energy. If it repairs a leak in its membrane, it needs energy. So within every cell are many sites where energy from food molecules can be released and stored.

All of these activities take place in a water-based fluid with just the amounts of minerals and nutrients necessary. This fluid is called **cytoplasm** ("cell" + "fluid"). You may also hear it called **protoplasm**.

Exercises:
1. Is a cell better described as a bag of reacting chemicals or as an orderly place in which many different chemical reactions constantly take place?
2. Which one of the following words could be used to describe each of the others?
   a. genome
   b. ribosome
   c. cell membrane
   d. organelle

5: *Cell Accessories*

Life would be pretty boring if everyone did things in exactly the same way. What if every girl carried the same purse and wore the same shoes and the same dress of the same color? Yuk. Life is far more interesting because different people do things differently. The fact that not all cells are alike also helps to make life more interesting. We can only begin to talk about the many differences among cell types, but we will focus on some of the biggies.

Some cells have a feature, called a **nucleus** (meaning "nut" or "kernel"), that separates the genetic material from the rest of the cell. The nucleus is a structure that keeps the genetic material out of harm's way. Its contents are separated from the rest of the cytoplasm by a **nuclear membrane**. It also has a fluid inside it, called **nucleoplasm**, that resembles cytoplasm.

The simplest of organisms, called bacteria and archaea, do not have a nucleus. Their genetic material is held among the rest of the cell's contents. Since these simple organisms lack a nucleus they are called **prokaryotes** [prō-KAR-ē-ōts] ("before" + "nut"). The genomes of these organisms are made up of a single large DNA molecule in the shape of a circle. The circle is twisted like a rubber band that has been grasped in two places and twirled in opposite directions. The molecule may then be "supertwisted" like that same rubber band if the twisted part then twists on itself.

Other organisms have genomes that are much more complex. Instead of a single circular genome, they may have several paired strands of DNA called **chromosomes**. Like the prokaryotic chromosomes, these chromosomes are twisted, but they are wound around a framework of proteins called **histones**. Organisms with cells having this more complex structure are called **eukaryotes** [ū-KAR-ē-ōts]. All organisms that are not prokaryotic are eukaryotic, including plants, animals, protozoa and fungi. Since more complex animals have a greater number of functions to carry out, they need this more complex genome.

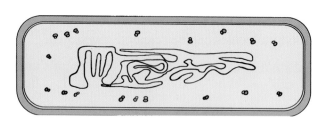

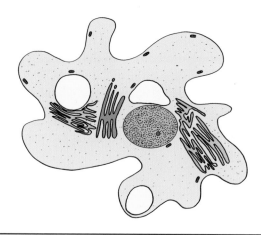

Bacterial cells are prokaryotic (that is, they have no cell nucleus). They are extremely small (about 1 millionth of a meter across) and have a cell wall that may be either rigid or somewhat flexible. Archaea are similar in structure and appearance to bacteria, but the makeup of their molecules is different.

Animal cells are eukaryotic cells perhaps a hundred times larger than bacteria and archaea. They do not have cell walls so they take on a variety of shapes and tend to be flexible. They are not photosynthetic, so there are no green chloroplasts or other pigments within their cells.

Some cells sport stiff outer walls for structure or protection. These cells include the bacteria, the archaea, plants and fungi. Each of these types of organisms has its own **cell wall** characteristics. Cell walls differ somewhat even within these groups. For example, bacteria are classified into two broad categories ("Gram positive" or "Gram negative") based on the type of cell wall they have. Animal cells do not have cell walls.

Cells of eukaryotes also have a complex inner membrane structure called an **endoplasmic reticulum**. This is a membrane (sheet) folded back and forth on itself to separate the cells into compartments and to provide a high surface area inside the cells on which to perform activities that need some attachment or separation. These more complex cells also require more organization of their energy generation. Energy generation is scattered throughout simpler cells; in these more complex cells, energy is generated in little chemical power plants called **mitochondria**, the "powerhouses of the cell."

Fungi are eukaryotic (that is, they have a nucleus which contains the cell's DNA) and have outer cell walls made of chitin (found nowhere in the plant kingdom). They are not photosynthetic and often lack a boundary between neighboring cells, causing them to run together into a large semisolid mass.

Plant cells have a rigid cell wall outside their membrane. They are eukaryotic and they have chloroplasts which contain the equipment needed for photosynthesis. When they have an abundance of food, they may store the extra food inside their cells as starch. The starch storage granules may be seen within the cell.

Exercises:

1. What do bacteria and archaea have in common?

2. Do animal cells have a cell wall?

3. In previous lessons we said that all of the work done by cells has to be paid for with energy. Name the structure where all of this energy is generated in eukaryotic cells.

6: *The Great Debate*

Now that we have had a glimpse at the basic organization of life, it would be good to get a taste of how evolutionists explain its origin from non-life. At the time when the general theory of evolution was first proposed, developed nations, especially in Europe and the Americas, consisted mostly of people who held a belief in the God of the Bible. Religion was powerful, and so religious leaders also tended to be powerful. These religious leaders unfortunately abused their authority. They made formal statements about the way things had to be in the universe in order to be consistent with their own views of God or the Bible. A few scientists were willing to challenge those public statements. Some of them came under threat by the churches and church leaders. These scientists were forced either to take back their comments or be punished. This began a feud between the religious establishment and scientists that has existed ever since.

The discipline of science has come to accept only **materialistic** viewpoints—viewpoints based on things that can be directly observed and tested. Many scientists of those early days set out in search of an explanation for the existence of the universe,

And God said, "Let the earth bring forth living creatures according to their kinds: cattle and creeping things and beasts of the earth according to their kind." And it was so. And God made the beasts of the earth according to their kind and the cattle according to their kind, and everything that creeps upon the ground according to its kind. And God saw that it was good. (Gen. 1:24,25) RSV

and for life on Earth, that relied only on observations and excluded anything beyond. In doing so they believed that they had eliminated all bias from their search for the truth. Little did they realize that even their "unbiased" approach itself involved a bias. Not all scientists accepted that bias, but it has gained general acceptance.

Once scientists began to look for purely physical explanations for the operation of the universe, and as the religious establishment lost power, scientists began proposing theories to explain how the universe and life might have come into existence without a Creator. Any such theory would require three main developments: the formation of the material universe, the origin of living things from non-living matter, and the evolution of all modern life forms from a simple original organism.

Today's most popular explanation of the first of these big developments, how the universe might have come into existence without a Creator, is often called the **big bang theory**. Since scientists have excluded God from their knowledge, the only explanation they can offer for the origin of life (the second big development) is to say that it came from non-living chemicals, so the second development is often called **chemical evolution** or **abiogenesis** [ā-bī-ō-JEN-es-is] ("no" + "life" + "beginning"). These terms refer to the formation of complex life-like chemicals from simple ones, and to the first organization of these molecules into something that acts like a living thing. Of course, the most important characteristic for this complex arrangement of chemicals is the ability to reproduce.

The third major step in the development of modern life from non-life must (according to theory) involve the evolution (change) of living things from a single living organism to all of the organisms that now exist, or have ever existed, including humans. This is often given the name **Darwinian evolution**, or **Darwinism,** after the man who most advanced it through his observations of nature. Since the time of Charles Darwin (1809-1882), the theory has taken one turn that most scientists consider to be a major change in the theory as Darwin proposed it. For this reason, the current version of evolutionary theory is often called **neodarwinian** (meaning "new" Darwinian). The following lessons will discuss in greater detail these steps in the supposed evolution of life.

Exercises:

True or false?

1. The big bang theory is proposed by scientists to describe how living things arose from non-living chemicals.

2. Neodarwinian theory contains changes that have been made to Darwin's theories since the time of his death.

3. Materialism considers only things that man can observe with his own senses.

4. Abiogenesis is a name given to the idea that living things have arisen from non-living chemicals.

7: *Bang?*

While believers in God have never doubted that there might have been a really big bang when God spoke the universe into existence, this is not what scientists mean when they talk about a big bang. By measuring the light from stars, scientists observe that the universe appears to be expanding in all directions. This leads them to suspect that at one time the entire universe was contained in a small space. There is also a certain electromagnetic energy present throughout the universe that they assume to have been left over from a great explosion. If all of the matter in the universe were contained in such a small space, there is no doubt that its expansion would be terrific. How it got there is anybody's guess, as there is really nothing to favor one theory over another. Perhaps a person could theorize that God put it there, but that would be breaking the rules of the materialists' "game." The theory continues that, as the universe expanded, this matter was distributed in all directions and eventually led to the gatherings of matter that account for galaxies, cosmic "dust," stars and planets.

There are problems in accepting the big bang theory. First of all, and perhaps most importantly, where did the matter that makes up the universe come from, and how did all of it get packed into a tiny spot like that? Anything that a person might imagine is certainly no less difficult to believe than the existence of a Creator. Second, if matter is in one nice smooth super-hot liquid ball, why did it spread itself out through the universe in such a messy way? The matter in the universe is organized into clusters of galaxies that are inconsistent with a random explosion of matter. Today's theories have no satisfactory explanation for this universal lumpiness.

Notice that no one has a real picture of what the universe would have been like at the time of the "big bang." The nicely painted portraits that you see in popular magazines are often artists' imaginations of what the big bang might have looked like. In most cases, you would be as well qualified as that artist to paint your own imaginings. Why not take some time and paint your belief about the origin of the universe?

Exercises:

Tell whether each of the following statements is true or false and take time to carefully explain your answer.

1. Pictures of the big bang that appear in popular magazines were taken by scientists at the time it actually happened.

2. The big bang is a well-documented scientific fact.

3. The big bang theory does not attempt to answer the question "Where did the matter in our universe come from?"

Your imaginations about the beginnings of the Earth, as long as they are well-educated, are as acceptable as anyone else's. No human was there to see the beginning.

8: *Abiogenesis*

In 1952 a man named Stanley Miller performed an experiment. He was a biochemist (one who studies the chemistry of living organisms). He believed that life could arise from purely physical processes, and he set out to perform an experiment to see whether his belief could be supported by evidence. He decided on a set of conditions that might produce "**biomolecules**"—the molecules making up living organisms. His test included a combination of the simplest chemicals. Obviously one must have a source of carbon, since most molecules found in living systems are made from carbon atoms, so Miller selected methane. One must also have a source of nitrogen, hence the ammonia. Water must also be abundant. If any chemicals formed are to last, oxygen must be absent, because if it is allowed, it will quickly react with and consume any products, so Miller excluded free oxygen. Then, to cause these chemicals to take on a higher level of potential energy, he zapped them with sparks generated by electricity.

Nothing living came out of Mr. Miller's experiments, but some basic biomolecules did—not the big ones, but several amino acids.

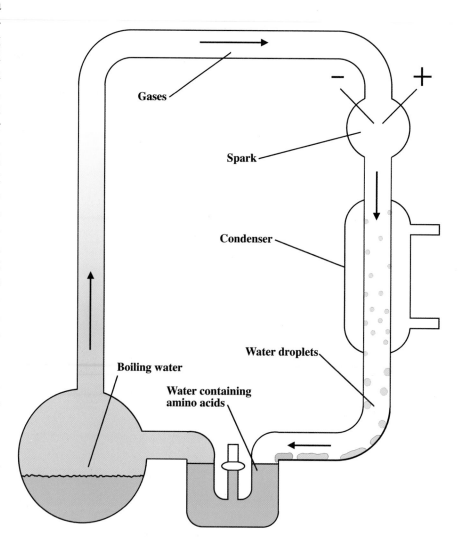

This is a diagram of an apparatus like the one used by Stanley Miller to show that certain organic chemicals can be synthesized in the absence of oxygen from selected gases using electrical energy.

This experiment has been performed under different conditions by several scientists, so that many simple biomolecules have been generated. Evolutionists are impressed with the fact that some of the parts of living molecules can be generated in this way; and well they should be. After all, this is equivalent to throwing a stick of dynamite into a room full of balls and having some of them land up on a shelf. The miracle is not that the balls land on the shelf, however, as the evolutionist might celebrate. The miracle is that there is a shelf in the room made for the ball to land on.

Since the time of this famous experiment, much has been written about the possibility of generating life from chemicals. So far scientists have obtained only chemicals from chemicals. It has now been more than 45 years since the original experiment was published, and no living thing has been generated or even closely approached. As time passes, it will be more and more difficult for other scientists to accept abiogenesis.

Another problem that is just as difficult for one who believes in evolution is the problem of **reproduction**. Suppose, by some stretch of the imagination, that an assembly of chemicals could come together to make a chemical of high organization (like a molecule of DNA). This big chemical will not be "alive" and will not be successful in evolving unless it can reproduce by making a working copy of itself. And this can't happen only once by chance in order for evolution to be successful; it has to happen consistently, time and time again. The notion that non-living things might function and create functioning copies of themselves challenges our most colorful imaginations.

Exercises:

True or false?

1. The experiment performed by Stanley Miller showed that some simple organic chemicals could be made from selected molecules under controlled conditions by adding energy.

2. The experiment showed that these molecules must have been present in the early atmosphere.

3. The experiment showed that life could possibly originate from non-living matter.

4. Scientists once created life in a test tube.

5. There is no such thing as a single-celled organism.

6. To be considered alive, a chemical must be able to make copies of itself.

9: *Making You Out of Apes?*

How does an evolutionist think a small molecule that makes copies of itself might develop into the diversity of life that we see on Earth today? The only possibility is for this molecule to become more complex without losing its ability to reproduce. But do things in our world tend toward greater or lesser complexity? By now you know that everything tends toward less complexity—that is, toward a lower level of potential energy. Being supplied with bursts of energy may cause an increase in that potential energy, but the results will be like building blocks that have been blown around with dynamite—less orderly and less likely to do anything useful. The more energy you blast the organism with, the less likely it is to reproduce.

You already have enough knowledge of chemistry and physics to understand how unlikely biological evolution is. Remember that everything we have observed tends toward a lower level of potential energy. Evolution from lower organisms to higher ones requires the opposite to occur—not just once, with a momentary blast of energy, but countless thousands of times. Each unlikely change must produce an organism that is more capable and highly organized than the one before it.

These days, you may read articles in any popular magazine about the presumed linkage between apes and humans. People are obsessed with the notion. But just remind yourself that there is no evidence that any such linkage exists. Certainly the human-like fossil remains that have been found are neither exactly like modern humans, nor exactly like modern apes. That in no way implies that they represent some relative of either one. Perhaps neither ape nor man is exactly what he was in the ancient past. History records people who lived much longer than they do today, and that life span would have to show up in the appearance of those ancient people. All animals have changed significantly in their appearance over time. There is no reason to believe, based on these fossil remains, that there is any common ancestry among separate groups of organisms. In fact, there is fossil evidence to the contrary.

Darwinian evolution is believed by many scientists to explain how people came into existence through a common ancestor with modern apes. In truth it makes apes out of a lot of people.

Exercises:

True or false?

1. Darwinian evolution is a fact that has been proven by modern science.

2. Darwinian evolution is believed, taught and even preached by modern scientists as though it had been proven.

3. Darwinian evolution is a theory which suggests that people share a common ancestor with modern apes.

4. At most universities—even religious ones—you are likely to be taught that evolution is a proven fact.

5. Fossil evidence shows that all organisms have evolved from a common ancestor.

6. Darwinian evolution attempts to explain the origin of the universe.

10: *Adaptive Evolution*

We have long known that organisms have the ability to change over time in order to become better suited to their environment. These changes are called **adaptations**. Although the word **evolution** is often associated with things that are untrue or unproven, the word itself merely means "change." There is no doubt that organisms can change and that these changes may be passed from generation to generation. Most of these changes do not affect the organism's ability to reproduce. Others may be harmful to the organism. In either case, the change is not evolutionary in the Darwinian sense.

Rarely, a change might bring about an improvement in a group of organisms that makes it better suited to its surroundings. For example, a slight change in the color of an organism might improve its ability to hide from a predator (an animal that eats it). After several generations there will be an increase in the portion of organisms having this color because of their greater ability to survive. We might accurately say that this is **adaptive evolution**, or change that makes an organism better suited to its environment. Don't confuse this small-scale change with the enormous changes that would be required for all organisms to have come from a common ancestor.

German shepherd

Golden retriever

Norfolk terrier

Briard

Afghan "blaze"

Chesapeake Bay retriever

Groenendael

Bulldog

Spaniel

Basenji

For centuries, people have taken advantage of this ability of organisms to change. For example, dogs have been bred that are specially adapted for war, for hunting, for pulling sleds, or for running. Plants have been specially bred to develop flowers having bold colors, striking color patterns, more beautifully shaped petals, or different sizes. However, nature does not favor these changes. If these organisms are returned to nature to breed as they will, they will quickly take on their old dull appearances. If you continue your interest in science, you will learn how such processes work.

In the following lessons we will survey the vast assortment of organisms that God has created for our wise use (and even for our amusement). You needn't memorize all of the mind-boggling names that you will encounter along the way (unless you intend to be a biologist, in which case, you might as well get started). But just relax and enjoy this marvel of diversity and stupefying intricacy. Notice the tremendous differences that can be brought about in animals of a single species by skillful selection of breeding pairs.

Exercise:

What might likely happen to all life on Earth if organisms did not have the ability to change in response to changes in their living conditions?

Hamilton stovare

Maltese terrier

Cocker spaniel

Japchin

Grand bleu de Gascogne

Chow

11: *The World of Microbes*

Everyone knows that many organisms are too small to be seen without a microscope. We call them "**microscopic**" organisms. What is confusing to most people is that there are so many different kinds of tiny organisms. People often think that these organisms (called **microorganisms**) are all alike. They lump them together and call them "germs" to include bacteria, yeasts, algae and viruses. Although they are all small, many of these are as different from one another as an elephant is from a coconut palm. Here is a rundown of the microbes:

Bacteria are tiny single-celled prokaryotic microorganisms. (Remember that a prokaryote doesn't have a nucleus in its cell.) They are found practically everywhere on Earth: in soil, water, air and the deep underground (as deep as anyone has ever drilled). They are also found in you: in your mouth, your nose, your ears, your stomach and your intestines, and on your skin. They are on your pillow and your towel, and even in your drinking water. Since you live in harmony with so many of these bacteria, they must be pretty friendly. In fact only a few bacteria are really troublesome, while many others are useful to us. The bad bacteria are the ones we hear most about, though. They include the disease-causing **pathogens** like those that cause whooping cough, tetanus, "strep throat," staph infections, cholera, botulism, anthrax, meningitis and pneumonia.

Bacteria can be controlled by the use of **antibiotics**. These are natural chemicals that are produced by other

These bacteria represent the smallest of all organisms. Magnified 1000 times, they are still barely large enough to be seen clearly. A few are harmful but many others are beneficial. They are the world's waste recyclers, taking dead plant and animal matter and using it to make their own energy by converting it to carbon dioxide and water.

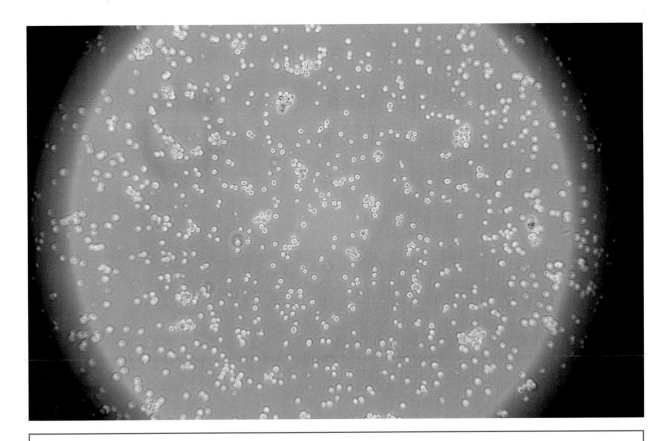

Yeasts are free-living microscopic fungi. They are much larger than bacteria. They are famous for their ability to ferment sugars. There are also some disease-causing yeasts, such as those that cause diaper rash in young children and urinary infections in women.

microorganisms. Once these chemicals were discovered, scientists learned how to change their chemical structures so that they attack different kinds of bacteria more effectively. Many antibiotic drugs are now being used. Over the years since antibiotics were discovered, bacteria have become adapted so that antibiotics are not as destructive to them. Scientists are now in a race against these **antibiotic-resistant bacteria**, trying to develop new ways of protecting people from them.

There is a group of organisms that look like bacteria, but are actually quite different. Until recent years they were thought to be bacteria, but when their DNA was compared to bacterial DNA it was discovered that these organisms are chemically as different from bacteria as bacteria are from us. These organisms used to be called archaebacteria, but are now known simply as **archaea**, which means "ancient ones."

Evolutionists once believed that these organisms were the first to occupy the Earth and that they were the organisms from which all others eventually evolved. This is because many of them share characteristics with plants, animals and bacteria. It is also because the archaea occupy some harsh environments thought by evolutionists to be similar to the environment of the young earth. For example, archaea live in the deep sea hydrothermal vents where temperatures can be hotter than boiling water. They are also found in hot springs, at pH values from 1 to 2 (very acidic). Now that the

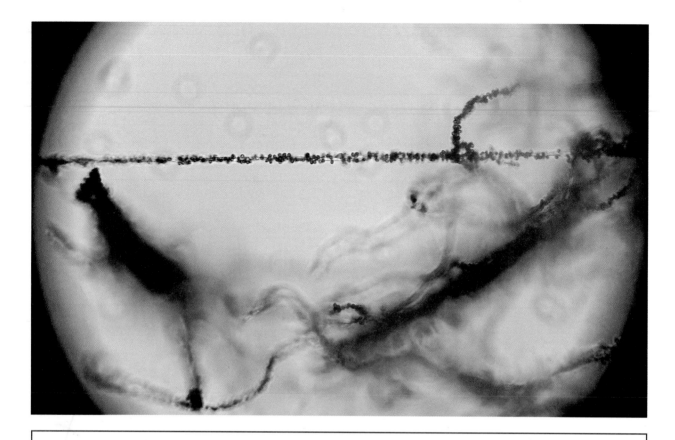

Molds are also fungi, but instead of living independently they usually grow in long strands called hyphae. *Many hyphae grow together to form a tangled mass called a* mycelium. *These organisms are famous for their fuzzy-looking growth, especially on bread, and as the source of penicillin—the first antibiotic.*

genomes of these organisms have been studied more extensively, however, the idea that other life forms evolved from archaea is difficult to support.

The prokaryotic organisms discussed in previous paragraphs—bacteria and archaea—are tiny, ranging in size from 0.5 to 5 micrometers. (A micrometer is one millionth of a meter, or one thousandth of a millimeter). Eukaryotic organisms (having nuclei in their cells) come in a variety of sizes. Take fungi, for instance. These include the yeasts, molds, slime molds, lichens, mushrooms and toadstools. You may recognize mushrooms and toadstools as **macroscopic** organisms (organisms that can be seen without the help of a magnifier). But yeasts are microscopic, and molds may be either macroscopic or microscopic. Even though they are small, microscopic yeasts and molds are still eukaryotic. They are 10 to 100 times larger than bacteria and archaea.

Although bacteria, archaea and fungi are not classified as either plants or animals, there are some plants and animals too small to be seen without a microscope. Microscopic plants are called **microphyta** (meaning "small plants"), while microscopic animals are called **microzoa** (meaning—guess what—"small animals"; you are so smart!). These organisms can be either single-celled or **multicellular** ("many" + "celled"). These microscopic organisms are considered by evolutionists to be among the **lower** plants and animals, meaning that they are less complex, and therefore "less evolved" than the **higher** plants and animals. You may hear some simple microzoa referred to as "protozoa." This term implies that they represent ancestors of higher animals. Actually, it's not as simple as evolution would have it. Many of these organisms have characteristics that we associate with both plants and animals, so it's difficult to decide whether they have closer family ties on one side or the other.

There are many organisms that are not easily classified into one group or another using the evolutionary model. The "blue-green algae" were for many years thought to be plants. Lately it has been realized that even though they have plant-like features, and they grow in strands like algae, their chemical makeup is more like the bacteria. They are now being called **cyanobacteria** or blue-green bacteria. But they are certainly odd bacteria!

These shelf mushrooms are examples of macroscopic fungi. Although yeasts and molds are much smaller, they are classified in the same kingdom because of their shared cell characteristics.

Exercises:
1. How many different types of microorganisms are named in the table?
2. If I wanted to look for bacteria, where could I find some?
3. Are bacteria harmful to us? Explain.
4. Colds are caused by viruses. Can a cold be cured through the use of antibiotics? Explain your answer.

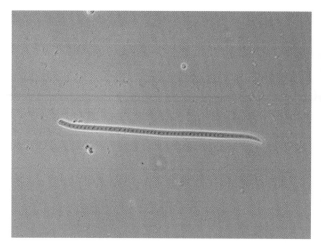 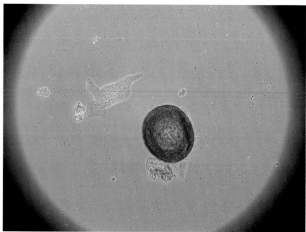

Plants (left) and animals (right) can also be microscopic.

TABLE: THE ROSTER OF MICROBES

Organism	Description
Virus	Not considered a "living organism" because it reproduces only at the expense of a living cell. Contains nucleic acid(s) and protein. An example is rhinovirus—the agent of the common cold.
Archaea	Prokaryotic organisms occupying harsh environments and sharing characteristics with organisms of various types. An example is the "extreme thermophiles" ("heat" + "loving") that live in water at 120°C.
Bacteria	Prokaryotic organisms occupying nearly every environment on Earth. Each has an external cell wall and a circular genome. Many believe the cyanobacteria ("blue-green algae") belong here, even though they have chlorophyll, like plants. Examples of bacteria are the deadly *Bordatella pertussis* which causes whooping cough and the harmless *Lactobacillus acidophilus* found in milk.
Microfungi	Eukaryotic organisms, in either single cells (yeasts) or long strands (filaments) having an external sheath. An example is baker's yeast used in making bread.
Microphyta	Tiny eukaryotic plants having chlorophyll and plant-like cell walls. May be either single cells or colonies; some have even higher organization. An example is a green alga (algae is plural).
Microzoa	Tiny eukaryotic animals having no cell wall. May be single cells or colonies; some have even higher organization. An example is a rotifer.

12: *Botany*

Botany is the study of plants. Why do people like plants? They can be beautiful, like some of the flowering plants. They can provide us with food, such as garden vegetables. They can provide us with protection from the sunshine and the wind. Trees are made mostly of cellulose, which is a sturdy molecule. It makes the wood hard and stiff and therefore useful for building. The chemical bond energy which is stored in wood can be released by burning, to keep us warm in the winter. Plants make good pets because they don't make noise or messes. Most of them don't bite, and all you have to do is water them and make sure they get their minerals.

To biologists, plants hold a special place in nature. Perhaps the most important reason is that they are at the bottom of the **food chain**. The food chain is the order of who eats whom. Lions eat zebras, and zebras eat plants. Plants don't eat anything, so they are at the bottom of the food chain. Whales eat shrimp. Shrimp eat **zooplankton** [ZŌ-ō-plank-tun] ("suspended animals"). Zooplankton eat tiny plants. But plants don't eat anything, so they are at the bottom of the food chain. I'm glad I'm at the top of the food chain, where I eat both plants and animals, but nothing eats me. I'm also glad that plants are at the bottom of the food chain because they don't have brains, so they don't care if they get eaten.

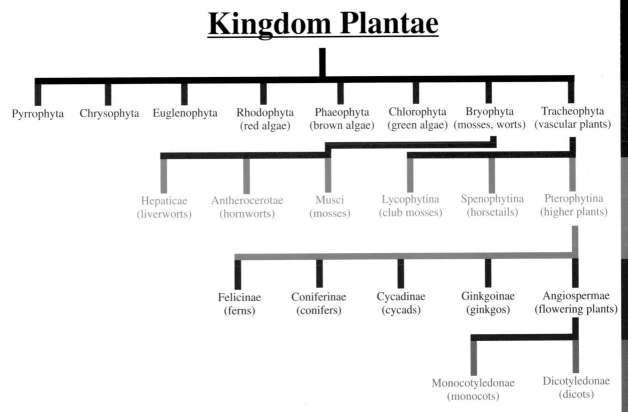

But if plants don't eat, and all living things require food, where do plants get their food? We have already learned that all living things are made mostly of carbon and that carbon is required to build more living things. The question is, where do plants get their carbon if not from eating other living things? We have also learned that we get our energy from oxidizing carbon-containing chemicals (like sugars and fats) to carbon dioxide. This reaction gives us energy. But if plants don't eat other living things, where do they get their energy?

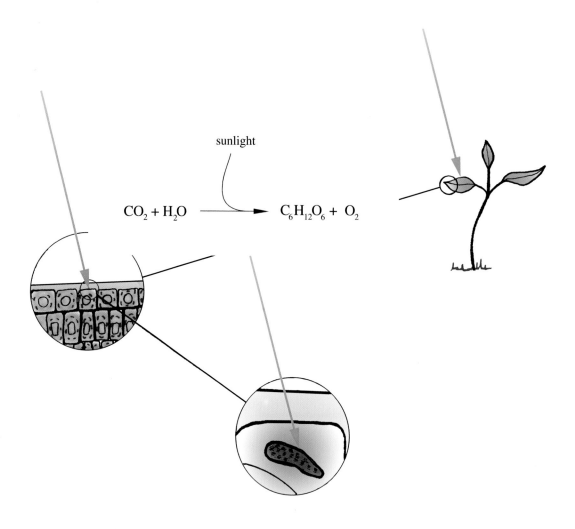

sunlight

$$CO_2 + H_2O \longrightarrow C_6H_{12}O_6 + O_2$$

Plants are called primary producers. *They grow using energy from sunshine and carbon from the carbon dioxide they bring in from their surroundings. They use these resources to make glucose by photosynthesis.*

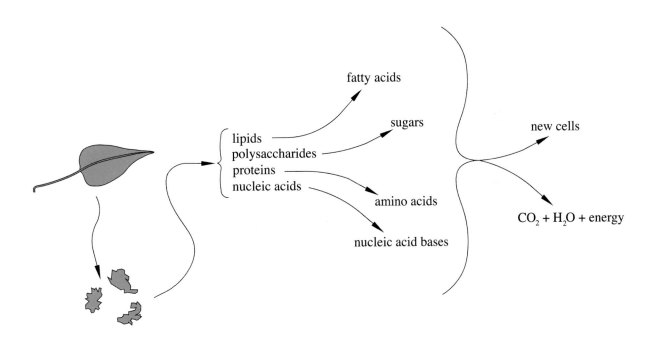

Because animals are not photosynthetic, they must rely on plants or on other animals that eat plants as their source of energy and carbon. An animal must have a digestive system to break down plant material into chemicals that can be used for carbon and energy.

The carbon that plants use for building comes from the atmosphere. They have the ability to take carbon dioxide out of the air and use the sun's energy to link the atoms of carbon together into simple sugars. These sugars serve as the plants' food. Taking an oxidized chemical like carbon dioxide and reducing it to make a sugar involves a shift from a state of lower potential energy to that of a higher one. As we have seen, such an upward shift requires two things. It requires a lot of energy input, and it requires a design that will direct the energy to where it can be used.

While animals get their energy from eating plants and other animals, plants get their energy from sunlight. The energy from the sunlight is used efficiently by plants to make chemical bonds. These chemicals are moved about inside the plant to the locations where the energy is needed. There the chemical bonds are broken, and the energy is released to pay for the plant's useful activities. The process by which plants obtain energy from sunlight to make sugars is called **photosynthesis** ("light" + "make").

Plants use chemical **pigments**—colored compounds—to capture the sunlight. The best known of these pigments is **chlorophyll *a*** which gives plants their green color. Plants use many other pigments as well, but chlorophyll *a* is common to nearly all of the higher plants. The colors we see in autumn trees as they lose their leaves are caused by the breakdown of chlorophyll to reveal some of these other pigments that are also in the leaves. As the pigments break apart, several products of the breakdown also contribute to this marvel of color.

Since evolutionists believe that life evolved from within the ocean, progressing onto dry land, they classify plants based on how different they are from an imagined ancestor that supposedly lived in the ocean. The algae that live suspended in water are considered to be lower plants. Plants that live on land in damp areas are placed somewhat higher on the evolutionary scale. So then, plants that live away from such abundant moisture and need ways to store water and move it around inside are classified as the highest on the evolutionary scale.

Exercises:
1. From where do plants get their energy?
2. From where do they get their carbon?

13: *The Tiny Plants*

We have already mentioned microphyta. These tiny plants inhabit moist environments. Among the microphyta are the **phytoplankton** (meaning "suspended plants") that live suspended in lakes, streams and oceans. Phytoplankton include the organisms shown in the following Figures. There are many organisms which make up each of the phyla introduced in this lesson. (See the Table for technical names.) We present only a few examples so that you can get a feel for the similarities and differences among the phyla.

TABLE: PHYLA OF MICROPHYTA (TINY ALGAE)	
Phylum	**Organism**
Pyrrophyta ("fire" + "plants")	dinoflagellates
Chrysophyta ("gold" + "plants")	coccolithophorids, diatoms
Euglenophyta ("good" + "eyeball" + "plants")	*Euglena* species (possess an eyespot)
Chlorophyta ("green" + "plants")	*Volvox* species, spirogyra

Some of the more famous phytoplankton include the dinoflagellates (sometimes called "red tide"). These little monsters can grow in great numbers within an area and produce toxins that kill fish and other animals. They can even be deadly to humans who swim in infested waters.

A second phylum includes many important phytoplankton. One group of these organisms, called coccolithophorids [KOK-kō-lith-ō-FOR-idz], die and settle to the bottom of the ocean. Their dead cell walls are made of calcium carbonate and accumulate into layers of chalk at the bottom of the ocean.

Another group in this phylum, called diatoms, consists of fascinating little organisms that build cell walls out of silica. Under the light of a microscope these "glass houses" of different shapes bend light, so they look colorful. Sometimes these organisms don't detach as they grow, so they remain stuck together, forming a variety of geometric patterns.

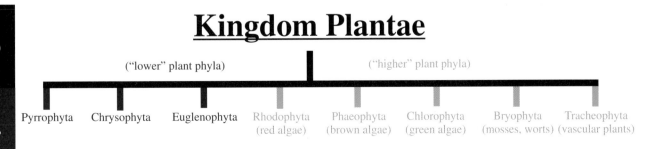

Kingdom Plantae

("lower" plant phyla)   ("higher" plant phyla)

Pyrrophyta   Chrysophyta   Euglenophyta   Rhodophyta (red algae)   Phaeophyta (brown algae)   Chlorophyta (green algae)   Bryophyta (mosses, worts)   Tracheophyta (vascular plants)

Phylum   Kingdom

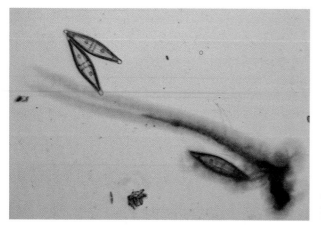

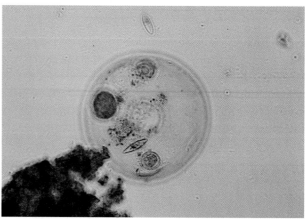

Diatoms *have outer cell walls made of the same silicaceous material (material containing silica) that glass is made of. They grow in lots of neat shapes.*

Volvox *are simple colonies of algae in the shape of hollow spheres that travel around using their flagella.*

A third phylum common in fresh water includes the *Euglena*. These organisms have lots of big **plastids** which are sacs that hold their pigments. Like many other microeukaryotes, they have an eyespot that senses light and a whip-like **flagellum** that they thrash to propel them through water.

The final group of microphyta consists of the **green algae**. Some of the most famous green algae are the *Volvox*, which are colonies of cells forming hollow spheres. Each sphere has two flagella that help direct its motion through water. Other organisms in this group include the slimy **filamentous** algae (algae that grow in long strands) that we see floating in the edge water of ponds.

Exercises:

1. In this lesson we begin a study of the plant kingdom according to the various phyla. How many phyla of microscopic algae are there?

2. Are all plants algae?

3. Are all algae considered to be plants?

14: *Up the Plant Ladder*

In the last lesson we mentioned the green algae. While these are **microscopic** in the sense that each filament is only one cell wide, they are **macroscopic** in the sense that they grow in masses that are big enough to be seen without the help of a microscope. This is just the first of the phyla of the macroscopic algae. There are two others, but they are found only in the ocean. They are the brown algae and the red algae. These two types of algae have their unique colors because they contain different kinds of pigments. Neither of these two groups has the characteristics of higher plants which would allow them to live on land.

Mosses, **hornworts** and **liverworts** are barely terrestrial. Because they have no way to carry water within them, they grow low to the ground and only in areas of shade and high moisture. You can find lots of mosses, hornworts and liverworts near waterfalls where the humidity is high. Mosses are often found on water-soaked rotten logs, and on the north side of trees, away from direct sunlight.

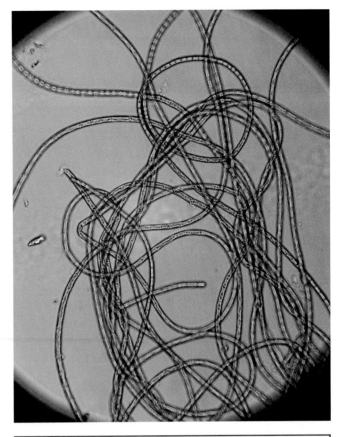

Green algae are aquatic plants that grow in long, thin strands.

Kingdom Plantae

("lower" plant phyla) ("higher" plant phyla)

Pyrrophyta Chrysophyta Euglenophyta Rhodophyta (red algae) Phaeophyta (brown algae) Chlorophyta (green algae) Bryophyta (mosses, worts) Tracheophyta (vascular plants)

Hepaticae (liverworts) Antherocerotae (hornworts) Musci (mosses) Lycophytina (club mosses) Spenophytina (horsetails) Pterophytina (higher plants)

Kingdom Phylum Subphylum

The **higher plants**, or **vascular plants** as they are sometimes called, are well-suited for life on the ground. Each of these plants has a series of tubes in a long stem for carrying water from its roots to its leaves. The leaves which are full of veins for distributing water from the stem to the cells, serve as food factories where photosynthesis takes place. The sugars that are produced by photosynthesis are sent back down to the roots (which are not photosynthetic because they get no light) through a second set of tubes, as if to say "Thank you for sending the water." Water is conserved in the plant by a waxy coating over the leaves. If it were not for this coating, the plant would surely dry out in the hot sunshine.

There are pores (called **stomata**, the plural form of the singular **stoma**) in the leaves that allow some water to escape along with the oxygen produced by photosynthesis; but the pores are open only during the day, and

Kelp is a type of brown algae that grows to be immense in large areas of nutrient-rich water called kelp forests.

Mosses are low-growing plants that grow in moist areas, often under heavy plant cover. Because they don't have veins to carry water, they must be protected from the drying rays of the sun.

then only if the plant has enough water. At night and during dry times the **guard cells** surrounding the stomata close, trapping water in the leaves.

The types of higher plants are many, but there are only a few divisions (subphyla) based on the plant structures and on the evolutionary way of thinking. The first division includes plants that are called **club mosses** (because they are low-lying plants that grow more or less in the shape of a club). The next group is the **horsetails** of which there are only a few now living. The third group contains all other vascular plants and is subdivided into many categories. These plants will be the subjects of the following lessons.

Horsetails are relatively uncommon plants showing some ability to transport water. To the evolutionist, they represent a transition from "lower" to "higher" plants.

Exercises:
1. Which of the following plants will be found only in water?
   a. algae
   b. mosses
   c. vascular plants
2. Which of the following plants will be found on land in the moist environments near water?
   a. hornworts
   b. vascular plants
   c. algae
3. Which of the following plants will be found on dry land, sometimes hundreds of miles from the nearest body of water?
   a. red algae
   b. mosses
   c. green algae
   d. vascular plants
4. Which of the following plants is not in the phylum Tracheophyta?
   a. club moss
   b. horsetail
   c. liverwort

15: *Higher Plants—Non-Flowering Plants*

The **pterophytes** [TĀR-ō-fīts] include several classes of vascular plants which we will introduce. First, I'd like you to meet the **ferns**. Ferns are vascular plants all right, but their leaves are small, so the veins are pretty simple. This gives the plants a "feather-like" appearance.

The ferns are an example of several groups of plants that have complex **life cycles.** Such plants live through several stages during which their appearances change dramatically. The two main stages are called the **sporophyte generation** and the **gametophyte** [ga-MĒ-tō-fīt] **generation**. The sporophyte generation is one in which the plant reproduces with **asexual spores**. "Asexual" means that the plants do not require male and female plant parts to reproduce. "Spores" are resting stages that are resistant to extremes of weather. They lie **dormant** until conditions are right for them to **germinate**. Germination is the process of coming out of dormancy and becoming active. The spores germinate to produce the gametophyte generation. During this generation, or stage, the plant uses male sperm cells and female ovary cells to reproduce sexually and produce the next sporophyte.

Most higher plants reproduce sexually and produce **seeds**. These seeds house the **embryo** or undeveloped plant until conditions are right for it to germinate and develop. (Some seeds have been known to germinate after waiting thousands of years for those right conditions.)

Now we're ready to meet one of the groups of seed-bearing pterophytes, the **gymnosperms**. The word *gymnosperm* means "naked seed." In the gymnosperms, the male **pollen** is produced in male cones. The female **egg cells** are produced inside female cones. The pollen is transferred to the female cone by the wind. In gymnosperms the seeds develop as scales on a cone. These fall to the ground, and under the right conditions, develop into new seedlings (young plants).

Kingdom Plantae

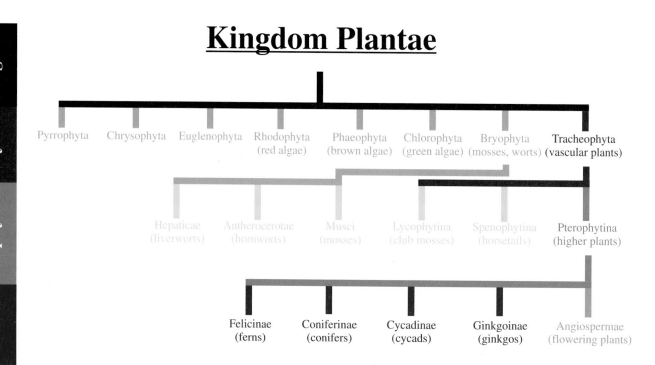

Ferns (top left) are vascular plants with tiny leaves. They reproduce by asexual spores (bottom left) located beneath their leaves. New growth of a fern plant uncoils in the form of a "fiddlehead" (right).

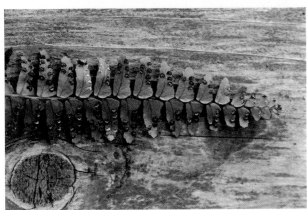

Gymnosperms reproduce with seeds that are borne on cones, and their leaves are needle-like.

The most common gymnosperms are the **conifers**. There are perhaps 600 different conifers, including the pines, cedars and firs. Pines are distinguished by their needle-like leaves. These leaves have the same basic features as the broad, flat leaves of the other higher plants. They have a stoma, a central vein, photosynthetic cells, and a waxy **cuticle** that conserves moisture.

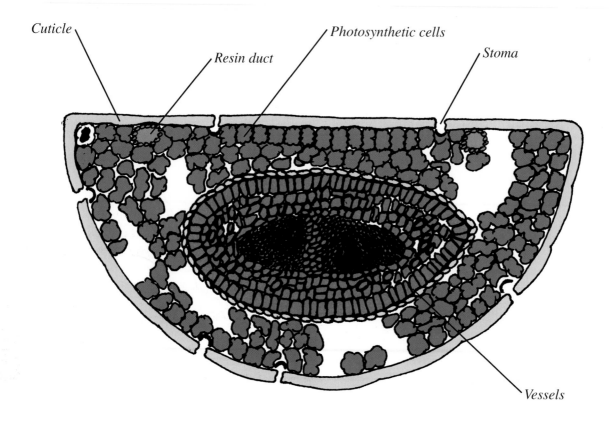

A needle of a gymnosperm has nearly the same features as the leaves of other plants, even though they look quite different.

Exercises:
1. From the table of the plant kingdom, tell whether ferns are in the phylum Tracheophyta.
2. Are pine trees and ferns in the same phylum?
3. Cedar trees reproduce using:

    a. spores (called asexual reproduction).

    b. sexual reproduction with cones (making them gymnosperms).

    c. sexual reproduction with flowers (making them angiosperms).

16: *Higher Plants—Flowering Plants*

All plants other than those of the types studied in previous lessons are **angiosperms**. These plants dominate the landscape, and you can thank God for that! These are the beautiful flowering plants that brighten the world with their color in the springtime, keep us in flowers all summer, and show spectacular color in the fall. The angiosperms are of two types: **monocotyledons** [mon-ō-cot-i-LĒ-donz] and **dicotyledons** [dī-cot-i-LĒ-donz]. Here's the difference: When the seed of a monocotyledon germinates, the plant's development begins as a single seed leaf breaking forth from the seed. The development of a dicotyledon seedling begins with two seed leaves breaking forth from the seed. (That's "mono-" for "one" seed leaf, and "di-" for "two." Makes sense, doesn't it?)

Monocotyledons are grassy plants. The veins in the leaves run parallel along the length of the leaf. These plants have growth in one major direction without branching. They include about 60,000 species. Dicotyledons are the plants with broad leaves having net-like or feather-like veins throughout. They may have growth branching out into a lot of different directions. They include nearly 200,000 different species.

The flowers of angiosperms are the sites of their sexual reproduction. We find the **petals** of the flower attractive, but they also attract insects by reflecting the ultraviolet wavelengths of sunlight which we humans can't perceive but which insects can. The flowers produce **nectar** (sugary liquid) that is used by the insects for food. As the insects reach inside the flower to retrieve the nectar, they

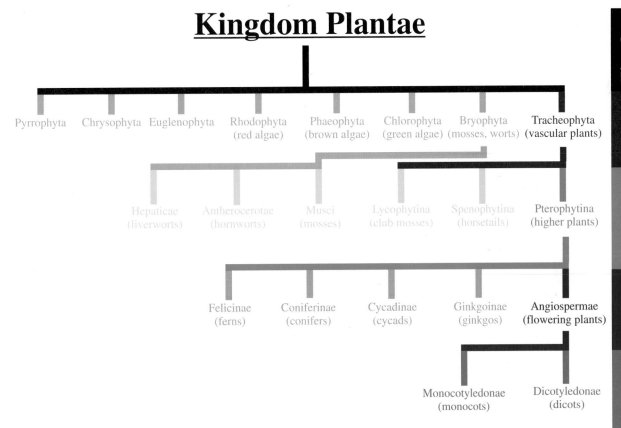

Kingdom Plantae

Flowers are supported by a green base called the calyx. The leaves of the calyx are called sepals.

pick up pollen from within the flower. The insects carry pollen from flower to flower, so the flowers are fertilized by the insect's action. (It's a good thing insects are not allergic to pollen like many people are, or their lives would be miserable!) The petals are supported from below by green leaf-like structures called **sepals**. The entire cup-like base of the flower is called the **calyx**.

Pollen forms on the surface of the **anther**, the thick structure on the end of the **filament**. Together these two organs make up the **stamen**—the male reproductive part of the flower. The female reproductive part is the **carpel**. It includes the **stigma**, the **ovary** and the **style**. The stigma receives the pollen for fertilization; the style is a stalk connecting the stigma to the ovary; the ovary is a hollow organ containing several **ovules**, each of which contains a single egg cell which can be fertilized to develop into a seed. While some flowers contain both male and female parts, other plants produce separate flowers with either male (**staminate**) or female (**pistillate**) parts.

The patterns of veins in the leaves of vascular plants are interestingly complex, but follow distinct patterns.

A stamen is composed of a long, thin filament capped with a bulb-like anther. The anther bears the pollen that is picked up by the wind or an insect and carried to the female reproductive organs. The pistil is composed of a stigma to receive the pollen from the anther of the male, the trunk-like style through which the sperm cells from the pollen must travel, and the ovary that contains the eggs (ova) to be fertilized. Multiple eggs may be fertilized, each to develop within its own ovule.

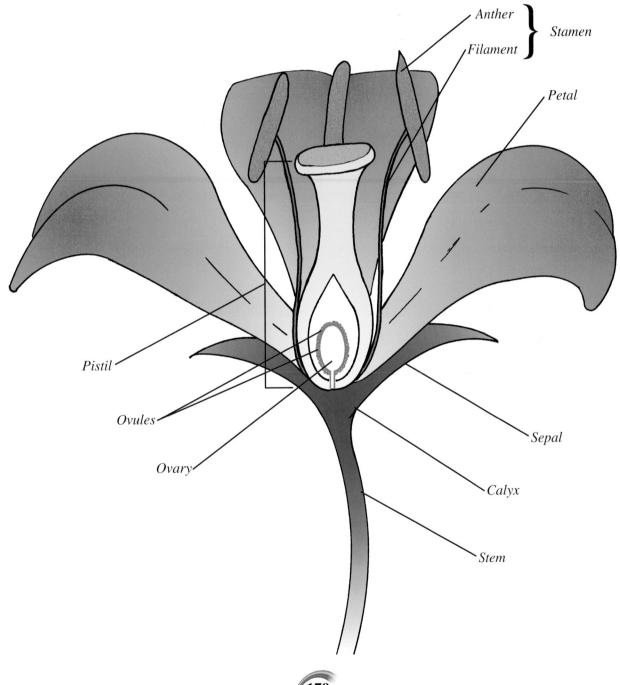

Anther
Filament
} Stamen
Petal
Pistil
Ovules
Ovary
Sepal
Calyx
Stem

A seed leaf is the first leaf to emerge from the ground when a seed germinates. A single seed leaf, like this one, indicates the plant is a monocotyledon.

Two seed leaves appear on a young dicotyledon.

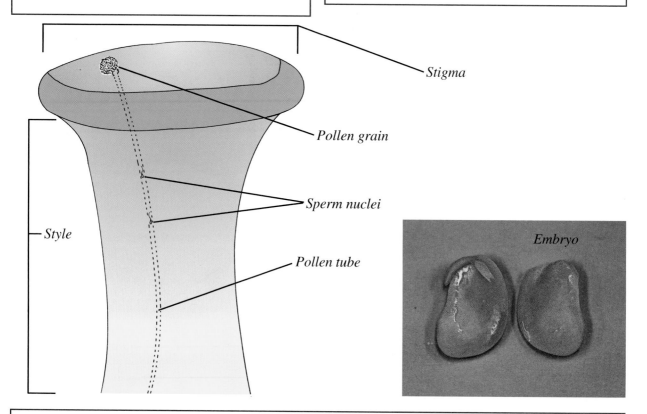

Stigma

Pollen grain

Sperm nuclei

Style

Pollen tube

Embryo

The fertilization process results in a seed that contains the plant embryo. If provided with a suitable environment, the seed will "germinate" and the embryo will develop into a mature plant.

The next two pages are photos of flowers containing both male and female parts. Can you identify the parts?

Exercises:

1. From the table of the plant kingdom at the beginning of the lesson, decide whether or not the flowering plants are in the phylum Tracheophyta.

2. The leaves of a corn plant have no veins, and the plants don't branch. Are corn plants monocotyledons or dicotyledons?

3. Name the parts of a flower that are considered female.

4. Name the parts of a flower that are considered male.

5. Name the parts of a flower that are neither male nor female.

17: *The Animals*

Zoology is the study of animals, which by scientific definition (and perhaps based on evolutionary thought) includes humans. Animals are special to us because they may have a brain, providing them with the capacity for senses and emotions. They may even act like us—for example, in forming attachments to people and to each other. They resemble people much more than do plants or microorganisms. All animals are consumers, and most of the higher animals eat and process food alike. (Did anyone ever tell you that you eat like a pig?) The body plans of higher animals are often laid out similarly, and many of them reproduce in similar ways.

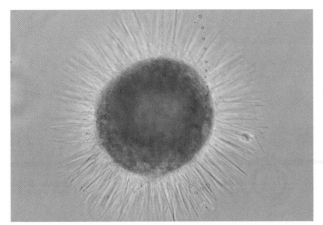 

The phyla of the animal kingdom may be divided into three groups—protozoa, mesozoa and metazoa—based on evolutionary theory. This protozoan (left) and metazoan (right) represent opposite ends of the scale of complexity.

But among animals there are obviously many differences, and how different they can be! (Nobody ever told me I eat like a squid!) In this study you will become familiar with both the variety and the similarity among the animals.

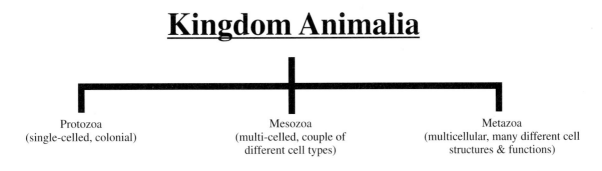

Kingdom Animalia

Protozoa	Mesozoa	Metazoa
(single-celled, colonial)	(multi-celled, couple of different cell types)	(multicellular, many different cell structures & functions)

Kingdom

The metazoa include all other animals—animals composed of different kinds of cells that perform different functions. By scientific definition, humans are in this group.

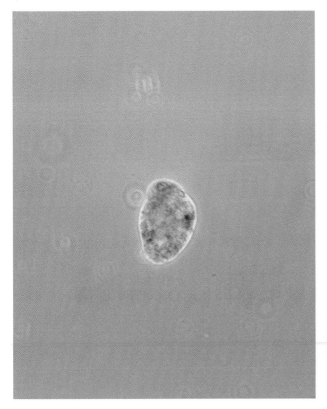 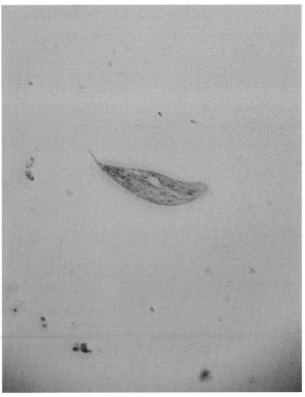

The protozoa may be either single-celled (left) or multi-celled (right), but all of the cells of the protozoa have essentially the same function. The cells of the mesozoa (not shown) may have different functions, but the differences in cells and cell functions will be only slight.

Let's begin with the "lower" animals. There are many microzoa, as we have already seen. The number of **species** living today is in the tens of thousands. (Sorry, we can't show pictures of each one.) These tiny animals range from the simple one-celled animals to organisms that are fairly complex, though small. The tiniest microzoa are often called **protozoa**, meaning "primitive animals." They are believed by evolutionists to be similar to the ancestors of all animals. These ancestors, according to evolutionists' assumptions, supposedly lived on Earth some 200 million years ago. Protozoa are either one-celled animals or **colonies** of similar cells that are attached to one another.

Exercise:
What feature makes a biologist call an organism a metazoan rather than a microzoan (or protozoan)?

18: *Phyla of the "Changed Animals"*

Climbing the evolutionary ladder from the protozoa we find higher levels of organization. Organisms are grouped into **mesozoa** and **metazoa** based on how organized they are. The simplest **multicellular** organisms (those having many cells) are the mesozoa ("middle animals"). These organisms are simple **parasitic** worms. Parasitic means that they live at the expense of some other organism. They often suck nutrient-rich fluids right out of the other organism, but they don't usually kill the organism or they lose their source of food.

The **metazoa**, meaning "changed animals" can be larger in size because they have different kinds of cells that work together to bring things in, take things out, protect the whole organism, and perform other duties that enable them to live in a wider range of habitats. Because of the various cell types, organisms at this level begin taking on a variety of shapes that are not possible among colonies of identical cells. The metazoa include all other phyla of animals from the simple to the complex.

A strawberry sponge of the phylum Porifera.

Kingdom	**Kingdom Animalia: Metazoa**									
Phylum	Porifera (sponges)	Coelenterata	Ctenophora	Platyhelminthes (flat worms)	Rhinochocoela (proboscis, nemertine & ribbon worms)	Nematoda (round worms)	Acanthocephala (spiny-headed worms)	Chaetognatha (arrow worms)	Nematomorpha (horsehair worms)	Hemichordata (acorn worms)

The next set of organisms in terms of their simplicity is the phylum **Porifera**—the sponges. There are many types of these animals that live in the sea and a few that live in fresh water. Sponges are made up of several types of cells. Notice that, in one big jump, we have gone from organisms that are groups of identical cells to organisms that are made up of several types of cells. The organisms that would bridge this gap in evolution are absent from the fossil record. This is another of the more important objections to the theory. Many such gaps exist.

Jellyfish, anemone, soft coral (or sea fan), sea pen and coral of the phylum Coelenterata. Most of these soft-bodied animals are built on a radial body plan, radiating from the center like spokes on a wheel.

Jellyfish

Anemone

Soft coral (sea fan)

Sea pen

Coral

Notice how each of the different phyla is identified by the basic body plan of the organisms making it up. The next two phyla, called **Coelenterata** [sē-LEN-tuh-RĀ-tah] and **Ctenophora** [ten-AH-for-ah], include animals that are laid out on the **radial** body plan. Radial bodies have a center and "radiate" from the center like the spokes of a wheel. These simple animals have many cell types that do different things. They are no longer groups of tissues but are arranged into simple systems, including digestive, nervous and muscular. Organisms included in these phyla are hydra, medusa (jellyfish), sea anemones [a-NEM-ō-nēz] and corals.

The next step up the supposed evolutionary ladder is composed of a large number (perhaps a hundred thousand) of different types of worms. Perhaps because radial symmetry is not a workable plan to support more complex digestion, the worms' body plan is what we call **bilateral**, or "two-sided." The left halves of their bodies are mirror images of their right halves (more or less).

Many "higher" organisms are bilaterally symmetrical. In the simpler ones, the body plan is like a sac that has a single opening through which everything enters and exits. In the more complex ones it's more like a drinking straw, where everything goes in one end and out the other.

These simple worms include flatworms, ribbon worms, the tiny rotifers, nematodes (which include several human parasites such as hookworms, pinworms and trichina worms), and several kinds of worms that are not well studied because they don't seem to have much impact on humans or

Comb jelly of the phylum Ctenophora. This is a football-shaped, translucent, jelly-like blob that glows in the dark. You would hardly think that anything fitting that description could be a living animal.

ecology. Because of the bilateral symmetry in the simple worms, evolutionists hold that they are our closer evolutionary relatives than sponges and jellyfish.

This is a photograph of a large, tropical flatworm of the phylum Platyhelminthes. This one is about 5 centimeters in length. Flatworms may be found under rocks in streams in North America, but they are best viewed under a microscope because they are usually only a fraction of a centimeter in length.

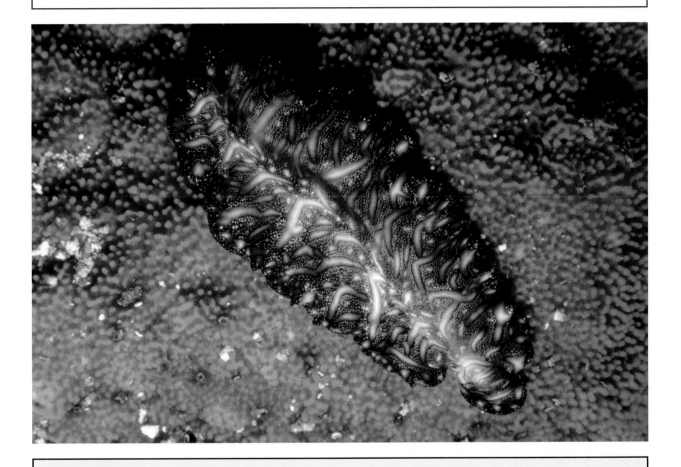

Exercises:

   True or false?

1. Metazoa include all animals that are not considered microzoa (or protozoa).
2. Mesozoa are a type of metazoa.
3. The terms protozoa, mesozoa and metazoa represent three different groups of organisms.
4. Metazoa represent a higher level of organization than protozoa.

19: *Do You Have a Cavity?*

The next step up is to those organisms that have a **body cavity**. A body cavity is extra space around the digestive tract where other organs can grow and develop. An organism with a body cavity has all features necessary for the placement of complex systems, including respiratory, circulatory, and reproductive. In lower animals, for example, a fluid that resembles blood may be squeezed into sacs in the outer tissues. This does the same things as, but is a very limited substitute for, the heart, veins, capillaries, and arteries that make up the circulatory systems of higher animals. Animals with body cavities—the so-called eucoelomate [ū-SĒ-lō-māt] animals—begin with those having few organs and simple systems, and extend all the way up the evolutionary ladder to humans.

The first several phyla of eucoelomates, which are not generally well known, have tentacles surrounding their mouths. They include the **Brachiopods**, also called "**lamp shells**." These still exist in a few hundred species but are much better known for their extinct forms. In the fossil record they number in the tens of thousands of species. Lamp shells have an outer shell consisting of either one or two parts. Their general shape is similar to that of a clam.

The next phylum, **Tardigrada**, is made up of animals generally less than one millimeter long. They are often called "water bears." Although they really don't have much to do with bears, somebody must have seen one and thought it looked cuddly. They are often found clinging to a small twig or fiber, as you might find a koala (which also isn't a bear!).

The phylum **Mollusca**, represented by 100,000 or more species, includes many well-known animals. It also includes some that are not as well known, such as **chitons**. These are **marine** animals (animals that live in the ocean). They are covered with hard plates that protect them, and feed on algae and other plants while moving along the floor of ocean shallows. Another of the lesser-known mollusks is the worm-like animal called a **solenogastre** [sō-LĒ-nō-gas-ter]. Better-known mollusks include the **gastropods**. These are mostly single-shelled animals whose shells are often coiled. Does this sound familiar? Gastropods include the snails, as well as abalone, whelks, slugs, periwinkles, and cowries. From single-shelled, gastropod mollusks, we move along to the double-shelled, pelecypod [pā-LĀ-si-pod] mollusks. These include marine and freshwater clams, freshwater mussels, and scallops.

Kingdom Animalia: Metazoa

Kingdom	Phylum	Class

Phylum level: Mollusca | Mandibulata | Brachiopoda (lamp shells) | Arthropoda | Annelida (segmented worms) | Chordata

Class level:
- Amphineura (chitons)
- Pelecypoda (bivalves)
- Scaphopoda (tooth or tusk shells)
- Gastropoda (snails, whelks, slugs)
- Cephalopoda (octopuses, squids, nautiluses)
- Archiannelida (simple marine worms)
- Polychaeta (worms with appendages)
- Oligochaeta (bristled worms)
- Hirudinea (leeches)

The last class of mollusks is the **cephalopods**. This class is best known for its well-developed head, which gives the group its name (*cephalo* = "head"). The group includes squids, nautiluses, cuttlefishes and octopuses. These animals have highly developed circulatory and nervous systems. The most striking feature of the nervous system is the eye, which in the octopus is surprisingly similar to that of a human. Although there are differences, the thought that two such similar organs could evolve separately in two such unrelated organisms is astounding. (Evolutionists do not consider octopuses and humans to be close relatives.) Evolutionary theory calls this process through which two organisms develop similar features **convergent evolution**, meaning that the two organisms "come together" in their characteristics by adapting to similar evolutionary pressures.

On the other hand, for those who acknowledge God as the Designer of the animals, the occurrence of similar design features in such distant organisms does not

This specimen is a beautiful worm—a polychaete (fan worm) of the phylum Annelida. Compare the beauty of this creature with the homeliness of its terrestrial neighbor, the earthworm. The earthworm is an oligochaete from the same phylum.

require imaginative theorizing; indeed it offers a strong argument for a single and purposeful designer. From this perspective God is seen to have used the same design basis for creating two distinct organisms, just as an engineer might borrow features from a car in designing a truck.

The next phylum of eucoelomates is **Annelida**. Animals in this phylum are worms with segments. These include the (mostly marine) **polychaetes** [PAH-lē-kēts] and the **oligochaetes** [AHL-i-gō-kēts]. It may be hard to think of a worm as beautiful, but the tentacle-like appendages that stick out from the bodies of many polychaetes can take on brilliant colors and sway with the wave movements of the sea. Fan worms are a particular example of the beauty of these animals. The oligochaetes include some famous worms like *Lumbricus*—the lowly earthworm. It may surprise you to know that there are earthworms that are not so lowly. They can reach nearly three meters in length and two centimeters across. (Lunch time!) The oligochaetes also include the leeches.

The animals on this page and the following are representatives of the phylum Mollusca.

Nautilus

Abalone

Cowrie

File shell

Cuttlefish

Terrestrial slug

Scallop

Sea slug (nudibranch)

Squid

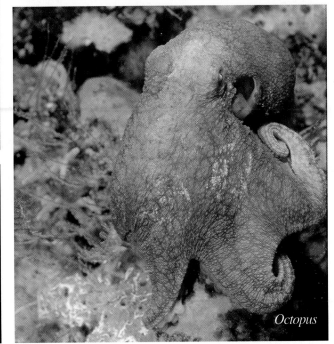

Octopus

Exercises:

1. Which of the following statements is more accurate:
   a. Tardigrades and mollusks are organized the same.
   b. Both tardigrades and mollusks are examples of eucoelomate animals, all of which have body cavities.
2. The distinguishing feature of eucoelomates is a body cavity that allows for the placement of sophisticated _____ (gosarn).

20: *You're Nowhere Without Joints in Your Legs!*

The most successful phylum of animals in terms of their numbers is **Arthropoda**. You can remember the name "arthropod"(meaning "joint" + "feet") if you know that arthritis attacks your joints and that podiatrists fix your feet. Arthropods have jointed legs that make them more efficient travelers than other animals. Of course higher animals have joints in their legs too, but the arthropods are the lowest animals in which we find this feature, so they get to keep the name.

The arthropods are "successful" in an evolutionary way of thinking. Evolutionists measure success by the abundance and **diversity** of a group of animals. "Abundance" means success in reproducing. If there are many of a particular type of organism, that organism has a high likelihood of survival. "Diversity" means that there is a lot of variety among the animals, so if conditions change, some of those animals will still be likely to survive. Arthropods include millions of species—more than all other species of animals combined. Some species of arthropods, like mosquitoes, are alive in countless numbers. Arthropods are also diverse, living in every environment on Earth: in the ocean, in fresh water, in the soil, in the air, in plants, in animals, in the presence and absence of oxygen, in high and low altitudes, in the desert, in cold and in hot regions.

The important feature of arthropods is their jointed legs. They also have an **exoskeleton**—a hard, outer case—for protection. This stiff structure provides the support for body parts that is necessary for the type of locomotion we see in arthropods. In most of them this exoskeleton is made of a stiff substance called **chitin** [Kī-tin]. The body of an arthropod is divided into two or three big sections instead of many segments like the annelids discussed in the last chapter.

One subphylum of arthropods is **Trilobita**, the trilobites. We would like to show you one, but we can't. As far as we know, they're all extinct. We know about them only because the fossil record contains lots of them. Trilobites were marine animals that had three body lobes (which is why they are "tri-lobe-ites" which means "three-lobed dudes").

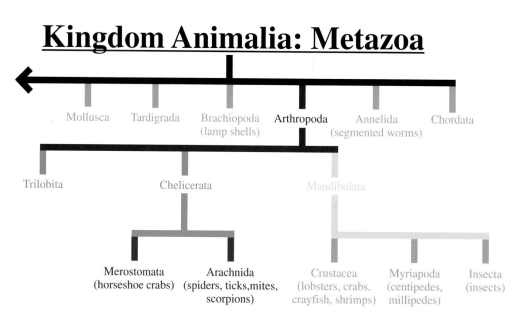

Kingdom Animalia: Metazoa

Kingdom

Phylum

Class

- Mollusca
- Tardigrada
- Brachiopoda (lamp shells)
- Arthropoda
- Annelida (segmented worms)
- Chordata

- Trilobita
- Chelicerata
- Mandibulata

- Merostomata (horseshoe crabs)
- Arachnida (spiders, ticks, mites, scorpions)
- Crustacea (lobsters, crabs, crayfish, shrimps)
- Myriapoda (centipedes, millipedes)
- Insecta (insects)

A second subphylum of arthropods is **Chelicerata** [kē-LIS-er-AH-tah], the chelicerates. These are animals that have chelicerae. (No joke!) Chelicerae are appendages (like arms) that have a pincher at the end of them for grabbing and crushing things, especially poor, unfortunate animals. The chelicerates include the horseshoe crab and the **arachnids**. The arachnids include our friends the scorpions, spiders, daddy-longlegs and ticks.

Arachnids, which include the spiders and scorpions, represent a single class of the chelicerate arthropods.

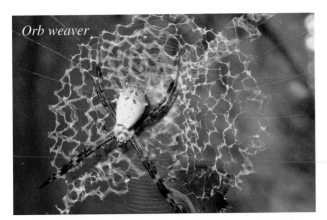

Orb weaver

Scorpion

Hunting spider

Exercises:

1. What feature is found in arthropods that allows them to be successful in many different environments?

2. Are spiders arthropods?

3. Were trilobites arthropods?

4. Were trilobites arachnids?

5. In organisms that will be discussed later, there is a bony skeleton that provides structure and support for the organism. What feature performs these functions in the arthropods?

21: *Mandibulates*

A third (and rather large) subphylum of arthropods is **Mandibulata**, the mandibulates [man-DIB-ū-lāts]. They are so named because they have mandibles, or jaws. They also have **antennae** which are used for sensing, and **maxillae** [max-IL-lē] which, in arthropods, are appendages around the mouth that are used for eating. One class of mandibulates is the **crustaceans**. These are mostly

These are myriapods. A representative of the Chilopoda (centipedes) is on the left and a member of the Diplopoda (millipedes) is on the right.

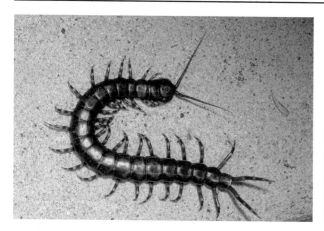

aquatic animals, meaning that they live in the water. You can learn to recognize some of them by name. They include the following small animals that are mostly **planktonic** (suspended in water): brine shrimp, water fleas, ostracods (also called seed shrimp), and copepods. Among these organisms are several parasites. They attach themselves to animals such as fish and lobsters and take their food from those hosts. Aquatic crustaceans also include barnacles, which are often found in clusters grow-

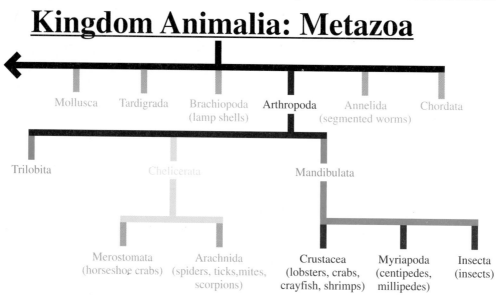

Kingdom Animalia: Metazoa

Kingdom

Phylum

Class

Mollusca · Tardigrada · Brachiopoda (lamp shells) · Arthropoda · Annelida (segmented worms) · Chordata

Trilobita · Chelicerata · Mandibulata

Merostomata (horseshoe crabs) · Arachnida (spiders, ticks, mites, scorpions) · Crustacea (lobsters, crabs, crayfish, shrimps) · Myriapoda (centipedes, millipedes) · Insecta (insects)

ing on any hard surface in the ocean. In order to cut smoothly through the water, ships regularly have to have barnacles scraped from their submerged surfaces.

Two orders of crustaceans built on the same body plan but looking terribly out of place among all these aquatic creatures are the **isopods,** which include sow bugs and pill bugs, and the **amphipods**, which include sand fleas. The order of crustaceans having the most species is the **decapods** ("ten" + "feet"). Among the decapods are shrimps, prawns, crayfish, crabs and lobsters. They don't really have ten feet, but they do have a whole bunch of appendages (usually nineteen pairs). Unless you are allergic to them, the best thing about decapods is that they taste great!

These are crustaceans.

Sow bug (isopod)

Lobster (decapod)

Hermit crab (decapod)

Shrimp (decapod)

Also among the mandibulates are **Myriapoda**, the myriapods [MIR-i-ah-podz]. "Myriapods" is a common name for organisms in several classes. These are arthropods with lots of legs and body segments. They include centipedes, millipedes, and the less well-known pauropods and symphyla [SIM-fi-lah]. Centipedes are **predators**, living on slugs, grubs, and other soft-bodied animals. Some larger centipedes can even eat snakes and small mammals. Centipedes (meaning "one hundred feet," which isn't accurate, by the way) have one pair of legs per body segment; those legs stick out from their bodies and can move quickly. (It's important to be quick if you have to kill things for a living.) Their first pair of appendages has special claws with poison glands; these claws can be used to kill prey.

Millipedes (meaning "one thousand feet," also not accurate), on the other hand, have two pairs of legs per body segment. Millipedes move slowly, on legs that are tucked underneath them. Can you guess what they eat? Right—things that are already dead! If they had to eat living things, slow-moving millipedes would starve. Dead things can't run fast, so they make good food for millipedes.

You might have heard of symphyla if you keep a greenhouse. These are pesky greenhouse dwellers.

The final class of arthropods is **Insecta**, the insects, also called **hexapods** (finally, a name that's accurate—they actually have "six feet"). Insect bodies are divided into **head**, **thorax** and **abdomen**. The head contains **antennae**, **compound eyes**, eye-like **ocelli** [ō-SEL-lī], and a **mouth** made up of perhaps six parts that move. The thorax is the part of the body that is mainly responsible for the insect's locomotion. It bears the insect's three pairs of legs (usually having six segments each) and sometimes two pairs of **wings**.

Insects are considered to be highly evolved because they have advanced circulatory, respiratory, nervous, excretory, muscular, digestive and reproductive systems. Space does not permit the mentioning of a large portion of the insect types, because there are so many, but the Table shows a few you should get to know—or may already know. Insects are the world's most numerous animals, with species numbering in the millions, many of which scientists have never described.

The following are insects (hexapods).

Grasshopper

Katydid

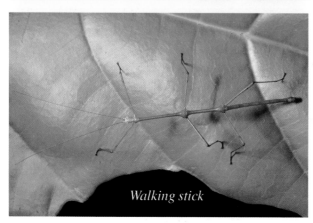
Walking stick

Praying mantis

Earwig

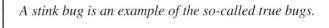

A stink bug is an example of the so-called true bugs.

Stink bug

Termites

Cockroach

Stone fly

Dragonfly

Damselfly

Dobson fly

Mayfly

The following are butterflies.

These two photos illustrate metamorphosis. They are the same insect at different stages in its life cycle. Not only butterflies, but most insects go through similar changes during their lifetime. To know the insects well, a biologist must not only know what the adult looks like, but must be able to recognize its other immature forms as well. Here we see the Monarch caterpillar and butterfly.

Black swallowtail

Quaderna hairstreak

Tropical leafwing butterfly

Pixie metalmark

TABLE : COMMON INSECTS			
silverfish	termites	lice	leafhoppers
crickets	dragonflies	true bugs	caddis flies
earwigs	damselflies	cicadas	moths
stone flies	mayflies	aphids	butterflies
true flies	mosquitoes	gnats	fleas
beetles	weevils	ants	bees
wasps	treehoppers		

Fly

Ladybug

Ants

Bee

Hornet

Hornets' nest

Ichneumon wasp

When describing the insects it is not sufficient to describe only the adults. The appearances of insects (as well as many other invertebrates) have different appearances at different stages of their lives. If a biologist is to be knowledgeable about insects he must be able to identify all of the different stages. The butterflies are often taken as striking examples of the different stages that insects go through during their life cycles. It is plenty for you now to learn to identify the adults; and, if you really want to be in the know, to be able to tell which caterpillars match which adults. The life cycles of some insects are quite complex, including eggs, pupae, larvae, nymphs, naiads, juveniles and adults in a single species.

Weevil

Clide beetle

Chafer

Exercises:
1. What is the name of the most widespread and numerous class of arthropods?
2. What features does the text identify that allow us to determine whether an animal is an insect (hexapod)?
3. In previous studies you learned that oxygen is necessary to burn fuel for generation of energy. Insects lack a sophisticated distribution center for oxygen. Insects' legs, which use a great deal of energy, are located on the thorax. In which body segment do you suppose their lungs would be located?
   a. abdomen
   b. thorax
   c. head

22: *You'd Walk Slowly Too if You Had Tube Feet*

The next phylum of animals on the evolutionary ladder is **Echinodermata**, the echinoderms [eh-KĪ-nō-dermz] (meaning "prickly skin"). Echinoderms start out bilaterally symmetrical when they are young, but develop into radially symmetrical adults. Unlike the crustaceans, they have **endoskeletons**—a system of bone-like supports inside their bodies. They also have an internal system for moving water around their bodies. This system allows them to control water pressure to their **tube feet** for locomotion. Tube feet are little dead-end tubes that move under water pressure, like a water balloon squeezed at one end. The motion of these organisms is slow, but they are nimble and can grip with amazing power, even pulling clam shells open to get their lunch.

The radial symmetry of these organisms makes them fascinating to look at. Some of the most famous echinoderms are the starfish, brittle stars and sea urchins. They also include crinoids, many of which we see in the fossil record, and sea cucumbers. Their prickly outer casings make them unattractive to many would-be predators. Personally, I can't imagine trying to eat a sea urchin.

These are all echinoderms.

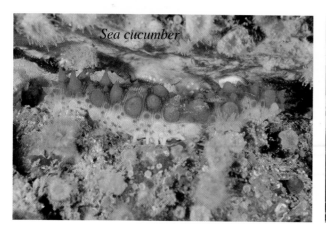
Sea cucumber

Starfish

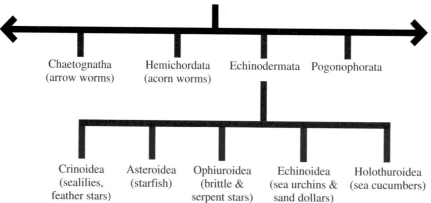

Kingdom Animalia: Metazoa

Kingdom · Phylum · Class

Chaetognatha (arrow worms) Hemichordata (acorn worms) Echinodermata Pogonophorata

Crinoidea (sealilies, feather stars) Asteroidea (starfish) Ophiuroidea (brittle & serpent stars) Echinoidea (sea urchins & sand dollars) Holothuroidea (sea cucumbers)

There are other phyla that we will not spend time with because they are unimportant to us. They include **Chaetognatha** (arrow worms), **Hemichordata** (acorn worms), and **Pogonophorata** (beard worms). These animals are not well known and are mainly of scientific and ecological significance.

Feather star

Sea urchin

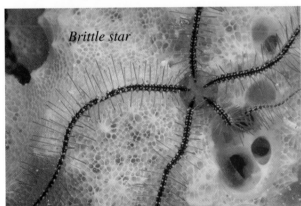
Brittle star

Exercises:
1. Of what use is prickly skin to an echinoderm?
2. The following is a list of statements speculating about the arrow worms, acorn worms and beard worms. Which one of these statements does not identify itself as speculative?
   a. I suggest that these organisms play an important role in the complex natural balance among organisms.
   b. One reason for creating organisms might be for the amusement and occupation of mankind. These organisms might perform that function.
   c. These organisms have significance that we do not yet fully understand.
   d. Perhaps these organisms performed a significant role in the past that we can no longer appreciate.

23: *Fishlike Animals with Cords*

Now we are left with only the "highest" forms of life—the **chordates** (in the phylum Chordata). At one time or another during its life, every chordate has a **nerve cord** down its back. In humans it

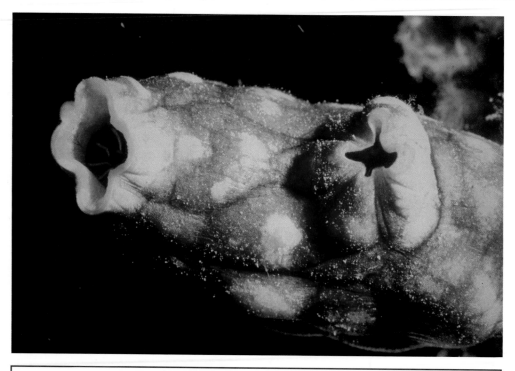

Tunicates have nerve cords without backbones.

Kingdom Animalia: Metazoa

Kingdom

Mollusca   Tardigrada   Brachiopoda (lamp shells)   Arthropoda   Annelida (segmented worms)   Chordata

Phylum

Tunicata (tunicates)   Cephalochordata (lancelets)   Vertebrata

Subphylum

Class

Agnatha (lampreys, nagfish)   Chondrichthyes (sharks, rays, skates)   Osteichthyes (bony fish)   Amphibia (salamanders, frogs, toads)   Reptilia (turtles, lizards, snakes, crocodiles)   Aves (birds)   Mammalia (mammals)

These are the Chondrichthyes or cartilaginous fish (fish with only cartilage rather than bones). The one on the left is a shark and the one on the right is an Atlantic Manta Ray.

develops into the **spinal cord**. Other chordates do not have a nerve cord so well developed as the human spinal cord, but they all have one. Two simple chordates do not have a bony **spine** (or backbone), but do have a nerve cord. These animals, called **protochordates**, are the tunicates and the lancelets.

From the protochordates we move on to the true **vertebrate** chordates, that is, chordates that have **vertebrae**, or backbones. From this point on we consider only animals that have a bony spine to protect their spinal cord. While you met many unfamiliar animals during our study of **invertebrates**, or animals without backbones, you will easily recognize most of the classifications of vertebrates.

The first group is the **fish** or fishlike organisms. These include the hagfishes and lampreys that can attach themselves to the side of a fish, wear a hole in its flesh and suck out its insides. (Yum, yum!) They also include the sharks, skates and chimaeras that look a lot like fish, but have no real bones. Instead they have only **cartilage**—soft, flexible bone-like structures.

Apart from a class of now extinct fishlike vertebrates, there remains only one class of fishlike animals, and that's the **bony fish**. Many of these are the ones you go fishing for: herring, salmon, pike, catfish, codfish, perch, sunfish, bluegills, crappie, sticklebacks and mullets. Some of these you don't go fishing for: garfish, sheepheads, various eels, sturgeons and paddlefishes, flying fishes and puffer fishes.

Exercises:
True or false?
1. All chordates have a spine.
2. All chordates have bones.
3. All fish are vertebrates.
4. Sharks have bones.
5. Protochordates are vertebrates.

These are all bony fish. Some have basically the same body shape while others (the eel and the sea horse, for example) are vastly different. What they all have in common are their body parts: scales, fins, gills and the hard bones that separate them from the cartilaginous fish, for example.

Sea horse

Flying gunard

Porcupine fish

Tilefish

Fairy basset

Stonefish

Mexican hogfish

Queen angelfish

Brown coney

Yellow queen angelfish

Spotted moray eel

Spotlight parrotfish

Spotted ray

Yellowtails

Rock beauty

Exercises:
   True or false?
1. All chordates have a spine.
2. All chordates have bones.
3. All fish are vertebrates.
4. Sharks have bones.
5. Protochordates are vertebrates.

24: *Slimy or Not, Mom Still Despises You*

Enough about fish; let's move on to the next large class of vertebrate animals, called **amphibians**. These are mostly animals that live part of their lives in and part of their lives out of water. They have glands that secrete a slimy substance to keep their skin moist. These are the slimy little animals your mother despises: frogs, toads, salamanders, and a few extinct and poorly known groups to boot. Amphibians are good swimmers even though they have lungs. Frogs, for instance, have webbing between the digits on their feet for navigating waters. Evolutionists see amphibians as the first animals to have made their way onto land from water. We see them as God's creation, especially made to inhabit moist environments.

Often confused with amphibians because mothers find them equally disgusting are the **reptiles**. Can you tell these two classes apart? While amphibians have moist skin, the skin of a reptile is quite dry and covered with tough scales. Reptiles are not at all slimy. They have more hard bones and less soft cartilage than amphibians. There are many differences. The reptiles include crocodiles, alligators, caiman, gavials, turtles and tortoises, tuataras, lizards, and snakes. They also include the ever-popular, ever-extinct dinosaurs. The Bible says that there was a time in our most ancient history when serpents were made to crawl on their bellies. What do you think a walking serpent might have looked like? A dinosaur?

Kingdom Animalia: Metazoa

Kingdom | Phylum | Subphylum | Class

Mollusca · Tardigrada · Brachiopoda (lamp shells) · Arthropoda · Annelida (segmented worms) · Chordata

Tunicata (tunicates) · Cephalochordata (lancelets) · Vertebrata

Agnatha (lampreys, nagfish) · Chondrichthyes (sharks, rays, skates) · Osteichthyes (bony fish) · Amphibia (salamanders, frogs, toads) · Reptilia (turtles, lizards, snakes, crocodiles) · Aves (birds) · Mammalia (mammals)

These are amphibians. Their skin is soft and moist, and they spend part of their life in the water.

California newt

Yellow tree frog

Red-eyed tree frog

Bullfrog

Yellow-eyed salamander

These are reptiles. Their skin is scaly and dry, and they are mainly terrestrial. A few (like the cottonmouth) live near water and eat aquatic creatures. Because their scales can seal water in, a few of these organisms (like the gila monster on the following page) can survive in the desert.

Pacific rattlesnake

Mojave rattlesnake

Cottonmouth

Ringneck snake

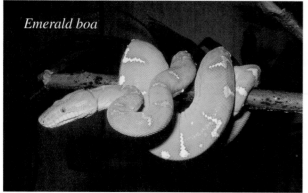

Emerald boa

Coral snake

Gila monster

Radiated tortoise

Green anole

Pink agama lizard

Exercises:

Knowing that each statement below describes either a reptile or an amphibian, which can you distinguish as one or the other?

1. I live in moist caves where my soft skin is protected from harsh sunlight.
2. I live near the water and feed on minnows.
3. I have hard bones and am often found living under rocks, even in harsh, dry climates.
4. I have webbing between my toes because I spend a great deal of my life in the water. As a juvenile I spent all of my time there.

25: *Up, Up and Away*

The next in the line of animals are the **birds**. Birds have skin that is covered with feathers. They have wings where other animals have forward legs, and their bones are mostly hollow. These and many other characteristics give most birds the ability to fly. The mouth of a bird has a hard beak. Different kinds of birds have differently shaped beaks for doing different things. Some beaks are made for picking bugs from tree bark, some for catching and killing small animals, some for sucking nectar from flowers, still others for catching fish.

Because flying requires rapid movement, it also requires a lot of energy. That energy comes from rapidly oxidizing chemicals, releasing chemical bond energy as they oxidize. And rapid oxidation requires plenty of oxygen to react with the chemicals and release the bond energy. All these requirements mean that birds must have an efficient way to get oxygen into the body. Well, guess what— birds have the most efficient of all respiratory systems in the animal kingdom. The degree of design that has gone into each animal to suit its own place of life and function is truly amazing. Not only do birds have specialized respiratory systems, bones, beaks, and **integument** (body coverings); they have specialized feet and spurs (toenails) as well.

Like every other kind of animal, birds have been grouped. There are many good books available to help you to identify the bird groups and individual species. If you are a nature lover and appreciate natural beauty, you will love finding and photographing birds of different kinds. The Table provides a complete list of the major categories of birds found in North America. As you can see, the diversity is overwhelming. Some people make a lifelong hobby out of watching and photographing birds. Besides the North American birds, look for these fantastic birds at your zoo: penguins, ostriches, emus, kiwis, parrots, toucans, and birds of paradise. Find out where these unusual animals live and what makes them so unique.

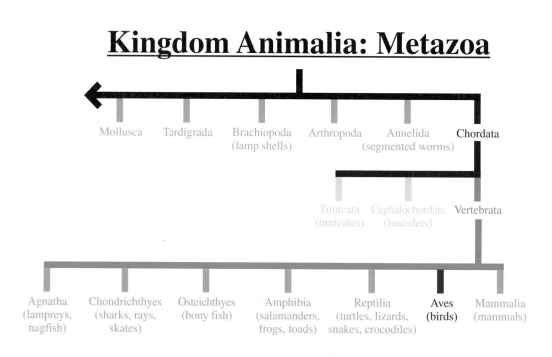

Kingdom Animalia: Metazoa

Scarlet macaw

Crowned crane

Red-winged blackbird

Great horned owl

Orange and black troupial

Snow bunting

Penguins

Bald eagle

Western gull

Latsan albatross

Mandarin duck

Cattle egret

Atlantic puffin

Evening grosbeak

Peacock

TABLE: CATEGORIES OF NORTH AMERICAN BIRDS

woodpeckers	petrels	cormorants	storks
hummingbirds	pelicans	herons	cranes
ibises & spoonbills	doves	roadrunners	nightjars
boobies & gannets	cuckoos	owls	swifts
shearwaters & fulmars	kingfishers	loons	albatrosses
waterfowl: ducks, geese & swans	pigeons	limpkins	trogons
perching birds: cotingas, flycatchers	rails		
songbirds: larks thrashers swallows mockingbirds orioles thrushes crows warblers jays wagtails pipits troupials shrikes seedeaters magpies creepers titmice babblers nuthatches dippers vireos bananaquits tanagers waxwings wrens wood warblers silky flycatchers	**shorebirds & gulls:** oystercatchers plovers sandpipers stilts & avocets phalaropes thick-knees skuas & jaegers gulls & terns skimmers auks	**fowl-like birds:** curassows guans chachalacas pheasants quails partridges guinea fowl turkeys	**birds of prey:** vultures hawks eagles ospreys falcons caracaras

Exercises:
1. Are birds vertebrates?
2. Are birds chordates?
3. Are birds reptiles?
4. Are birds and reptiles in the same class? Phylum?

26: *You Big Hairy Animal!*

The last class of vertebrate chordates is the **mammals**. Mammals are known for their hairy skin and for the fact that their young get their nourishment from milk produced by the mother in special glands called **mammary glands**. Mammals live in almost every habitat on Earth. While most are terrestrial, dolphins and whales are **marine** (living in the ocean). While most are earth-bound, bats take to the air. Mammals may be **subterranean** (living underground) or they may occupy trees, mountains, forests, grasslands and deserts. Some even live in the arctic circle (polar bears, seals and whales). There are about 4,000 different species of mammals. Here you will learn the names of many you have never heard of before.

A few really unusual mammals called **monotremes** are found only in the region around Australia. These animals are odd sorts. They include the spiny anteaters and the duckbilled platypus. These animals are curiosities because no others are quite like them. The platypus, for instance, has a bill and webbed feet like a duck, but hair and mammary glands like a mammal. There are a handful of animals like these that seem to have characteristics of two distinct groups of animals. We see these as animals that have been created by a Designer who selected from a variety of different design plans and used them throughout the animal world to make unique creatures for our amusement.

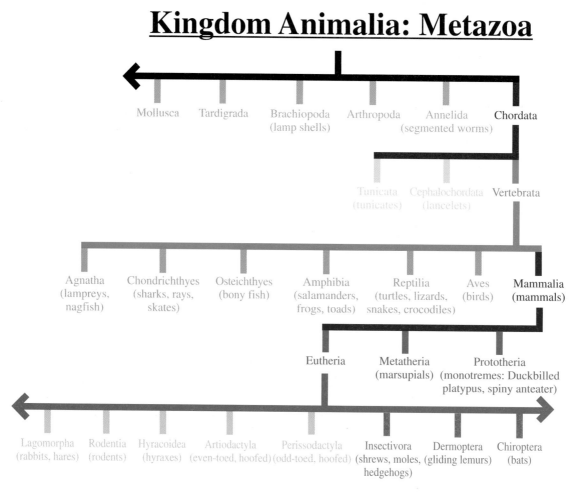

Kingdom Animalia: Metazoa

Kingdom — Phylum — Subphylum — Class — Subclass — Order

Phylum: Mollusca, Tardigrada, Brachiopoda (lamp shells), Arthropoda, Annelida (segmented worms), Chordata

Subphylum: Tunicata (tunicates), Cephalochordata (lancelets), Vertebrata

Class: Agnatha (lampreys, nagfish), Chondrichthyes (sharks, rays, skates), Osteichthyes (bony fish), Amphibia (salamanders, frogs, toads), Reptilia (turtles, lizards, snakes, crocodiles), Aves (birds), Mammalia (mammals)

Subclass: Eutheria, Metatheria (marsupials), Prototheria (monotremes: Duckbilled platypus, spiny anteater)

Order: Lagomorpha (rabbits, hares), Rodentia (rodents), Hyracoidea (hyraxes), Artiodactyla (even-toed, hoofed), Perissodactyla (odd-toed, hoofed), Insectivora (shrews, moles, hedgehogs), Dermoptera (gliding lemurs), Chiroptera (bats)

TABLE 1: MARSUPIAL ANIMALS

marsupial wolves	marsupial moles	banidicoots	koalas
marsupial mice	numbats	cuscuses	wombats
marsupial rats	opossums	phalangers	kangaroos
wallabies & wallaroos	marsupial cats	devils	caenolestids

Several mammals give birth to young that are immature. The young finish their development outside the mother's body. This subclass of mammals, called the **marsupials**, includes the animals shown in Table 1.

All of the remaining mammals in our discussion are orders of the subclass **eutheria** which give birth to more mature young. They are called **insectivores** ("insect munchers") because they eat mostly insects. They include the types shown in Table 2. Gliding lemurs make up the next order by themselves. These unique animals live in trees in the far east.

The spiny anteater is of the subclass Prototheria. Animals of this group are called monotremes *and their features tend to be a bit* ex-treme.

TABLE 2: INSECTIVORES

hedgehogs & gymnures	golden moles	shrew moles	moles	tenrecs
elephant shrews	otter shrews	shrews	solenodons	desmans

You will recognize the next group of mammals. These winged mammals are **nocturnal** (active at night rather than during the day; the opposite of nocturnal is **diurnal**). They find their way through the night sky by sonar—sending sound waves and receiving them back. What are they? Bats. The more than 800 different species of bats around the world have been divided by scientists into the groups shown in Table 3.

These animals of the subclass Metatheria are called marsupials. They give birth to premature young which they carry in a marsupium (pouch). The young are held and nursed in the marsupium until they reach greater maturity.

Opossums

Wallaby

Kangaroos

Koalas

Although bats will never win any beauty contests, they are most useful in keeping the insect population in check. Many bats sweep the nighttime skies preying on insects.

TABLE 3: BATS

new world leaf-nosed	old world leaf-nosed	mouse-tailed	vampire
New Zealand short-tailed	hollow-faced	sheath-tailed	horseshoe
new world sucker-footed	false vampire	free-tailed	smoky
old world sucker-footed	vespertilionid	fish-eating	fruit

Exercises:

1. The prefix pro- means "early," meta- means "changed," and eu- means "good" or "complete." In the evolutionary way of thinking, which of the three—Prototheria, Metatheria or Eutheria—is the least "advanced"? (Notice the similarity of these terms with the Protozoa, Mesozoa and Metazoa discussed back in Lesson 5.)

2. Which of the three subclasses of mammals includes most modern mammals?

27: *Miscellaneous Little Fuzzy Things*

The next order of mammals has large claws used for either digging or hanging from trees. They seem to be missing a lot of their teeth, so they are called **edentate** (meaning "out" + "teeth"). They are the anteaters, tree sloths and armadillos. Each of these is a curiosity in itself.

One small and unfamiliar mammal is in an order by itself. It is called a **pangolin**, and it lives in Africa and southeast Asia. It reminds us a lot of an armadillo because it has a long head and is covered with armor-like plates. This animal has no teeth at all.

From the pangolins we take a big jump to the rabbits, hares and pikas. Together they make up the **lagomorphs**. They are best known for their large ears, short tails and big front teeth (**incisors**). Most people don't know that they also have a smaller set of teeth directly behind the front ones.

The next order of small mammals is **Rodentia**, the rodents. These are known for having incisors that continue to grow throughout their lives. They keep those incisors small by munching on hard things. These famous animals are also known for being pests. They are often found in houses, munching where we don't want them to munch, on such things as our woodwork, wallboards and the food in our cabinets. A list of rodents is provided in Table 1.

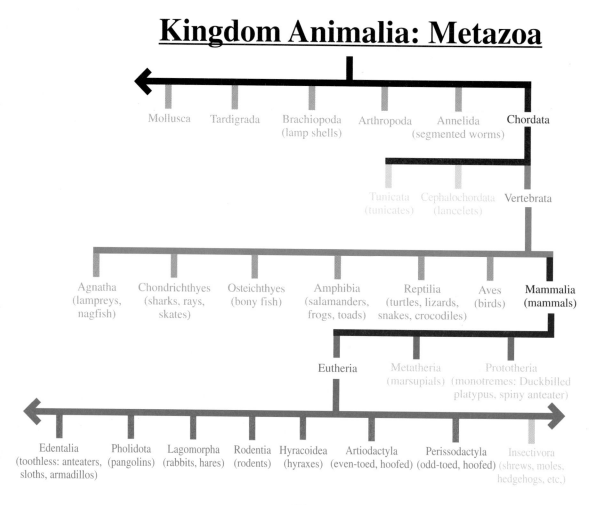

Kingdom Animalia: Metazoa

TABLE 1: RODENTS

pocket gophers	cane rats	dormice	spiny rats	tuco-tucos
mountain beavers	mole rats	jerboas	chinchillas	cavies
kangaroo rats	bamboo rats	rock mice	viscachas	capybaras
African mole rats	old world rats	mice	coypus	squirrels
chinchilla rats	old world mice	jumping mice	springhares	agoutis
old world porcupines	pocket mice	false pacas	hutias	pectinators
new world porcupines	spiny dormice	pacas	octodonts	beavers
scaly-tailed squirrels	desert dormice			

The **hyraxes** are next. These are small climbing mammals that live in Africa and parts of Asia. They are **herbivores** (that is, they eat only plants). They don't have much of a tail and look like woodchucks, but they have hooves on their feet.

The many common and well-known **hoofed animals** (Table 2) are usually divided on the basis of whether they have odd-numbered or even-numbered toes. The two orders are listed separately in the Table.

TABLE 2: HOOFED ANIMALS

Odd-toed:	Even-toed:	
horses	swine	giraffes
tapirs	peccaries	okapis
rhinoceroses	hippopotamuses	pronghorns
	camels	cattle
	llamas	antelope
	chevrotains	sheep & goats
	deer & other deer-like animals	

These animals are rodents.

Groundhog (also called a woodchuck)

A guinea pig is a cavy—a particular type of rodent. In this case, a particularly friendly type. Guinea pigs make excellent pets.

Chipmunk

Marmot

Capybara

Squirrel

Beaver

Porcupine

Wood rat

Rabbits are lagomorphs.

The rhinoceroses (left) and zebra (right) are odd-toed, hoofed animals called Perissodactyla.

These are even-toed, hoofed animals called Artiodactyla.

Oryx antelope

Bison

Giraffe

Ram

Exercises:

1. The small mammals are categorized into many orders. The best known of these animals are among the _____ (somarghpol) and the _____ (deonrts).

2. Are all of the animals in this lesson among the Eutheria?

3. Are they vertebrates?

4. Are they chordates?

5. Are they fungi?

28: *Was Jonah Swallowed by a Mammal?*

There are some famous mammals that resemble fish and live in the ocean. These are the whales, porpoises and dolphins. On the surface, these don't look much like mammals at all. They have no hair, and their nostrils are on the tops of their heads. (I'm glad I'm not made that way. I'd drown in the shower.) They don't have external ears, and their limbs look like flippers. Some of them can get big. How big? How about 30 meters long? But inside they have a lot in common with other mammals. They give live birth to young animals that they nurse from mammary glands. Their internal organs and systems resemble those of other mammals, too.

There is another order of mammals that live around water, but these don't look as much like fish. They're called **pinnipedia** ("baby ears") because of their tiny ears. They also have big eyes that make them look really cute. Many of them live in cold regions and have lots of blubber to keep them warm. They include sea lions, seals, hair seals, earless seals and walruses.

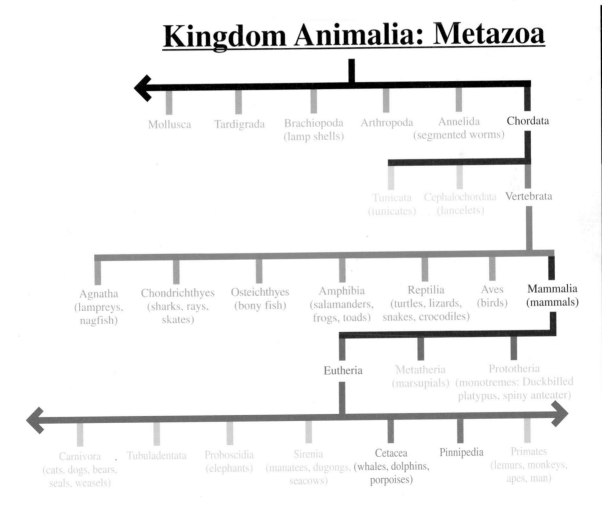

Kingdom Animalia: Metazoa

These are Cetacea.

Blue whale

Common dolphin

These are Pinnipedia.

Walrus

Baby seal

Adult seal

Exercises:

   True or false?

1. Pinnipedia are the only animals that have blubber to keep them warm.
2. Whales are pinnipedia.
3. Porpoises are fish.
4. A mammal may be a fish.
5. Sharks are mammals.

29: *I Wouldn't Say You're a Dog, but You're Still Ugly!*

Carnivores (meat eaters) are also pretty famous. If you will notice, what makes an animal famous is its size, its abundance, or the effect it has on people. Small animals that are rare are not usually famous, but everyone knows the large animals (like elephants), and the small ones that are all over the place (like mice and rats). (If you are interested in animals, make it your business to know the less famous ones and to know how to tell different animals apart.) The carnivores are large mammals, and many of them are common, so we recognize them quickly. For example, there are dogs (including foxes, coyotes and wolves), bears, giant pandas, raccoons, mustilids, civets, hyenas, aardwolfs and cats (including the big cats like lions, tigers, cheetahs and pumas).

The mammals seem to include more than their share of odd-looking animals, and the next order is a good example. The aardvarks are as funny looking as their name is funny sounding. They are squatty animals with long heads and a snout at the end of a long nose. They have long ears but short legs. They also have eating habits that match their name and their looks; their favorite foods are insects. These strange animals live in Africa.

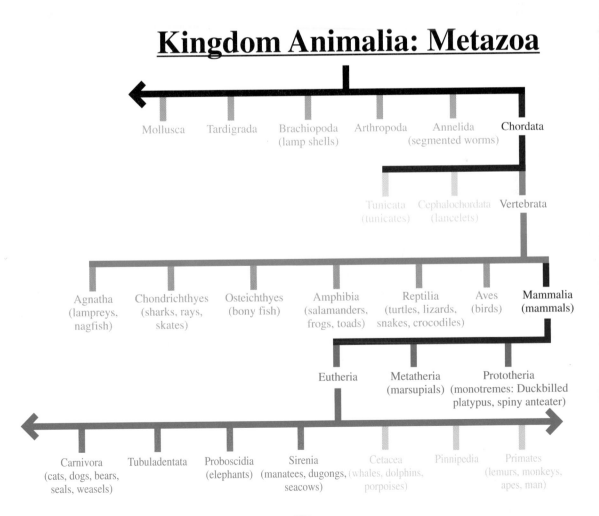

Kingdom Animalia: Metazoa

These are Carnivora ("carnivores").

San Joaquin kit fox

Timber wolf

Coyote

Most of us have seen enough elephants that we are used to their long snouts and big floppy ears. These largest of all land animals live in parts of Africa and Asia. They are prized for the long, hard teeth that curve up and out of their mouths to form **tusks**. Sometimes people kill the whole, big, beautiful animal just to get the teeth. This has happened so much that the animals have become **endangered** of extinction. Now governments count and protect the elephants from people who might kill them.

Another large and somewhat homely order of animals is the **sirenians**: manatees, dugongs and sea cows. These water-loving animals are large and extremely fat. Instead of hind limbs they have tail flippers, and they have a pair of frontal flippers where we have arms. They don't have a visible outer ear, and they look like your dad after he has gone a few days without shaving—they have coarse bristles around their mouths.

Cougar

Bobcat

Lynx

Grizzly

Polar bear

An elephant (left) is a proboscidian. The manatee (right) is a sirenian.

Exercises:

Please make a list of the carnivores that are mentioned in the text and underline the ones you are familiar with. Look at the list of unfamiliar carnivores. The next time you are at the library you might like to familiarize yourself with the ones you don't know. Look them up in an encyclopedia or a good book on vertebrate zoology.

30: *You and Me, Baby*

The next order of mammals is well known for its rather large brain, **opposable thumbs** (thumbs that can meet with the other fingers, allowing them to hold a sandwich), flat nails on their digits, and excellent mobility with special **ball and socket joints**. These are the primates, and they include tree shrews, lemurs, woolly lemurs, aye-ayes, lorises, galagos, tarsiers, larger new world monkeys, marmosets, old world monkeys, anthropoid apes, you and me. How does it make you feel to be classified as an exceptionally smart ape?

Without pause, the evolutionist classifies us as higher animals. He does so because he has no appreciation of a clear difference between us and any other animal apart from the sizes of our brains. A good Bible student knows the difference.

If you want to study something in detail, one way is to cut it apart and study the pieces. We all like to know about ourselves, so we begin by studying our **anatomy**. The word *anatomy* literally means "a cutting apart." Now we're not really going to cut apart any people, but we will study the parts. The

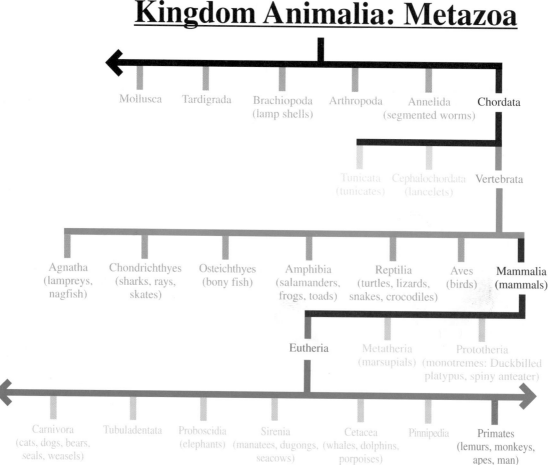

Kingdom Animalia: Metazoa

Kingdom

Phylum — Mollusca | Tardigrada | Brachiopoda (lamp shells) | Arthropoda | Annelida (segmented worms) | Chordata

Subphylum — Tunicata (tunicates) | Cephalochordata (lancelets) | Vertebrata

Class — Agnatha (lampreys, nagfish) | Chondrichthyes (sharks, rays, skates) | Osteichthyes (bony fish) | Amphibia (salamanders, frogs, toads) | Reptilia (turtles, lizards, snakes, crocodiles) | Aves (birds) | Mammalia (mammals)

Subclass — Eutheria | Metatheria (marsupials) | Prototheria (monotremes: Duckbilled platypus, spiny anteater)

Order — Carnivora (cats, dogs, bears, seals, weasels) | Tubuladentata | Proboscidia (elephants) | Sirenia (manatees, dugongs, seacows) | Cetacea (whales, dolphins, porpoises) | Pinnipedia | Primates (lemurs, monkeys, apes, man)

These are among the primates.

Mandrill baboon

Orangutan

Celebus Ape

Gorilla

Chimpanzee

These organisms are among the great apes. They can be quickly distinguished from the other primates by their lack of a tail.

Bush baby

Patas monkey

Lemur

Exercises:

1. As you did for the previous lesson, make a list of all the primates, then underline the ones you are familiar with. Pick up an encyclopedia or a book on primates and see what you can learn about the others.

2. Complete this paragraph using words from the word list below. Each word in the list will be used only once if the paragraph is completed correctly.

A human is made up of _____ which are groups of _____ that function together. The latter are made up of _____ which are composed of similar cells. Cells have tiny _____ that carry out the cell's functions. These are made up of many different types of _____ including the large biomolecules that we studied in chemistry. Of course, those are made of _____, (the smallest stable form of matter) which are made of _____, _____, and _____. Atoms having the same number of protons are atoms of the same _____.

neutrons, atoms, molecules, tissues, organs, electrons, element, systems, organelles, protons

31: *Them Bones, Them Bones*

The first system we will consider is the **skeletal system**. You can probably guess what this is. Have you ever seen a skeleton? Of what is it made? The skeletal system is made of **bones**. Except in unusual circumstances, as when a deformity or an accident causes a change, every human has 206 bones. These include 28 skull bones, 1 hyoid bone in the neck, 26 back bones that make up the **spine** or vertebral column, and a **rib cage** (25 bones) made up of 12 pairs of ribs and a sternum (breast-bone). The number of ribs is the same in both males and females.

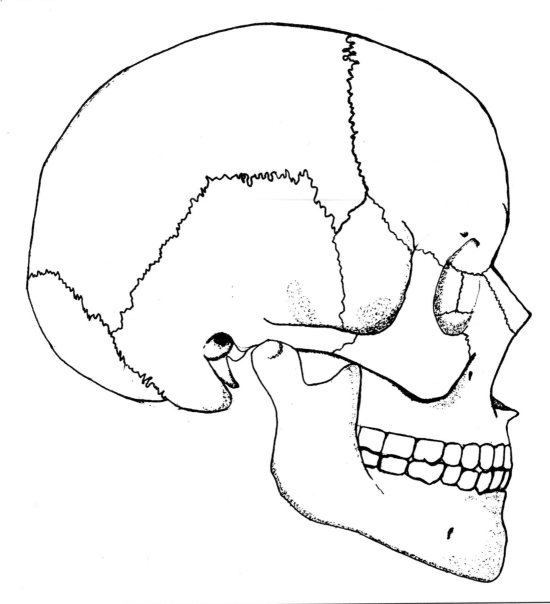

Notice how the skull is made of many bones that fuse together into non-moveable joints. This is critical for protecting its delicate contents.

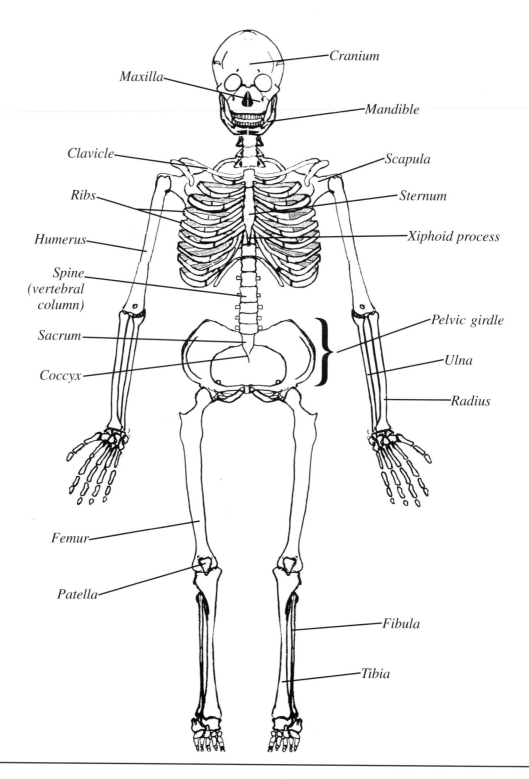

Cranium

Maxilla

Mandible

Clavicle

Scapula

Ribs

Sternum

Humerus

Xiphoid process

Spine
(vertebral
column)

Pelvic girdle

Sacrum

Ulna

Coccyx

Radius

Femur

Patella

Fibula

Tibia

The skeleton is the frame of the body. The bones making up the skeleton provide support and protection. Joints between the bones provide the mechanical basis for motion.

Sixty-four bones make up the **upper appendages**. The **shoulder girdle** consists of collar bones and shoulder blades which suspend the arms. The arms are called **upper extremities**; these include the upper arms, lower arms, wrists, hands and digits (fingers). There are 62 bones making up the **lower appendages**. The **pelvic girdle** is composed of pelvic bones that suspend the legs. The legs are **lower extremities**, which include the upper legs, lower legs, ankles, feet and digits (toes).

What would a person be like without bones? Bones are to humans what a frame is to a house. Without them we would just be blobs of muscle, fat and organs. We would have no particular shape, and we would not be able to direct our movements. If an arm muscle moved, the blob would just slither. If a leg muscle moved…more slithering. We would be like octopuses out of water. So you see, bones are a critical part of what makes us as we are. They give us structure and allow us to direct our motions.

The **joints** connect the bones and allow them to work together. There are several kinds of joints making up the human skeleton. They are designed specifically for the job they have to do. Some move freely, like the **ball and socket** joints in the hips and shoulders. Others move in only one direction, like the **hinge** joints of the knees and elbows. There are **saddle** joints where our thumbs connect with our wrists. These important joints allow our thumbs the great range of movement that is important in the ways we use our hands. There are **pivot** joints that allow us to twist our forearms and lower legs. **Gliding** joints, such as those in our wrists and ankles, give our hands and feet the freedom to rotate. On the other hand (so to speak), there are several joints that are quite stiff by design. Some bones (backbones, for example) are joined together with stretchy **connective tissue**. These joints stretch just a little, allowing us to bend over while still protecting the organs inside of us. After we reach adulthood our skull bones join together in a way that prevents them from any movement and provides protection for the brain.

In addition to the bones, we also have some **cartilage** that helps to fill out some of our features. The tips of our noses and our ears are examples of body parts containing mostly cartilage. Cartilage is like bone, but it doesn't have the minerals that make bone hard. So cartilage is soft and rubbery. Play with your ears for a minute and see what cartilage feels like. Okay now, stop playing with your ears! Because cartilage is soft and smooth, it also serves at the ends of bones to keep their rough, hard surfaces from grinding against each other. Cartilage is one type of connective tissue. Other types are the strong **tendons** and soft, stretchy **ligaments**. These connective tissues hold the bones of our skeletons together.

Exercises:

1. What purposes do bones serve?
2. Joints between bones often act like a type of machine that was introduced in Red Lesson 7. Name the type of machine.

32: *Muscles*

By themselves, skeletons have to be hung up. In fact, you could fold one and place it in a suitcase. They can't stand without support because they have no strength to hold themselves up. **Muscles** give strength and motion to our skeletons. They also give bulk to our bodies. Without them we would be "all skin and bones." Muscle is the soft tissue that fills out our arms and legs. It's the meaty part of animals, the part we eat.

Every motion that we can perform requires a muscle which either contracts (shortens) or relaxes (lengthens). One pair of muscles closes our jaws when we need to shut up (sometimes). Other muscles pull the lower jaw left or right. Some muscles allow us to blink; others allow us to squint.

See if you can get a feel for which muscles cause you to do what. Flex your upper arm muscle by raising your elbow and pulling your fist toward your head. The bulge in your upper arm is your biceps muscle. Now stretch your arm straight out. Notice that the muscle on the back side of your upper arm tightens. This is your triceps muscle. Lift your leg forward and point your toes away from you. Feel the calf of your leg tighten. This is your gastrocnemius muscle. Notice that the muscle causing a particular action is usually located right above the joint that moves, and that it's located on the side toward which the motion goes. That's because, as wonderful as muscles are, they all work the same way. They pull something toward them by making themselves shorter. When they make themselves shorter they naturally get fatter, and that's what causes them to bulge.

Muscles respond to electric signals from the brain. If you decide you want to move in one direction, the brain sends signals to the appropriate muscles telling them to contract, without your having to think about each one. Aren't you glad you don't have to consciously think and tell each muscle exactly what action to perform? One motion, like getting up from a chair, may require the actions of dozens of different muscles.

Right now we are considering only the **skeletal muscles**. There are other types of muscles that are not part of this system—like the **smooth muscle** tissue surrounding your blood vessels, muscle which regulates the size of those vessels. Skeletal muscles are the ones attached to your bones. Smooth muscles control those actions that you don't deliberately decide to do, such as the narrowing of the pupils of your eyes in bright light.

Exercises:

1. What purpose do muscles serve?

2. Explain how bones and muscles together allow a person to do work as defined in Red Lesson 7.

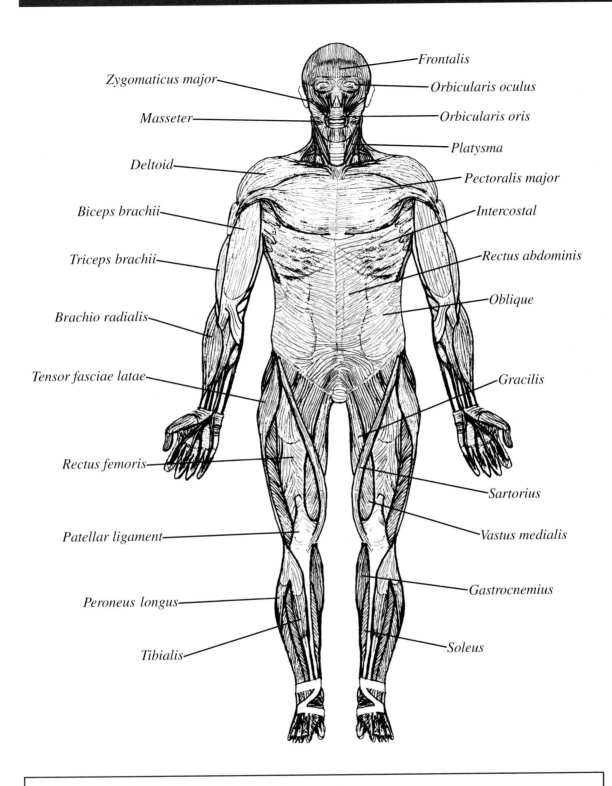

Zygomaticus major
Masseter
Deltoid
Biceps brachii
Triceps brachii
Brachio radialis
Tensor fasciae latae
Rectus femoris
Patellar ligament
Peroneus longus
Tibialis

Frontalis
Orbicularis oculus
Orbicularis oris
Platysma
Pectoralis major
Intercostal
Rectus abdominis
Oblique
Gracilis
Sartorius
Vastus medialis
Gastrocnemius
Soleus

The muscular system is the engine of the body. It gives motion to the bones and other organs of the body that allow the entire organism to function.

33: *Digestive System*

In the chemistry section you learned that our bodies operate on energy which we get from the chemical bonds in compounds that make up the food that we eat. But we can't send our bodies' cells a whole chicken! How could they bring it inside and use it? It's bigger than the cells themselves. Obviously we have to send our cells something much smaller than they are. But we can't bite off molecule-sized bites of food. Somehow our bodies have to take in food and break it down into molecules that our cells can use. This is the function of our digestive system; it's a big food processor.

We put bites of chicken into our mouths and chew. This does three things: it reduces the size of the pieces of food, it increases the surface area of the food, and it mixes **saliva** into the food. Saliva is the liquid substance in your mouth that comes from glands located around your mouth. Teeth don't make the food molecule-sized, but they do break it into smaller pieces to get started. Teeth have a variety of shapes that allow them to perform different functions. The front **incisors** are for cutting, the pointy **canines** are for holding and tearing, and the **premolars** and **molars** are for crushing and grinding.

Surface area is important in digestion because the chemicals that **digest** or break down the food can't do their jobs if they can't reach it. The chemicals have to be on or close to the surface of a food

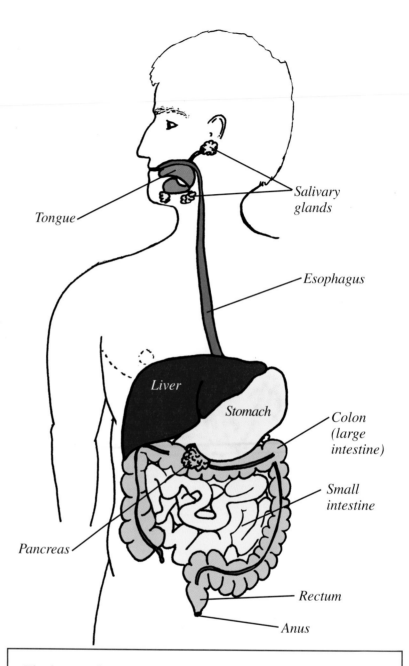

Tongue

Salivary glands

Esophagus

Liver

Stomach

Colon (large intestine)

Small intestine

Pancreas

Rectum

Anus

The human digestive system receives food and breaks it down into smaller and smaller pieces, then into individual molecules that can be used by the body's cells. The mouth, stomach and small intestine are the processing chambers. The liver, gall bladder and pancreas add chemicals (acids, enzymes and emulsifiers, for example) that help in the digestion of various types of food. The large intestine receives and processes the solid waste. The rectum receives the waste and holds it until it is passed through the anus to exit the body.

particle. This is why your mother always tells you to chew your food well. You can't digest big wads of food very efficiently. Big wads go right through your digestive system because the insides of the wads aren't exposed to the chemicals that can break them up.

Remember when we said that enzymes are important proteins in human cells because they make chemical reactions take place so fast? Enzymes are used to break the chemical bonds in a small piece of chicken to make it fall apart. Many enzymes take part in digestion; the first ones are found in your saliva and are mixed into the food while you chew.

Next, with a push from the back of the tongue, your food leaves your mouth and is directed into your throat. Your throat is like a funnel that leads into a tube. In an adult the tube, called the **esophagus**, is about a foot long. It has muscles along the path that push the food downward from your throat to your **stomach**. If you get something in your stomach that your body rejects, these muscles work in the opposite direction to get rid of it. The stomach is a stretchy bag surrounded by muscles and chemical-releasing glands. It is a reaction chamber where chemical reactions continue to break down the food into molecules. Digestive juices high in enzymes are added to the food in the stomach. Yellow-green **bile** comes from your **gall bladder** into your stomach. This is an **emulsifier** to bring the hydrophobic ("water-fearing") chemicals such as oils into contact with the digestive juices. The **pancreas** also adds digestive fluids to the stomach. Contraction of the muscles surrounding the stomach helps the process along by continually mixing the chemicals. Acid is released into the stomach to help break down the chemicals in foods.

After the stomach is finished adding these chemicals, mixing them, and giving them time to react, it squeezes all of the digested materials into the **small intestine**. The intestine is a curved tube approximately six meters long and two to three centimeters in diameter—with about the same amount of surface area as a tennis court. How can a tube with these dimensions have such a huge surface area? The inside walls of the intestines have little folds in them that greatly increase the surface area of the inner wall, just as the fibers on a carpet have more surface area than a flat floor. With all of this surface area the chemicals that were released and continue to be released for digestion are taken up by the intestinal walls where the blood waits to take these chemicals away to the body parts that need them. But the digestion is not yet complete. The blood carries these chemicals to the **liver** where sugars can be stored until they are needed.

Any undigested food passes from the small intestine into the **large intestine**, also known as the greater bowel or colon. The colon is the body's recycler and waste handler. It is a somewhat larger tube about six centimeters in diameter and about 1.5 meters in length. It receives the waste materials from digestion, pulls out and absorbs the water, wraps the waste in mucus (slime), and squeezes the waste into the **rectum** where it awaits passage from the body. This is the waste that is eliminated to the toilet when we have a bowel movement. The **anus** is the muscle which surrounds the opening that empties the rectum.

Exercises:
1. What is the purpose of digestion?
2. If muscles are the organs that provide motion to the bones, then they must require lots of energy. What part does digestion play in giving muscles the energy they need?

34: *Respiratory System*

One thing that humans need a lot of is **oxygen**. We use oxygen to oxidize organic molecules for energy. Our cells store that energy in a few special chemical bonds and then use it as needed to fuel their activities. We take oxygen right out of the air using our **respiratory system**. Our respiratory system begins with the mouth and nose because through them air enters our bodies. The air entering the mouth goes to the throat. Air entering at the nose has a more twisted path through the **nasal passages**, which empty into the space right above the throat. The throat is the place where those two air streams come back together. From the throat they pass through the voice box (also called the **larynx**) [LAR-ingks]. The voice box has two folds of flesh that come together and vibrate against each other to produce sounds, the sounds we make when we talk, sing or hum.

From the voice box the air travels into a tube that looks something like a vacuum cleaner hose. That tube is called the **trachea**. A vacuum cleaner hose is made of a series of plastic rings that give it strength and keep it from

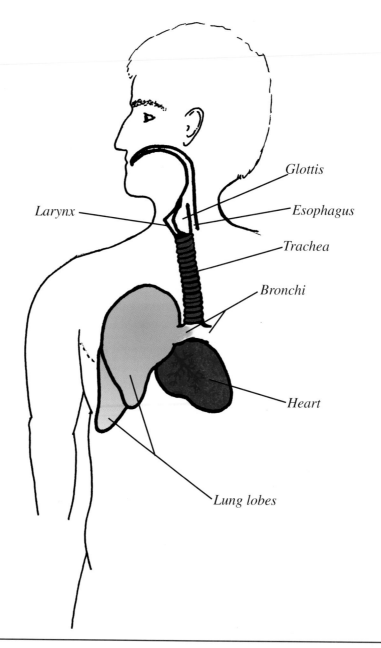

The human respiratory system delivers oxygen to the blood so that it can be distributed to the rest of the body. It also accepts waste carbon dioxide from the blood to remove it from the body. Air enters the mouth and nose and travels through the airways to the lungs. The cells of the lungs form tiny sacs, called alveoli, that have thin walls to exchange oxygen and carbon dioxide with the blood. Oxygen passes from the lungs to the bloodstream while carbon dioxide does the reverse.

collapsing, while also giving it some flexibility. The trachea is made of a series of rings of cartilage joined together. Because of this ring structure it is both flexible and strong. It is situated right in front of the esophagus, and both tubes (the trachea and the esophagus) originate in the throat. When we swallow food we have to close off the trachea so we don't get food "down the windpipe." The trachea is that windpipe.

The trachea divides into two smaller but similar tubes called **bronchi** [BRON-kī]. The bronchi split the flow of air between the two lungs. When we have a severe infection in the air passage, these tubes become **inflamed** (or irritated and swollen). We call such a condition bronchitis (meaning "inflammation of the bronchi"). The bronchi branch out into several **bronchioles** as they enter the lungs. These bronchioles break up the air flow into smaller and smaller streams which then enter the **alveoli** [al-VĒ-ō-lī]. The alveoli are small sacs from which oxygen crosses a thin layer of tissue and enters the blood. At the same time oxygen is passing into the blood vessels, carbon dioxide from the blood leaves through the wall of the blood vessels and passes into those little sacs so that it can be sent out of the body when we exhale.

Blood cells contain a special complex chemical compound called **hemoglobin**, which likes oxygen. Hemoglobin can hold loads of oxygen until it can be delivered to the cells that need it. If hemoglobin liked oxygen too much, it wouldn't let go when it came close to the cells needing some. On the other hand, if it didn't like oxygen well enough, it would let go too soon, before reaching those cells. For these reasons, the exact design of the hemoglobin molecule is extremely important. Carbon monoxide poisoning offers an example of how disastrous a problem with hemoglobin can be. Cars produce a small amount of carbon monoxide (CO) in their exhaust. These molecules have a tremendous liking for hemoglobin. Once they combine with hemoglobin, they will not let go; as a result, the hemoglobin can't accept oxygen molecules as it normally would. People who have been exposed to enough CO to fill a large portion of their hemoglobin will die of suffocation, even if they are given plenty of oxygen, because their hemoglobin can't get rid of the CO to accept the oxygen.

Lungs are like stretchy bags. They are enclosed inside the chest cavity. When the chest cavity is made bigger, it creates a vacuum on the outside surfaces of the lungs. As the lungs expand to fill the vacuum, air is drawn down the trachea from the mouth and nostrils. When the chest cavity relaxes, the stretchiness of the lungs makes them go back to their original shapes, forcing the extra air out. Take in a deep breath and notice how the expansion of your chest brings in air through your mouth and/or nose.

Exercises:

1. What is the purpose of the respiratory system?

2. In Yellow Lesson 17 you learned that food molecules are used as fuel for the body. But a substance is reacted with the food molecules to release the energy. What is the substance, and what does this have to do with the lungs?

35: *Urinary System*

All life is connected with water. Water dissolves the nutrients organisms need, and water is the medium in which life processes take place. Your body is about 90% water. Not only is water itself necessary, but the amount of water is also critical. For this reason organisms must have a way of controlling the amount of water that they have inside. If they have too much, they have to get rid of some. If they have too little, they have to be able to bring in more. This is true of every organism from the lowly bacterium right up to humans. It is just as true for plants as it is for animals.

> *The human urinary system removes waste products from blood. The blood is filtered by the kidneys to get rid of excess ions and molecules that are not easily used by the cells of the body. The waste material sent out by the kidneys passes through the ureters to the urinary bladder. There it collects until the bladder is emptied. When a person urinates, the urine leaves the body through the urethra.*

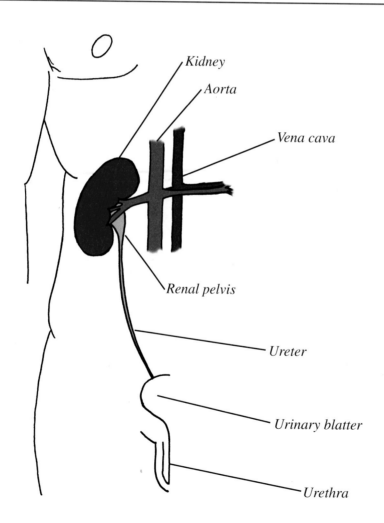

Kidney

Aorta

Vena cava

Renal pelvis

Ureter

Urinary blatter

Urethra

Humans have many uses for water. They use it to sweat and cool down when they get too hot. They use it as a carrier for nutrients. They use it as a carrier for wastes. They also use it to control their internal pressures, like blood pressure and the pressure on the brain.

We have already described how we get water: The body takes it in through the mouth and removes it from food. But in order to control the amount of water we have inside us, we must also have ways of getting rid of excess. This is one purpose for the **urinary system**. It removes excess water from our systems.

Another purpose is to remove waste materials that the blood carries away from our cells. In order for it to give up excess liquid and dissolved wastes without losing blood cells and nutrients, the blood has to be filtered. The **kidneys** do this filtering. Kidneys can be thought of as complex filters that remove waste products from blood while leaving the good stuff. After the waste is filtered out of the blood, it collects in the inner part of the kidney (the "renal pelvis") along with just the right amount of water. Then the liquid travels down tubes called **ureters** and into the **urinary bladder**. The bladder is like a balloon that stretches as the fluid collects. When your bladder reaches a certain fullness, it begins to over-stretch. It sends messages to your brain that you need to empty it.

At the exit of the bladder is a muscle which regulates outflow, a muscle children usually learn to control when they are more than 18 months old. When this muscle is relaxed, the fluid, called **urine**, flows out of the bladder through a tube called the **urethra**. The urethra is the small tube that carries the liquid outside the body.

Exercises:

1. What two purposes does this lesson assign to the urinary system?

2. In Yellow Lesson 15 you learned that water is a product of the release of energy from petroleum fuel. It is also a product of the release of energy from food. What role does the urinary system play, then, in this process of fueling the body's activities?

36: *The Race for the Egg*

Every creature on Earth has a way of reproducing. Otherwise, when the first organisms died, their types would simply have ceased to exist. All of human life would have ended with Adam and Eve if they had not been given a way to reproduce. Clearly, God planned for people to reproduce, or there would be no history, no story of His people. If humans are always to have access to food, other organisms must continue to survive and reproduce as well. Human reproduction is sacred because it involves the ability to create more humans. If humans were simply animals, it would make no long-term difference whether they survived or not. But because humans have a connection with the Creator that continues after death, human life is of indescribable value.

The way humans make new life is not so terribly different from the way other higher mammals reproduce. Each **sex**, male and female, has a set of cells called **gametes**. The male gamete, called a **sperm** cell, contains half a genome (that is, half of the genetic material required to direct the formation of a new organism). Sperm cells are active swimmers, having a tail that whips to propel the sperm cell along.

The female gamete, called an **egg** cell, also contains half a genome. These specially prepared eggs are released, in humans about one every 28 days, into the **oviducts**—the tiny passageways from each of the two ovaries to the **uterus**. The uterus is also called the **womb**. At the time the egg is released, it begins traveling by the action of the oviduct toward the uterus. The oviduct is lined with tiny hair-like structures that beat in a wave pattern, pushing the egg along the surface of the duct. When an egg cell and a sperm cell come together (usually in the oviduct), they combine to form a **zygote**. The zygote contains the half genomes from the two gametes which contribute to a complete genome of a new organism. The zygote, a young **embryo**, is then whisked along into the uterus where it attaches to the inner lining and draws nutrition from the mother.

God made male and female bodies to fit together in such a way that the male sperm cells are placed within the female at a place where they race to the female's egg cells. Millions of sperm cells are placed there at once. The sperm cells then begin a race through the female's reproductive system to the place where the egg is located. With the help of the female's body and chemical signals being sent out by the egg, the sperm cells swim toward the egg. The single strongest and fastest sperm cell (of the 300 to 400 million placed within the female at one time) taking the most direct path to the egg cell will reach it before the others and **fertilize** it.

If the egg is not fertilized within about three days, the inside lining of the uterus, along with the egg and some blood, is pushed out of the uterus. This cycle of preparing a new egg for fertilization and the wasting of an unfertilized egg lasts about 28 days in most females. It is called the **menstrual cycle**. The bleeding and ridding of the female's uter-

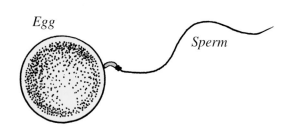

Egg

Sperm

The encounter between a sperm cell and an egg cell is called fertilization. *The sperm cell releases enzymes that wear away the protective coating on the outer surface of the egg. This allows it to enter the egg and release its DNA into the egg where the DNA from the egg can combine with that of the sperm. At this point the new cell formed from the other two is called a* zygote. *This is a new individual—no longer a product of either father or mother alone, but a product of the two—a new person.*

ine lining is called **menstruation**, or her "period." When the period is over, the next cycle of egg preparation begins. In most women the egg is prepared for fertilization about halfway through the menstrual cycle. The time when the egg is prepared for fertilization and released to be fertilized is called **ovulation**.

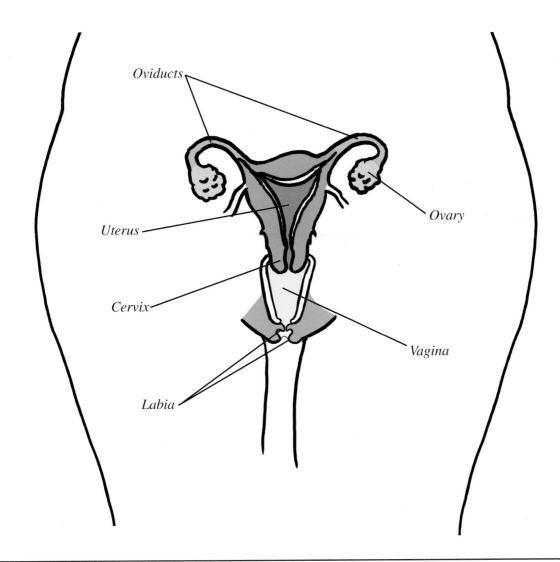

The female reproductive system consists of ovaries that produce egg cells. The egg cells are released— usually one per month—into an oviduct. The wall of the oviduct is covered with hair-like cilia. The cilia beat in wave-like patterns to push the mature egg cell along the oviduct toward the uterus. If there are male sperm cells in the female's reproductive system during this journey, the egg will usually meet a sperm cell and be fertilized while in the oviduct. After its fertilization the tiny new human will continue to travel until it reaches the uterus where it will imbed itself in the uterine wall and continue its development.

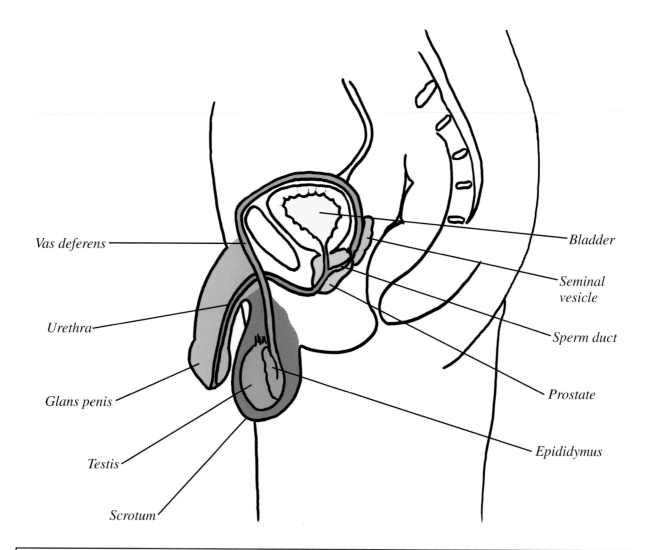

Vas deferens

Urethra

Glans penis

Testis

Scrotum

Bladder

Seminal vesicle

Sperm duct

Prostate

Epididymus

The male reproductive system consists of testicles that produce sperm cells that are then stored in the epidydimus until they are ready for use. At that time they are "ejaculated" from the epididymus through several feet of tubing. The tubing passes through the man's body cavity and through several organs that add fluid to make the sperm cells live longer in the female's body. This "seminal fluid" then empties into the urethra where it leaves the male's body through his penis. The seminal fluid, containing the sperm cells, is deposited in the female's vagina near the cervix—the opening through which the cells enter.

Exercises:

1. What is the basic purpose of reproduction?

2. How long would life on Earth last if not for reproduction?

3. If a living cell formed from non-living chemicals, but that cell lacked the ability to reproduce, what would come of it?

37: *Circulatory, Lymphatic and Immune Systems*

How do all of the internal organs receive food, water and oxygen? They depend on a pretty efficient distribution system. In fact, the circulatory system is that system, and it is quite efficient. Blood carries all of these goodies not only *to* the organs but also *through* them. The heart pumps blood to the major **arteries**. The arteries divide into smaller arteries and even smaller **arterioles** down to the **capillaries**. Capillaries can be so small as to allow only one or two blood cells to pass at a time. The thin outer walls of these tiny blood vessels allow nutrients and oxygen to cross through and come in contact with the cells that need these materials. After releasing their goods and collecting the waste, the blood returns to the heart through small **venules** and increasingly large **veins**.

Once returned to the heart, the blood is pumped to the lungs to gain oxygen and get rid of the extra carbon dioxide waste that it picked up at the cells. The newly oxygenated blood is returned to the heart to be pumped throughout the body.

The blood cells themselves can't get into the small spaces within the body's tissues. They remain in the blood vessels. There is liquid within these tissues that doesn't contain any blood cells. This liquid is called **tissue fluid**. It goes between the cells and keeps them bathed in the nutrients that they require. This fluid collects in special collection vessels called **lymphatics**. The fluid that collects in the lymphatics is called **lymph**. It is similar to **blood plasma**, which is just the liquid part of blood without the blood cells.

Within the circulatory and lymphatic systems, higher animals and humans have an **immune** system. The immune system protects from intruding organisms that come in to harm our bodies. These include the tiny viruses and bacteria, the worm-like parasites, fungi and other organisms that harm our bodies in their own attempts to survive. Designed right into our own bodies is the ability to tell the difference between our own cells and the cells of intruders. The immune system marks these alien cells as bad guys; it then attacks and kills them without mercy.

Exercises:

1. Place the following in proper order of diameter starting with the largest and ending with the smallest:

       a. capillary
       b. artery
       c. aorta
       d. arteriole

2. Answer each of the following questions about the body's systems with one of these answers: circulatory, immune, or lymphatic.

       a. Which of the body's systems provides a liquid of the correct makeup to be an ideal environment for most tissues to live in?
       b. Which includes arteries and veins?
       c. Which is responsible for identifying and destroying intruders?
       d. Which distributes oxygen from the lungs throughout the entire body?
       e. Which has pumped fluid?

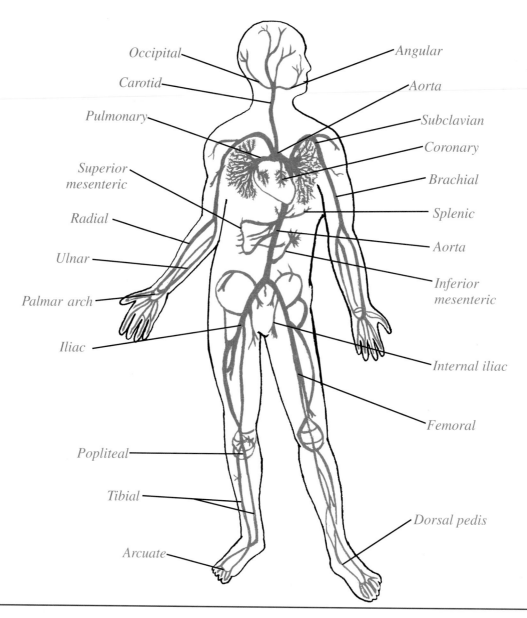

Occipital

Carotid

Pulmonary

Superior
mesenteric

Radial

Ulnar

Palmar arch

Iliac

Popliteal

Tibial

Arcuate

Angular

Aorta

Subclavian

Coronary

Brachial

Splenic

Aorta

Inferior
mesenteric

Internal iliac

Femoral

Dorsal pedis

The human circulatory system is the body's pipeline to distribute oxygen from the lungs and nutrients from the intestines. The central organ is the heart that sends blood to the rest of the body. The blood passes from the heart through the aorta to the major arteries. Those arteries get smaller and smaller as they get farther and farther from the heart. Smaller arteries called arterioles pass blood from arteries to even smaller vessels called capillaries. Capillaries allow passage of nutrients and oxygen through their thin walls directly to the tissue fluid around the cells and of waste materials from tissue fluid into the blood. Small venules receive the blood from the capillaries and carry it, along with the waste products it now contains, to the veins. The major veins empty blood into the vena cava which delivers it back to the heart. The heart sends the blood to the lungs where it discharges carbon dioxide and picks up more oxygen. The blood then returns to the heart for redistribution throughout the body. This diagram shows the system of arteries, but the system of veins is not shown.

38: *You Are a Bundle of Nerves*

We introduced the **nervous system** when we said that each muscle receives signals from the **brain** telling it when to contract. The nervous system is the great conductor of the symphony that is constantly going on inside your body, whether you are asleep or awake. It tells your heart to keep pumping and your respiratory system to keep drawing air either faster or slower. It tells your blood vessels how far to open or close in order to raise or lower the pressure on the system. It tells you when your food and water levels are low.

Our brains control many things we don't even know are happening. For example, our brains call for the growth hormone to stop being released at the time we have reached full height and are ready to stop growing. It tells the **adrenal glands** above the kidneys to produce adrenaline when we get excited, afraid or angry. This prepares us for the "fight or flight" response that gives us the energy to either fight our enemy or run away.

The nervous system consists of a brain—the master control center—a **spinal cord**, **nerve cells** to link the various parts of the body back to the spinal cord, and **sensory endings** or **receptors**. The sensory endings are of many different types. They allow us to sense pres-

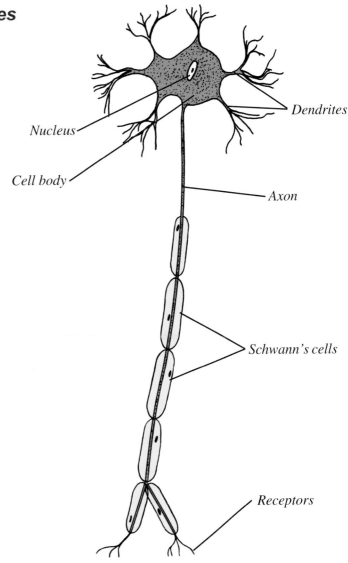

Nucleus

Dendrites

Cell body

Axon

Schwann's cells

Receptors

A nerve cell, or neuron, is one of the cells that carry electrical signals throughout the body. This network of cells is like the wires in a telephone connection except that it is made of living tissue.

sure, warmth, lack of heat ("cold"), and pain. There are also receptors deep inside muscles, tendons and joints that sense position, vibration, deep pressure, and deep pain. There are receptors inside the organs that sense **nausea** (a need to vomit), hunger and pain. And there are receptors in our sensory organs that give us special sensory abilities: the light receptors in our eyes, the wave detectors in our ears, the chemical taste receptors in our mouths, and the chemical smell (**olfactory**) receptors in our noses.

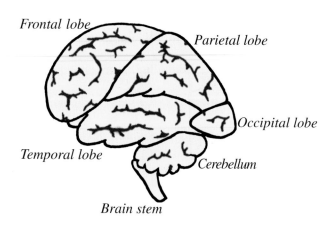

Frontal lobe
Parietal lobe
Occipital lobe
Temporal lobe
Cerebellum
Brain stem

The human nervous system is a series of links that carry electrical signals from all parts of the body to the brain and back again. The sensory endings accept inputs (such as pressure or heat) from the person's environment and send a signal of electrical energy to neighboring nerve cells. The electrical signal is passed from cell to cell up the spinal cord and eventually to the brain. The brain processes all of these signals that constantly come into it from different parts of the body and replies with its own electrical signals. These signals go back down the spinal cord and out to the muscles and other organs that are involved in the body's response. The time required for this entire process is a fraction of a second.

The sensors give us the ability to perceive the environment and react to it. This may seem simple, but it is really complex. We can see a sight that we have never seen before, like a tornado or a tidal wave, and realize that it means danger to us. Our brains can tell us to be afraid of situations that we don't really understand. We should listen to those signals and react with fear when we don't feel comfortable. God put those fears in us to protect us. However, if we understand a situation and realize that it is harmless, we have the ability to be unnecessarily afraid as well. Talk to adults about the things you fear. They can give you good advice about fears and what to do about them.

Exercises:

1. In the following paragraph insert the words from the word list below it that complete it accurately. Don't worry if all of the questions were not answered in the text. You can figure them out anyway.

   _____ endings receive input from the environment. Those endings send signals to nearby _____ which relay the message to the _____ _____ _____ or CNS. The CNS is primarily made up of the _____ and _____ _____. The CNS processes the information and sends out a signal, setting off the body's responses. The signal goes from the brain, down through the spinal cord and then through motor neurons to the muscles that take part in the response.

   brain, neurons, central nervous system, spinal cord, sensory

2. What type of energy is used by the nervous system to send signals? (This type of energy was the focus of several Red Lessons and was first revealed in Red Lesson 11.)
3. Do human bodies obey the laws of physics?

39: *Genetics*

When we introduced cells in Lesson 4, we mentioned that cells have a genome made of DNA. DNA is a large complex molecule that contains a lot of information stored in a code. The code is made up of chemical units in the same way words are made up of individual letters. These complex codes contain the directions for making all of the cell's products and for performing all of the cell's duties.

In bacteria a new cell is formed by making an exact copy of the parental DNA. The cell divides into two pieces, and each new cell gets half of the old DNA molecule and half of a new copy. So each has DNA that is exactly like the parent's DNA. In higher organisms the situation gets much more complex. The DNA from a mother combines with the DNA from the father in an unpredictable way to get an **offspring** that is quite different from either mother or father. This gives the possibility of much greater variation among offspring.

In the 1800's an Austrian monk by the name of Gregor Mendel did a series of experiments that started the discipline that we now know as **genetics**—the study of inheritance. Mendel's experiments showed that if you know certain things about the parents' characteristics, you can make some accurate predictions about the characteristics of their offspring. From these observations scientific disciplines have arisen that use genetic information to predict and even change the characteristics of offspring. By **selective breeding**, breeders of money crops like cotton, potatoes, corn and soybeans can produce plants improved for specific purposes like insect resistance and ability to stay fresh. Cattle breeders can breed more beef-productive cattle.

More recently it has been shown that DNA can be chemically changed, causing organisms to take on certain desired characteristics. This process, called **genetic engineering**, is producing an explosion of new ideas and uses. It is also producing an explosion of problems and questions. For example, should we apply these techniques to "improving" people? Should we select what features people should be allowed or not allowed to have? Many people feel that genetic engineers are taking on tasks that should be left only to God.

Exercises:
1. Which of the following is an example of selective breeding and which is an example of genetic engineering?
    a. selecting pairs of males and females who are likely to have children with extremely large noses and forcing them to marry each other
    b. finding a gene on the human genome for nose largeness (we'll call it the *nos z* gene) and chemically patching it into the DNA of a human embryo
2. From reading the second paragraph of the lesson, tell why selective breeding won't work in bacteria? (Don't say "Because they don't have noses!")

Gregor Mendel realized that specific features of offspring can be predicted by the features of their parents. This opened up the science of heredity called genetics. By understanding genetics you may learn what traits can be inherited from one or more parents and how likely a given trait is to be expressed by the offspring.

40: *Ecology*

Ecology is the study of the interactions among organisms and environments. This is an important study because all of nature is in a certain balance. Anything that is done to affect one organism or its environment has an impact on other organisms. We have tried, for example, to make life more pleasant by exterminating insect pests, not realizing that the insects we regarded as pests were food for other creatures. By eliminating insects we unintentionally hurt other creatures and lost some indirect benefit the "pests" brought us. Such efforts have taught us a great deal about nature's balance; we have a new awareness nowadays of our own effects on ecological balances. Only through increased understanding can we hope to give the proper emphasis to ecology in relation to other human goals.

The next several lessons will discuss specific topics in ecology. The first interaction for discussion is **pathogenesis**.

Have we mentioned that there are certain bad little guys that go around sucking the guts out of poor defenseless fish? Have we also mentioned that there are other organisms, like nematode worms, that prey on poor people like us? It turns out that there are many different types of organisms that prey on other animals. When our sheep, cattle, dogs, cats and horses are affected, they are seen by a **veterinarian**. When these organisms come after us, we go to a **physician**, a person who has studied diseases and has learned how to control many of them and completely knock out some of them.

We have to realize that there are many kinds of human pathogens (meaning "sources of suffering"). These are organisms that make themselves healthy and happy while making us suffer. Fortunately, when the human immune system is working properly, it can attack and eliminate many of these pathogens before they cause great harm.

One common group that includes many pathogens is the **viruses**. These are not really even "organisms," because they do not seem to be "alive" by our definition. A virus is smaller than a bacterium. In fact, some viruses infect bacteria and are called **phages** (short for **bacteriophages**). There are viruses that cause all kinds of disease in humans, from simple **colds** to the complex and deadly **acquired immune deficiency syndrome (AIDS)**. Viruses are not considered to be organisms because without the help of a host organism, they don't act as though they are alive. They don't eat food, excrete waste, reproduce, maintain themselves or carry out any other life process. But when they infect a living cell, they *appear* to come alive. They take over a cell's DNA to reproduce, and they usually destroy the cell in the process. Right now scientists are working hard to develop new **antiviral** drugs that kill off viral infections.

Human pathogens can also be found among the bacteria. Not all bacteria **infect** people (or attack them from the inside), but several bacteria are well-known infectors. **Antibiotics**, chemicals that kill bacteria, were first used in the 1800's and early 1900's to fight bacteria which animals' immune systems had trouble stopping. Humans began to be treated successfully with antibiotics in 1939. The use of antibiotics proved so effective for several decades that few bacteria were a serious threat to the health of people to whom antibiotics were available. But bacteria have changed since then. A small but growing number of bacteria have adapted to antibiotics so that the drugs are now less effective than they used to be. When people are attacked by one of these **antibiotic resistant** bacteria, they often die, especially if their own immune systems are not effective at killing off the organism.

Another group of pathogens is found among the **fungi** (i.e., among the yeasts and molds). A common human yeast pathogen is *Candida*, the organism that causes diaper rash. Several molds, like the athlete's foot fungus *Epidermophyton*, are also troublesome. These organisms are typically more difficult to treat than bacterial infections because their cells are more like our own. They are more like us in the sense that they are eukaryotic, and they do not have the same kinds of cell walls that bacteria have. These cell walls, along with the prokaryotic properties of bacteria, have been the targets of many of the drugs that have been successful against them. It's harder to find targets for drugs in cells that are like our own. Drugs we use to kill the pathogenic cells may be harmful to our own cells as well.

There are also pathogenic worms, especially among the nematodes we learned about in Lesson 19. Fortunately, medicines are available for ridding us of these pests, which often come from un-cooked or poorly cooked meat. One common example of worm infection is **trichinosis**. This disease comes from the parasitic **trichina worm** found in pigs, so we get it from poorly cooked pork.

 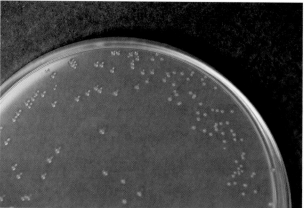

Here are examples of growing colonies of mold (left) and bacteria (right). There are organisms from each of these groups that are pathogenic (harmful) to humans and to animals and plants. Some microorganisms even attack other microorganisms.

Exercises:
1. What is ecology?
2. Based on this definition, which of the following would you consider to be a study in ecology?
    a. the doctor's study of the effects of fungi on people
    b. the laboratory scientist's study of a single plant enzyme
    c. the agronomist's study of the effects that bacteria in soil have on the roots of plants
    d. the geologist's study of the effects of solid waste generated by humans on the quality of underground water

41: *Food Web*

One profound way in which I can affect an animal is to eat it. That also has an effect on me. I live; it dies. A while back, we talked about the fact that humans are at the top of the food chain. We eat other things, but nothing eats us (usually). But this food chain is really not so much a chain as it is a complex web.

At the center of the web are the **primary producers**. They don't eat anything, but several animals feed on them. The primary producers are photosynthetic plants. They convert carbon dioxide from the air into the organic molecules that make up living organisms. Animals that feed on plants are **primary consumers**. That is, they are the first in line that are actually consuming another organism. The primary consumer can be a simple organism like a bacterium consuming dead leaf material that

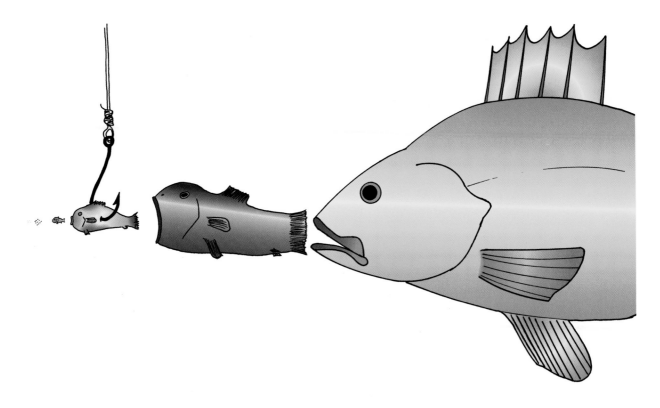

The food chain consists of a series of organisms, each of which feeds on another in the chain. The first organism in any food chain has to be a photosynthetic organism, because it does not require consumption of another organism to live. Every other organism is a consumer.

---

has fallen from a tree. It can also be a higher animal or even a human sitting down to eat a salad. Since not many humans are eaten by animals, humans are at the outside of the food web. However, when they die their bodies are consumed by bacteria and converted once again to carbon dioxide.

At the outside of the web are the **ultimate consumers**. These are organisms that convert organic matter from living things (or dead things) to carbon dioxide. Once organic matter is converted to carbon dioxide, nothing can consume it again. It can be recycled into living things only if a primary producer captures it and converts it to sugar ("fixes" it) through photosynthesis. Bacteria are ultimate consumers. Although they themselves may be devoured by organisms such as other bacteria, some fungi or some microeukaryotes, they convert about half of all the carbon they consume to carbon dioxide. This places them near the outside of the food web.

To demonstrate how many consumers can line up in a single thread of the web, let's start with a primary consumer, like a phytoplankton in the deep ocean. The phytoplankton fixes carbon dioxide to make its **biomass** (living material) and uses sunlight for energy. The biomass of the phytoplankton dies and is consumed by bacteria. The bacteria are eaten by rotifers. The rotifers are then eaten by copepods, and copepods are eaten by shrimp. The shrimp are eaten by fish, which in turn are eaten by larger fish. The larger fish are eaten by a shark. The shark dies and its body falls to the bottom of the ocean where it is eaten by a sea turtle. The turtle dies and falls to the bottom where its body decays and is consumed by bacteria, but the pieces of the sea turtle that are not consumed are resuspended by waves and eaten by oysters and worms. The oysters fall prey to a starfish, while the worms are eaten by fish.

It should be clear to you by now that any carbon that starts out as carbon dioxide and enters the food web when it is fixed by a primary producer can be cycled and recycled and recycled for years and years and years. Someday it will go to a consumer that will convert it back to carbon dioxide. These cycles continue endlessly.

Exercises:

1. If you were the only organism on earth, and no other organism (or organic matter) had ever come before you, would you have to be a producer or consumer in order to survive? Explain your answer.

2. Is it possible that you are made of some of the same carbon atoms that made up Moses? Explain your answer.

42: *Can We Get Along?*

There are many other types of relationships among organisms. Please don't try to memorize all of these words, but if you ever need them, they are here in the book for you. You will benefit just from knowing that these words, and especially the relationships they name, exist. The diagram on the following page should be helpful to help you understand the organisms relationships with each other.

Organisms can simply coexist without having much, if any, effect on one another (**neutralism**). There can be a selfish relationship from which one organism benefits and the other doesn't (**commensalism**). A relationship can be beneficial to both organisms but unnecessary to either one (**synergism**). A relationship may be both beneficial and necessary (**mutualism** or **symbiosis**). Organisms may compete for resources, resulting in a harmful effect on the loser (**competition**). A relationship may have a harmful effect on one organism without affecting the other (**amensalism**). Or, as we have said, a relationship may involve one organism either eating the other (**predation**) or sucking some good stuff out of it (**parasitism**). We presume this relationship to be bad for the one that turns out to be the other's meal or for the one that has its stuff sucked out.

These relationships not only affect the well-being of a particular organism, they also impact the overall balance of the entire community. While their effect on a particular organism may be negative, the effect on the general population may be considered positive. For example, protozoa may feed on bacteria within a community of microbes. This has a negative impact on the bacteria, but among the organisms consumed are dead bacteria as well as live ones. The nutrients contained in these dead cells are recycled into the community of living organisms, so the effect on the entire community is positive. Not only is the impact on the community different than the impact on an individual organism, but the magnitude of the impact can also be quite different. That's what makes ecology such a challenging field. Scientists are often left to decide what effects are likely and which of the possible effects are preferred.

Exercises:
1. Termites have bacteria living inside their guts that break down wood so that they can use it for food. Without these bacteria they would die. The bacteria also benefit from living within the protective body of the termite and getting regular meals of wood to eat. This is an example of:
   a. commensalism
   b. synergism
   c. symbiosis
2. There are five science students and only one candy bar. All of you are fifty yards from the candy bar when you find out it is there. Because you are selfish slobs, you run to the candy bar as fast as you can. The one who gets to it first gobbles it down, leaving none for anyone else. What kind of ecological relationship do you have with the other slobs—I mean *students*?

Ecology is the study of the interactions of organisms with one another and with their environments. There are many ways that organisms can affect one another as illustrated in these diagrams. Don't try to memorize the words. Just be impressed by the fact that all these different kinds of interactions have names and real-life applications.

In predation, a predator kills and consumes its prey for food.

In parasitism, a parasite lives at the expense of its host organism. While this relationship is often harmful to the host, the host usually continues to live (for at least the duration of the parasite's life cycle).

In synergism, the relationship is mutually beneficial but unnecessary.

In commensalism, one organism benefits and the other doesn't.

In neutralism, neither organism is affected by the other.

In symbiosis, the relationship is both mutually beneficial and necessary

In amensalism, one organism is harmed while the other is unaffected.

In competition, one organism wins out over another for a limited resource such as food or oxygen.

43: *Population Dynamics*

We have already noticed that all organisms on Earth reproduce. If they didn't, they would become extinct in one lifetime. Some organisms reproduce quickly, while others reproduce slowly. For instance, bacteria may double in number every 15 minutes. If we started with just one bacterium, and it divided into two cells after 15 minutes, then each of those cells divided into two cells in 15 more minutes, in 30 minutes we would have four cells. But notice what happens afterwards. Within 40 hours we would have generated enough bacterial cells to fill the whole volume of the Earth!

Then why don't bacteria take over the Earth? It seems like a simple question, but the answer turns out to be fairly complex. Nature has a built-in balancing effect that keeps these kinds of hazards in check. We could talk about any organism here, but since we started with bacteria, let's keep on.

The first reason bacteria don't take over the Earth is the effect of **nutrient limitation**: there isn't enough food to go around. As bacteria grow, they remove all of the food from their immediate surroundings. Because that food comes into their surroundings at a specific rate, if the rate at which they consume it ever exceeds the rate that it comes in, the food source will become scarce, and the growth of the bacteria will not be supported. It will slow down. If you noticed, we were talking about nutrients coming in from other places. This represents the second reason bacteria don't take over: even if the food supply were unlimited, the food isn't right where it needs to be when it is required. This is the problem of **nutrient distribution**.

The third reason bacteria don't take over the Earth is because when there are limited nutrients and the number of organisms exceeds the availability of nutrients, bacteria have to compete with each other for nutrients. Some bacteria are good competitors, and others are poor. Only the good competitors will reproduce quickly, and the poor competitors will reproduce slowly, if at all. So **competition** for a nutrient source is an important factor in limiting the growth of an organism.

Another important reason that bacteria don't take over the Earth is their limited length of life. One factor that we must consider when we think about taking over is that we all die at some time. Sometimes organisms die at a rate higher than the rate at which new life is generated. In these cases the total number of organisms living at a given time actually decreases. We have to compare the **growth rate** with the **death rate** to see if the population is growing, shrinking or staying about the same.

There are many reasons why organisms die. One reason is **senescence**, that is, old age. Many cells reach a certain age and simply stop maintaining themselves. They get old, and they die from poor upkeep. Another reason for death is **starvation**. Many cells simply can't get the nutrition they need, so they can't maintain themselves properly. As we know, life exists at a high potential energy; keeping us up there costs a lot of energy. If we can't obtain enough fuel molecules to supply that energy, then we will return to our ground state—our molecules will become disorganized or "degrade."

Another reason organisms die is from **predation**. That is, they are eaten by other organisms. This happens a lot with bacteria. If a bunch of them grow close together, ciliate organisms (microzoa that *love* to eat bacteria) notice, and *whammy*—they start a feast. Before you know it you have a lot of fat, silly ciliates and we're back to just a few bacteria. The ciliates will graze on bacteria until the bacterial numbers are too low for the ciliates to be interested in hanging around; then the ciliates will go away until the numbers come back up.

Other organisms die from **disease** or damage caused by outside influences (like chemical toxicity), harsh environments or parasites (even bacteria can have them). These influences can wipe out an entire population living in a certain area. They are especially problematic in areas already stressed from starvation or senescence.

Back in the 1970's there was a scare generated by the scientific community and the media because the world's population was increasing so rapidly. The fear was that we would soon become so numerous that we would overpopulate the Earth. Some people predicted that tragedy would strike as early as the 1980's. The year 2,000 is now upon us and our numbers are still growing, but there is no immediate fear in North America of tragic overgrowth. The reason the so-called "**population explosion**" didn't happen is because of the food distribution problem. Those areas of highest population growth began to suffer from malnutrition causing the **birth rate** to slow down and the death rate to increase from starvation and disease. The length of life decreased in those places, too. As long as these forces continue to act, malnutrition will continue to be a problem, and so will disease and low birth rate, but overpopulation is less threatening.

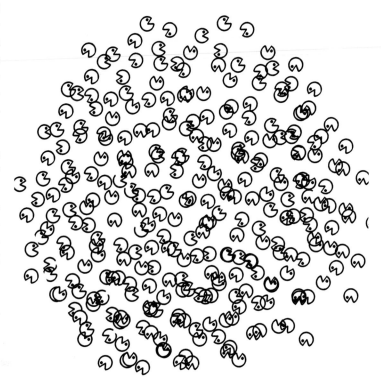

Were it not for limitations present in the environment and for competition for these limited resources, a single bacterium could divide to fill the volume of the earth in less than two days.

Exercise:

People eat fish, fish eat worms, worms eat microbes, microbes eat decayed plant matter, decayed plant matter comes from plants, and plants make their own biomass using carbon dioxide and energy from the sun. If the global temperature increases, plants will make more biomass, feeding more microbes, worms, fish and people. However, diseases spread more readily in moist environments than in dry ones. With more disease-bearing microbes, disease will spread more rapidly and people and animals will die at younger ages. Can you determine the effect of global warming on the human population? No—I can't either. Have a nice day!

APPLICATIONS OF THE RAINBOW

Our environment is our surroundings. At a given time we might be surrounded by the ocean or the sky. A few humans have even turned up in outer space. Although most of us can't go yet, with the help of a telescope we can see far beyond our immediate environment to remote areas of the universe. In one way of thinking the universe is our environment. In a narrower way of thinking our environment is the **biosphere** of Earth—the locations on Earth where life exists. In order to get to know our dwelling place, we start with the big picture. We look from the center of the Earth to the edge of the universe, then break this down into smaller pieces so we can understand in greater detail those places where we spend most of our time. But first, we look at the way scientists study their surroundings. Now please proceed immediately to Lesson 1.

1: *Scientific Method*

Just as science is a collection of knowledge, **scientific method** is a way of collecting knowledge so that the results can be trusted. There are accepted ways of confirming results. Although the word

science is an old word (and not looked upon favorably at times), what we now call the scientific method is relatively new, being, at the most, only a few hundred years old. Despite the clear-cut methods laid down in many textbooks, there is no simple set of rules that make up scientific method. Instead, any method that is logical and provable will be accepted by scientists.

In order to prove something, an **experiment** will generally be found to consist of a comparison be-

An experiment is an objective comparison between a treatment subject and an experimental control subject. The treatment subject is intentionally modified in some way, while the experimental control subject is left unmodified. This photograph shows the effect of several different levels of toxic mercuric chloride on the growth of bacteria. All of the tubes to which mercuric chloride were added are treatment subjects. The experimental control subject had no mercuric chloride added to it. It is otherwise identical to the treatment subjects.

tween a **treatment** and a **control** in order to answer a simple question. For example, what effect does ammonia have on the growth of corn seedlings? This is a basic question to which we would like an answer. I called it a *basic* question because it is simple. An example of a complex question that would be difficult to answer is: What effect does ammonia have on the stock market? The problem with a question like this is that so many factors affect the stock market. If there were any effect, it would be hard to demonstrate above those of other factors that affect the stock market. But we can set up a simple experiment to test the effect of ammonia on the growth of corn seedlings. All we have to do is:

1. Grow some corn seedlings.
2. Weigh them.
3. Place them in test tubes under controlled lighting and temperature.
4. Add water (which has no ammonia in it) to the test tubes.
5. Add a known amount of ammonia to some of the test tubes—these are our experimental subjects ("the **treatment group**").
6. Be sure to leave some of them without ammonia—these are our control subjects ("the **control group**").
7. Allow them sufficient time to grow, checking their weights periodically.
8. Compare the results from the treatment group with the results from the control group to see if they are different.

If there is an effect, and if the effect is not too tiny to be seen by our method of comparison, the test will have answered our question. That's the scientific way. Every experiment has a control (or controls) to which we compare our experimental subject (or subjects). The answer to our question is in the comparison.

Now that you see how easy it is to be a good scientist, all that's left is learning a few terms. We started out with a simple question. What effect does ammonia have on the growth of corn seedlings? We must have had a reason for asking that question. From the start we suspected that ammonia would have some effect on the growth of corn seedlings. Because we know that plants require nitrogen and that ammonia contains nitrogen, we *suspected* that adding ammonia to a plant's water would increase its growth rate. We even suspected that a plant without added nitrogen would have a hard time growing at all. So we formed a **hypothesis**. A hypothesis is an educated guess. Based on my education, I guessed that adding ammonia to a corn seedling's water would cause it to grow faster (unless I added too much and it killed the plant).

The second term is familiar to most people. The term is *experiment*. The scientific definition of this word is: the test of a hypothesis.

The third word for your learning describes what makes you able to form a hypothesis. You are able to do so because you have some background information to go on. A lot of information is known about the growth of just about every plant, but if that information were not available there would have to be something in your mind telling you to try adding ammonia. In other words, there must be some **model** for plant growth in your mind that suggests to you that nitrogen would be helpful. That model is called a **theory**. A theory is a mental picture of how a system will work. If you think your model is a good one, you'll share it with others so they can have a mental picture too. Together you can learn the answers faster and check each others' answers. If you work for a company, a mental picture of how a system works can be among the company's top secrets. The company officers may prevent you from ever explaining it to anyone!

To summarize, a test is done when a scientist uses his mental picture (theory) to come up with a hypothesis. The hypothesis being tested is a simple statement that is determined to be either true or false by comparing a treatment (experimental subject) with a control subject. In order to conduct a test you must have an **objective** way to measure the results. You can't simply say, "Yep! Just as I thought; this one looks bigger than that one." Instead there must be a method that does not depend on your opinion. **Subjective** testing is not sufficient because it can lead to bias in your results. That doesn't mean that scientists are always objective thinkers. In fact, scientists often hold to opinions that are wrong. That's why the test has to be objective, so that the scientist's opinion is not reported as a fact when it is actually wrong.

Anytime a scientist presents a theory as a fact, he is no longer acting as a scientist. If you ever hear someone talking about the theory of human evolution as though it were a fact, tell him you are not interested in his opinions. Tell him to present only the facts and let you decide for yourself. Chances are, he won't even know the facts. If he does know some facts, you probably won't find them convincing.

Exercises:
1. For each pair of measuring tools, choose the one that provides an objective measurement.
   a. for measuring heat: feelings of warmth; a thermometer
   b. for measuring your weight: a bathroom scale; sensation of fullness after a meal
   c. for measuring time: a stopwatch; feelings of tiredness
2. Which of the following is **not** a useful scientific test?

   a. determining the effectiveness of a medication by taking it for a week to see if you feel better

   b. determining the effectiveness of a medication by administering it to five subjects while administering an identical pill of no medical value to a second group of five subjects and comparing their health by some objective measure after a period of time considered adequate for the medication to have an effect

   Explain what is lacking from the useless test.

3. Which of the following best describes a theory?
   a. a model formed in the imagination to help in explaining results of previous experiments and in guiding future experiments
   b. a well-supported series of facts that can be used for making important decisions
   c. a fantasy
4. An _____ (xienpertem) is defined as the test of a _____ (pteysoihhs).

2: *The Earth*

In our journey to the outer reaches of our environment, perhaps the best place to begin our observations is close to home—right here on Earth. The Earth is a large ball measuring 8,000 miles in diameter. Since it is nearly a sphere, you can use its diameter to calculate its circumference ($c = \pi d$) and come up with something close to 25,000 miles. We don't know what the Earth is mostly made of because we have never experienced much of anything more than a few miles beneath its surface. However, there are a few things that we know about its insides. When the earth cracks, molten rock comes out. This means there are some super hot spots in there, and probably a lot of rock. **Rocks** are large hunks of dense crystalline mineral material thought to have been formed by the cooling of the material that the Earth was composed of at the time it was formed.

Most scientists believe the Earth is hottest near the center. Rock melts to become **magma** when it reaches something close to 2000°C. Water in the deep ocean is sometimes carried below the ocean floor where it is superheated under pressure. This water then comes blasting out of the earth at temperatures that may be several times the boiling point of water. When it comes out it carries dissolved minerals from deep inside the Earth. By studying this water we can learn a little more about the chemistry of the deeper earth.

The Earth is thought to be composed of three internal layers: (1) an inner **core** of magnetic metal surrounded by magma which was formed from molten core material, (2) a thick **mantle** of dense crystalline rock surrounding the core, and (3) a thin (but not light and flaky) **crust**.

In comparison with the deeper earth, we are much more familiar with the crust. It is up to 40 miles thick, although it varies from place to place, and contains all of the Earth's oceans, rivers and streams. It also contains the mountains, plains, valleys, ridges and plateaus. It is made up of layers of rock, **sediment** (settled material) and **soil**. (Later, we will define soil and talk about it in detail.) Although we think of the oceans as several in number (Indian, Arctic, Atlantic, Pacific), they are actually one continuous body of water. We might refer to it as "the ocean" rather than the oceans of the world. The ocean bottom is covered with geological formations that appear similar to the mountain ranges, valleys, plains and other surface features of the land. It also has deep cracks, called **trenches**, that form the ocean's greatest depths. The greatest depth is in the Mariana Trench which is in the western Pacific basin. Although nobody has ever reached the bottom of the trench at the location of its greatest depth, it reaches approximately 6.8 miles beneath the ocean's surface.

The bottom of the ocean is covered with sediments containing living things and the remnants

We have never seen another planet quite like ours. It is largely covered by water, and the surface of the dry land has soil in which plants can grow. You will see how both of these features are absolutely critical to our survival.

of life (such as dead animal and plant matter) that settle down from the water above. Much of the deep ocean is largely unexplored because of the difficulty involved with such extreme conditions. It

> *The ocean floor is not unlike the dry land. It has many geological features that match land features. These include volcanoes, mountain ranges, plains and deep fissures (cracks). However, the most significant of these features are located in the deep ocean and remain largely unexplored. Pictured below are the following: a crevice (top left), a wall (top right), a hill (bottom right) and a cave (bottom left).*

is mostly cold (averaging about 1°C) and dark (sunlight is unable to penetrate that much water), and the weight of the water at the bottom is crushing to all but the most sturdily crafted vessels and animals designed for deep-ocean survival. At its greatest depths, the water pressure of the ocean is as high as 8 tons per square inch.

Dry land is composed of layers of soil that lie atop solid rock. Although nobody saw it happen, soil is presumed by most geologists to have formed by the wearing away, or **erosion**, of rock. Erosion is what happens when wind and water cause particles to grind against each other, reducing larger particles into smaller ones. Those small particles are carried away by wind or water, and tend to collect in low-lying areas. Freezing and thawing cycles are also thought to play a part in soil formation by causing large rocks to fracture into smaller ones. Living things, especially bacteria, are believed to help this process along by producing acids that seep into the minerals of rocks and dissolve them, weakening the rocks' structures.

People who rely strictly upon physical processes to explain the Earth's existence determine that it has taken billions of years to arrive at the Earth's present condition from what it is believed to have been in the past. We who believe in the Creator are not restricted to this model for the explanation of what we see. Today, most of us maintain that the age of the Earth is not known with any degree of certainty. We have no doubt that the Genesis account of creation, although necessarily unscientific (because it was written before scientific method was developed), is as good a representation of how

Soil is made of particles of mineral material that is often similar in mineral content to the large clefts of rock beneath. It often occurs in layers that suggest different conditions on the face of the Earth when these different layers formed.

the Earth came into existence as could be devised to be understood and believed across time and nations. This account has been accepted by a great many people in every generation since it was written 3500 years ago.

But the Genesis writings do not teach us the technical detail of the Earth. Scientists want to know this information so we can use it for understanding and predicting. For this reason we try to investigate to understand the actual ways in which the Earth (and, indeed, the universe) was formed.

Erosion is thought to be responsible for many surface features of the Earth. Because God is excluded from the picture, scientists are left to speculate that these features must have required billions of years to reach their present state.

Exercises:

1. If you wanted to sample the mantle of the earth, how deep would you have to drill?

2. If you could ride a bicycle at 25 miles per hour in a straight line around the circumference of the Earth without slowing down or stopping, how long would it take to go around the whole Earth? Give your answer in hours, then give it in days.

3. If you wanted to go around the world in 80 days, you would have to travel:
   a. about half that speed.
   b. about twice that speed.

3: *Earth Tantrums*

Some of the most violent situations on Earth are thought to arise when large plates underlying the continents (**tectonic plates**) collide or separate. It is these events that are believed to cause materials usually held within the Earth's mantle to push their way to the surface of the Earth. For example, pockets of gases and hot, molten rock (**magma**) collect below the Earth's surface. When the pressure builds they explode through the Earth's crust to form **volcanoes** (mounded holes in the Earth's crust) at the surface. These explosions can blow matter many miles into the air. Smaller particles, especially light **ash**, may be carried for hundreds of miles in the Earth's upper air currents, depositing on houses and lands, even in other countries. The ash darkens the sky such that weather patterns can be affected for months or years.

Volcano

The danger of volcanoes is due to the violence of the explosion that lofts large fragments of earth for miles around. Also associated with these explosions is the hot magma, called **lava**, once it reaches the ground surface. More hazardous to life are the gases that are released by volcanoes. In low-lying places around the volcano, large areas can be completely engulfed in the carbon dioxide, carbon monoxide, hydrogen and sulfur dioxide. These gases will suffocate any living thing in their path that relies on oxygen to live. Mud slides can result, especially in areas where **permafrost** at the tops of snow-capped mountains is melted by the heat of the volcano. These massive mud slides carry entire communities of houses with them and crush them under thousands of tons of mud.

Another hazard associated with movements of the Earth's plates is **earthquakes**. Earthquakes are thought to result from sudden movements and collisions of large "plates" of the Earth's crust. The enormous potential energy that is built up in the land masses is released in such a tremor that solid structures may be completely destroyed. The amount of kinetic energy released by an earthquake is measured on the **Richter scale**. The scale runs from 1 to 9, with 9 being the highest activity ever seen in a quake. Each increase by one unit amounts to a factor of 10 increase in energy, so an earthquake that measures 7 is 10 times more energetic than one that measures 6, and 100 times more than a quake that measures 5. A scale like this one that changes factors of 10 to single digits is called a **logarithmic** scale.

When a quake occurs in the ocean, a **seismic wave** can be formed. These are caused by seismic (earthquake) disturbances at sea. They are also called by their Americanized Japanese name "tsunami" [soo-NAH-mē]. Seismic waves are often mistakenly referred to as **tidal waves** which are caused by the gravitational pull of the moon on sea water. Both types of waves can become large enough to do great damage. Seismic waves 15 meters high can form, involving enough water to destroy an entire coastal village.

Lava

Permafrost

Earthquakes and volcanoes happen frequently along a 32,500 kilometer string of activity surrounding the Pacific Ocean called the **Ring of Fire**.

Exercises:
1. Earthquakes, volcanoes and seismic waves tend to happen together. Why?
2. Tidal waves do not coincide with earthquakes. Why?
3. Why do earthquakes and volcanoes tend to happen in the same places time after time?
4. How much more energy is released by an earthquake measuring 6 on the Richter scale than one measuring 5?
    a. twice as much
    b. six times as much
    c. ten times as much

4: *Collections of Water*

Approximately 70% of the Earth's surface is covered by water. Most of that water (about 99%) is contained in the world's oceans, while a small portion runs across or stands on the surface of the ground. A larger portion (but still small in comparison to our oceans) is located in soil and rock beneath the ground surface. We call this **ground water**, and it is the source of the water that is pumped up from underground for drinking.

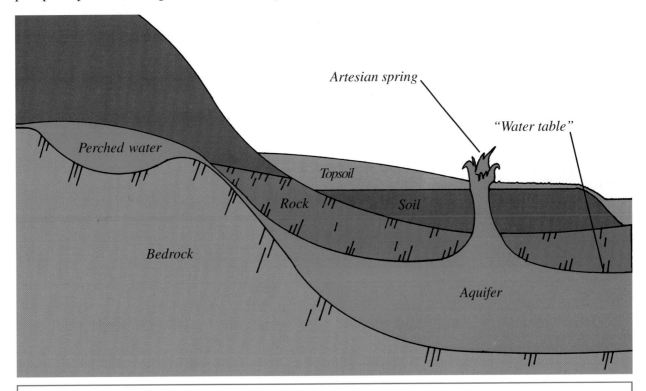

Ground water is simply water underground. It lies on bedrock within soil as if it were held in a thick sponge. It can stretch for miles, forming itself with the curves of the rock beneath. It can also form large lakes beneath the ground surface in hollow places in rocks or dissolve its way through limestone making an intricate underground tunnel system. Occasionally it surfaces, forming an above-ground stream or spring. If it is under pressure from water on higher ground it may form an artesian spring, continually shooting into the air.

Light from the sun warms the surface of the Earth. If you'll remember from your study of physics, three things may happen to light when it strikes an object. It may be (1) absorbed ("soaked up"), (2) reflected ("bounced off"), or (3) transmitted ("passed through"). Well, the Earth is too thick and absorptive to allow the passage of light, so that leaves only two things that can (and do) happen to light from the sun. The light that is absorbed by the Earth is converted to heat. Because most of the Earth's surface is covered with water, much of that heat goes to increasing the energy level of the water molecules. When a water molecule absorbs too much heat to remain liquid any longer, it leaves the water phase and becomes water vapor. We say it "**evaporates**." So a large portion of the sun's energy is used to convert liquid water to water vapor in the atmosphere.

An impoundment is a storage for water made by damming a river to allow the water to collect. From overhead, impoundments tend to branch out upriver from the dam. They don't look as neatly rounded as natural lakes.

This evaporation is absolutely critical to life on Earth. If not for the evaporation of water, the sun would be free to heat up the Earth to unbearable temperatures. The evaporation of water keeps the Earth in a tolerable range of temperatures to support life. Evaporating water takes heat away from the Earth in the same way it takes heat away from our skin when we sweat.

The warm water vapor rises from the ground and mingles with the air. The farther from the warm earth the water rises, the cooler it becomes. As the water cools, it **condenses** by forming little droplets. These droplets form bigger droplets as they continue to cool. When they become too big to be carried by the air any longer, they fall under the pull of gravity, growing in size by picking up additional water as they fall. When they are far from the earth these falling droplets may freeze to make snow, sleet or hail. If they thaw again as they fall through warmer air, they reach the earth as rain.

When rain falls from the sky, it lands over a large area. The rain soaks the soil, then begins to run down the slopes of the land in tiny streams that come together to make slightly larger streams. Continuing under gravity to even lower lands, the streams come together to make creeks which flow downward and together to make rivers, which flow into larger rivers. The large rivers flow back toward the ocean. Sometimes streams don't lead to rivers or oceans. Instead they come to a dead end at higher ground, so the water can't flow downward anymore but collects into a **basin** and forms a

There are few things in the world that can make a person feel so small as an unobstructed view of the ocean.

lake or pond. The water remains pooled in the lake until it is evaporated by the sun or until enough accumulates to flow over the edge of the basin so the stream can continue.

People have also learned to make artificial lakes, or **impoundments**, to store water by building **dams** in rivers and streams. The impounded water can be used to water crops, serve as drinking water for a community, grow fish to serve as food for the community, or generate electricity from the force of the waterfall that is created at the dam.

The branch of science that studies lakes and other fresh surface waters is called **limnology**. **Ocean-ography**, of course, is the study of oceans. Besides being nice places to go swimming and boating in the summertime, lakes and oceans are unique habitats for an enormous portion of the world's population of living things.

Exercises:
1. Why are people who live close to lakes especially affected by flooding after a heavy rain?
2. Does a person have to live in a place that is actually receiving rainfall for his yard to get flooded?

5: *Big Collections of Water*

Because we rely on fresh water resources for life, we place a great deal of importance on this water, even though it accounts for less than 1% of the water on Earth. The vast majority of the Earth's water is to be found in the ocean as salt water. The salt content is 3.6%. This is saltier than most any food. We can't drink water having this much salt because it is saltier than our own bodies. Drinking water this salty actually *removes* water from our bodies.

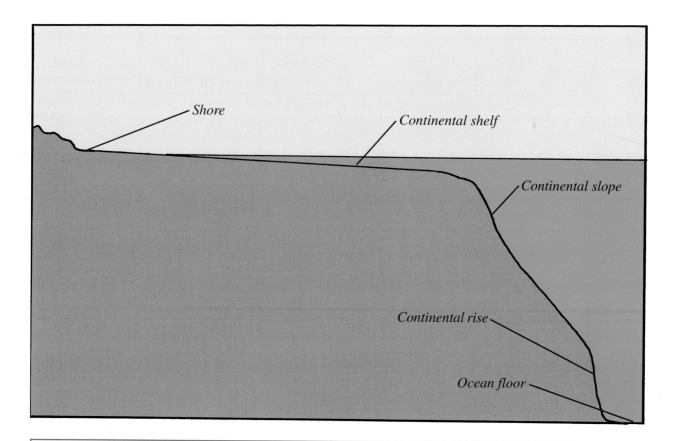

Although the look of these features changes from place to place, every continent is bounded by a shelf with these basic features.

In some desert countries there is no fresh water available. The people in those countries have to take water from the ocean and **desalinize** it (take the salt out of it). They do this by pushing the water through a filter. The filter is fine enough to keep the larger salt molecules on one side, while the smaller water molecules are pushed through. Although this effectively removes the salt, it requires a lot of electric power to do the filtering, and it makes the water expensive, especially when you have to desalinize enough water to serve a whole country. Anyone who could think of a less expensive way to remove salt from water would quickly be famous and would probably win a Nobel prize.

Each of the world's continents has a **continental shelf** that extends out into the water for perhaps 75 km. Above the continental shelf the oceans waters are shallow. The greatest depth at the end of the shelf is perhaps 200 meters. The shelf ends abruptly at the **continental slope** which dives 3,500 meters. At the base of the slope is the **continental rise** which dives another 600 meters to the ocean floor. In the center of the ocean floor between continents lies the **mid-ocean ridge**. This ridge is an extremely long mountain chain that extends all over the globe separating each of the continental masses. It is as though each continent is riding on a huge scaly plate that has crumpled against each of the other plates to form the large ridges of crust between the plates. In the areas of these mountains are volcanoes and earthquakes. Volcanoes add land mass to each of the continental plates as they drift farther apart. This drifting action is called **continental drift**.

We have already spoken of the importance of the oceans' waters in cooling the Earth, but we haven't talked about the other reasons why the oceans are so important. Not only do they provide water for rain and evaporation, but they also provide aquatic life for food, amusement and to support the ecology of the world. Because the oceans cover so much of the Earth's surface, and because there are algae at the surface collecting sunlight, the ocean is responsible for a large portion of the planet's primary production. If you recall, this is the production of biomass from the carbon dioxide in the air by photosynthesis. So the ocean is the beginning of a large portion of the Earth's food web.

The ocean floor is covered with **sediment** that is an average of 500 meters thick. The sediment consists of mineral matter, shells of dead animals, and decaying organic matter from dead plants and animals. Because sediments are high in organic matter, they make good habitats for **detritus feeders**. These are organisms that live off dead matter. Ocean currents may cause waters high in organic content from nearer the ocean floor to be brought to the surface. The areas where these **upwellings** occur are areas of plenteous nutrients for organisms living at the surface. These are areas famous for fishing, shrimping, and various other food-gathering activities. Animals recognize this as well, so the large animals that feed on the small fish show up in hoards.

Because the ocean is the source of most of the water in our atmosphere, the ocean has a great impact on the **weather** and climates all over the world. Our location in relationship to oceans decides in part how much rain we get. Not only does this water provide rain, it also controls temperature changes. The ocean has so much capacity for heat that lands surrounded by the ocean tend to have temperatures that are fairly constant throughout the year. The Hawaiian Islands are a tourist's haven because of the year-round moderate temperatures that are provided by its tropical location and the fact that it is surrounded by the world's largest body of water—the Pacific Ocean.

The oceans' waters range in temperature from approximately 25°C near the equator to -2°C at the poles. While this is below the freezing point of pure water, the salt in the water lowers its freezing point, keeping it liquid at otherwise freezing temperatures. These temperatures are experienced only at the surface. Most ocean water is at approximately 1°C. There is a zone of rapidly changing temperature, called a **thermocline**, between the warm surface water and the large body of cooler water

Exercise:
    Besides providing a great place to swim, of what use is the ocean?

6: *The Greenhouse Effect*

The Earth itself and the water on the Earth are not the only things standing in the way of the sun's light. The **atmosphere** (the gases that are being held to the Earth by gravity) also absorbs light. The shorter, more energetic wavelengths of light tend to bounce off and get scattered about. That's why the sky appears blue. It is this scattered light that our eyes pick up as we look into the sky. The longer wavelengths of light, like the yellows, greens and reds, come through to the Earth. That's why the sun appears to be yellow-white. That color is the strongest to our eyes. At night as the sun goes down, more of these middle-range wavelengths get filtered out because there is more atmosphere between the sun and our eyes to scatter those shorter wavelengths. The wavelengths that travel best through the atmosphere are the last to be filtered out. That's why the sun appears red as it goes down. Red is the most penetrating component of visible light.

It's a good thing the atmosphere is there to protect us from the sun's rays. If it were not, the ultraviolet light from the sun would surely kill us. Most of the sun's ultraviolet radiation is reflected away from us when it hits the outer atmosphere. The warming infrared rays pass all the way through to be absorbed by the Earth. These rays are absorbed by the soil and water, and their heat is passed back to the air above the ground bringing warmth to the Earth's inhabitants.

We've all noticed that a car sitting in the sunshine will be warmer inside than it is outside. This is an important observation that we call the **greenhouse** effect. The long warm wavelengths of light pass right through the windshield of the car and strike the car's interior—the dashboard, the seats and the carpet. These textiles absorb the light and become warm. The windshield holds the heat in, so the inside of the car can be quite warm, even in the wintertime when outside temperatures are frigid. The Earth's atmosphere acts like the

A greenhouse is designed to let in light so plants can capture it while continuing to hold in heat. The atmosphere has this same effect on the surface temperature of the Earth.

windshield of a car. It too can hold the heat in close to the Earth. This is the same thing that happens in a greenhouse which brings extra warmth to plants during cold seasons.

Lately scientists have caused quite a stir about the overproduction by industry of certain gases, especially carbon dioxide, that hold in heat. They call these gases "**greenhouse gases**" because they increase the greenhouse effect on the Earth. This contributes to increased warming of the Earth. The fear is that all of this warming will cause the ice at the polar ice caps to melt and raise the levels of water in the ocean, flooding several coastal cities throughout the world. Often the Earth's ability to lessen the severity of these problems is not fully appreciated. Time will tell.

Exercises:

The text explains what might happen during the daytime without the atmosphere to protect us from the sun's ultraviolet rays. What do you think would happen to us at night if it were not for the atmosphere and the greenhouse effect?

7: *Geology*

Geology is the study of the Earth, and as you can imagine it includes a lot of different studies. The Earth is composed of mineral matter at the surface, while little is known of its internal structure. As we noted before, we haven't ever seen anything deeper than a few kilometers beneath its surface, so we are left to wonder about much of its composition.

In the surface of the Earth we find layers (or **strata**) of sediments that are presumed to have been laid down in order, since they contain a **succession** of living forms. This means that the different strata have different groups of organisms represented within them, and that these organisms seem to follow a sequence. The succession progresses from lower animals (by the evolutionary definition) to higher animals. The study of the history of life within the geological record (**fossils**) is called **paleontology**.

Besides the study of the history of life, geology also includes **mineralogy**, a study of the minerals within the Earth. This study is especially useful for gaining information in order to find important mineral deposits. These deposits may include elements such as gold, silver and platinum; precious stones, such as diamonds, rubies, sapphires and emeralds; or the so-called **fossil fuels** such as petroleum, natural gas and coal. These are called fossil fuels because they are **organic** (having carbon-based structure) and are thought by most scientists (based on the evolutionary model) to have formed from the aging of dead plant and animal materials. Many people take up rock collecting because of their appreciation for the beauty of different kinds of minerals they find in the earth.

One area of challenge to people who believe that God is the Creator of the Earth is the field of **geochronology**, or Earth dating. If certain portions of the Old Testament of the Bible are to be taken literally, they imply that the Earth is only a few thousand years old. This is in obvious disagreement with most modern geochronologists who date the Earth back some 4.5 billion years, and date modern man as having occupied the Earth for some 200,000 years. These dates are based on special techniques involving radioactive elements in the earth. The dates are based on several important assumptions. In order to understand more clearly how to deal with these inconsistencies, ask your teacher to explain to you the section in the Teacher's Helper about the agreement and disagreement between science and the Bible.

There are other areas of study that are included under the study of geology, and these will be the subjects of the lessons that follow.

Exercises:
1. The field of geology is at the center of the creation-evolution debate. Why?
2. Petroleum companies hire lots of geologists. Why?
3. The U.S. Geological Survey is a government agency whose employees have traveled all over the surface of the U.S. (and much of the world) charting the types of minerals and features of the Earth. Why might geology be of such interest to the government?

This is the geological column as seen by most modern geologists. It is based on evolutionary assumptions.

Table: Geochronology

Named divisions of time and proposed time periods based on geochronology methods and assumptions. First appearances of flora and fauna in fossil record are listed in their associated periods.

Era	Period	Epoch	Beginning (mil yrs ago)	Fauna	Flora	Other
Cenozoic	Quaternary	Recent	0.2	Modern humans		
		Pleistocene	1.5	Humans		
	Tertiary	Pliocene	7	So-called "hominids"		
		Miocene	26	Large marine mammals		
		Oligocene	38	Apes		
		Eocene	53	Horses		
		Paleocene	65	Carnivores		
Mesozoic	Cretaceous		136	Marsupials, insectivores		Extinction of dinosaurs
	Jurassic		195	Birds, flying reptiles		
	Triassic		230	Dinosaurs, mammals		
Paleozoic	Permian		280		Conifers Angiosperms	
	Carboniferous*		345		Reptiles	
	Devonian		395	Amphibians		
	Silurian		440		Terrestrial plants	
	Ordovician		500	Fish		
	Cambrian		600	All invertebrate phyla		
Precambrian			4500			Few prokaryotes**

*Often broken down as Pennsylvanian and Mississippian periods.

**Most so-called fossils from Precambrian formations remain contested.

8: *How to Make Soil*

Rain washes over the surface of the Earth, dissolving minerals from rocks and washing small particles from the highlands down into the valleys. The small particles carry organic matter from partially degraded plants attached to the rocks' surfaces. The lowlands collect these small particles that are rich in organic matter, and these collections make excellent, rich **soils** for growing plants.

Other soils are also thought to have formed from this so-called **weathering** of rocks. Soils appear to be made up of minerals from the major rock formations lying underneath them. When geologists consider the age of the Earth they consider, in part, the length of time that must have been required for layer upon layer of soil to form by the weathering of rock, assuming that nothing has happened over the years to speed things up. This assumption has taken such an important place in the field of geology that it has its own name. It's called the **assumption of uniformity**. It has also been accepted more generally by the scientific community that uniformity is assumed unless there is a reason to assume otherwise. This is known as **uniformitarianism**.

This doctrine of uniformity has come under attack in recent years by scientists who recognize that the uniformity principle has led to errors in the interpretation of geological data. For example, not even the most generous estimates on the age of the Earth would allow for the slow, uniform accumulation of the great chalk formations in England. Only a **catastrophic** event (an event that was relatively short and dramatic) could explain such a formation within a reasonable time frame. If we know that there are some formations that do not fit the assumption, then we can be sure that other conclusions have been affected by the same error. In order to more clearly interpret the information contained within the Earth, these subjects will have to be approached more objectively. By the Genesis account, the creative activities of God undoubtedly included some degree of soil preparation, as we have the first people occupying a garden that had been prepared for them. Such a creation would clearly be considered catastrophic by the scientific definition. Exactly what parts were played by God and nature in bringing the Earth toward its present state are matters of speculation, since we were not there to observe and record the changes, and few written records exist for us.

Soil consists of a number of strata of minerals that are generally like the rock below or like the minerals from which they presumably eroded. Soil minerals can be carried for great distances (even thousands of miles) by wind, water, and, in some periods of history, by ice. In many cases the origin of a particular stratum is not clear. Streams of water are nearly always in a valley, bounded by sand, with a silty flood plain lying higher and farther away. This is because, when floods occur, the heavy sand particles deposit near the bank. The lighter silt particles wash over the bank and settle out of the water more slowly. Clay will deposit only in those areas where water stands for a long time because the particles are tiny and light, so gravity doesn't pull them down quickly through the water.

Soil is an important natural resource because the type of soil decides which plants can grow and which cannot. Since the soil is the greatest source of minerals for land plants, and since land plants are the greatest source of primary production (food) for land animals, and since land plants and animals are the most important source of food for humans not living near oceans, I'd say soil is important. Without good soil or access to ocean life, people quickly start getting hungry. The field of **agronomy** is concerned with the uses of soils for agriculture. It considers the complex relationships between soils and plants.

The Law of Moses contained in the Old Testament of the Bible required the Israelites to provide a Sabbath rest for their land. Every seventh year they were to allow their land to lie fallow. This protected the land from overuse. Today, amidst modern technology, we have forgotten the basic laws provided by God for our protection, and our land is suffering from overuse. Someday it is likely that our farmlands will no longer be fit for farming; then they will have their rest.

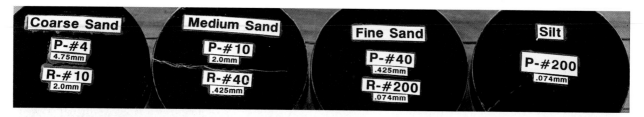

This soil has been passed through a series of screens to separate out particles of different sizes. All soil is a combination of different sizes of particles. Many think this is a result of weathering—erosion and effects of microbes.

Exercises:

With the help of the dictionary and the previous lesson as well as this one, fill in the blanks using the words below. (Not all of the answers will be found in the text.)

1. _____ is the study of the Earth, especially with regard to its large formations.
2. _____ is the study of the soil in relationship to agriculture.
3. _____ is the study of the minerals that make up the Earth's rocks and other features.
4. _____ is the study of the age of the Earth and its various formations.
5. _____ is the study of the fossil record.
6. _____ is the study of the layers of rocks and sediments in the earth.

mineralogy, geochronology, agronomy, stratigraphy, geology, paleontology

9: *Water in the Soil*

We have already talked a little about ground water. It is the water that fills the **pore spaces** in the soil and rocks beneath the surface of the Earth. Did you ever think about where rain water goes after it falls on the ground and gets soaked up by the soil? Does it go all the way through the Earth to the Indian Ocean? No, it goes down under the force of gravity until it hits something that makes it stop. Imagine what would happen if you dug a hole in the ground and placed a bowl in it, then filled the hole with soil again. When the rain fell, the soil would soak up the water, and the water would get

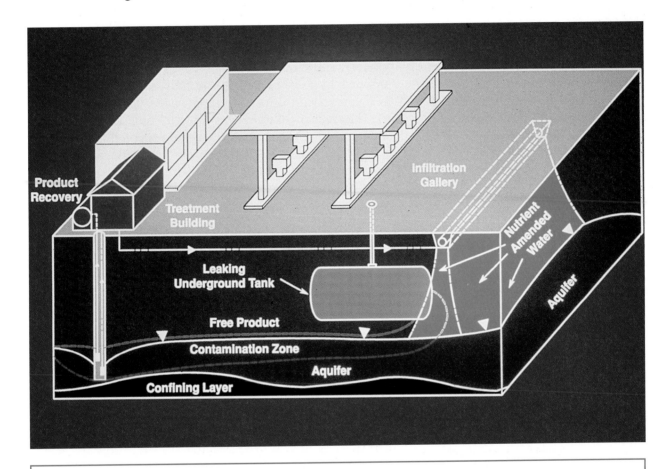

Throughout the developed countries, including the United States, hundreds of thousands of underground fuel-storage tanks have leaked their contents into water. Cleanup of a single contaminated site might cost hundreds of thousands of dollars. This diagram shows an underground fuel spill and a typical cleanup operation.

pulled deeper into the ground by gravity. It would continue to go downward until it hit the bottom of the bowl and would collect there until the bowl was full. Then it would overflow the bowl and continue down into the ground until it hit something else that changed its direction.

You see, ground water is not mystical or magical. It does what water does everywhere. It flows downward until it hits something, and then it spreads itself over whatever it hits. If it hits a surface, it collects there. If the surface is sloped, it travels over the slope to the lowest point. The difference between ground water and surface water is that ground water moves more slowly because it has to travel through soil, and the soil slows it down. In fact, most ground water will travel only a few feet per year.

So when you are walking on the Earth's surface, you can realize that below your feet is a large zone of rain-soaked soil that is slowly, but constantly, moving toward lower ground. This ground water is a great source of drinking water because there is a lot of it—more than ten times the combined amounts of water in our rivers, streams and lakes. It is usually fresh water, not salt water, so it is **potable** [PŌ-tuh-bul] (good for drinking). The soil acts like a natural filter to remove particles, and harmless bacteria living in the soil can destroy many contaminants, so ground water tends to be purer than surface water. Recently we have come to realize that a portion of our ground water has become contaminated by industrial, agricultural and government activities and is no longer fit for drinking. In some of the areas where this has happened, efforts are underway to clean up the water.

Exercises:
1. Clay particles are tinier and pack more tightly together than sand particles. Which will water pass through more quickly—a layer of sand or a layer of clay?
2. If you were standing on a spot of soil that was composed of pure sand that went 10 meters deep with solid granite bedrock beneath, where would rainwater collect?
   a. in the air above the ground
   b. at the ground surface
   c. on top of the bedrock
   d. beneath the bedrock

10: *Atmospheric Science*

The atmosphere is the name for the entire mass of gases surrounding the Earth that are held there by gravity. This mass is made up of layers, each having its own makeup giving it its own characteristics. The layers of atmosphere include the **troposphere**, **stratosphere**, **mesosphere** and **thermosphere**. The troposphere ("touching" + "zone") is about 6 miles thick above the northern to central United States, and thicker (about 10 miles thick) at the tropics. Commercial airline jets cruise near the boundary between the troposphere and the stratosphere. The stratosphere ("layer" + "zone") is a good place to fly because it is above the bad weather that can make it difficult to fly an airplane.

The thermosphere ("heat" + "zone") is a layer of high energy because it is constantly bombarded by X-rays, electrons, and ultraviolet radiation from the sun. These energy inputs convert many of the gas molecules into reactive ions, so the inner layer of the thermosphere is called the ionosphere. The outer layer of the thermosphere has little gas because there is no gas weighing on it to compact it. Some of the high-energy molecules can escape the Earth's gravitational field into outer space from here. This outer, low-density layer is called the exosphere ("outer" + "zone").

Unless you're weird (and maybe even if you are), you live near the ground where the atmosphere is made up of approximately 78% nitrogen, 21% oxygen, and less than 1% of argon, carbon dioxide and other gases. Water vapor is also a significant part of the air. Of course, it changes a lot from day to day, but at any given time there is ten times more water in the atmosphere than in all of the world's rivers. At 30°C, air that is **saturated** with water (that is, holding as much as it can) can hold 4.2% of its weight in water. This mixture of gases and water vapor under the warming influence of the sun creates our living environment.

The atmosphere does many things for us. First, it provides protection from the sun. Twenty-five percent of the sun's light (including most of the harmful high-energy rays) is reflected back into outer space, leaving the less harmful rays for us.

Second, it warms us like a blanket. The heat generated by the sun would escape back into outer space without the atmosphere to capture it and hold it near the Earth.

Third, it provides the gases we need to live. None of the other planets or moons in our solar system provides an atmosphere that is suitable for humans. Ours has the right concentrations of all the right gases for us and for the plants that provide us with oxygen. This is an amazing and critical balance without which we could not live. Because of the mass of the Earth and the intensity of its gravity, the atmosphere also provides a suitable amount of pressure on us to give us a concentration of these gases high enough at the surface of the Earth to keep us alive, yet low enough to prevent us from being damaged by the oxidizing effects of oxygen. At the same time, it provides us with a pressure low enough so that we are not crushed under its weight.

Fourth, the atmosphere is responsible for our weather patterns. Now, we often complain about the weather, but believe me, it could be much worse. How would you like a 2000°C day with sulfuric acid rain or a night that drops to -100°C under an atmosphere of ammonia gas? That's what we might get if we lived on a different planet in our solar system! We, on the other hand, get the necessary light and dark cycles, wet and dry seasons, and warm and cold seasons that are necessary to support the marvelous diversity that we see in our plant and animal life. Our atmosphere also allows the unnecessary but appreciated beauty that comes to us as a bonus with these changes of season.

Imagine yourself in a rocket ship blasting off from the earth. Let the words below guide you on your trip beginning in the troposphere. The descriptions below tell you what you would experience as you travel through the atmosphere.

Exosphere

The density of gases in the atmosphere continues to decrease as your distance from the earth increases. In the exosphere there is little protection from the damaging rays and particles given off by the sun. The atmosphere will get thinner and thinner until the number of atmospheric gas particles fades to near nothingness. From here, a chance particle that gets energized by the sun's rays might jump free from the Earth's gravitational field into interplanetary space (the space among the planets).

Exosphere (650 km & upward)

Thermosphere

Even in your air-conditioned spacecraft you begin to sweat. You look at your temperature gauge to learn that the temperature of your aircraft is climbing wildly. The temperature of the thermosphere will increase to a maximum of $1,500^{\circ}C$ because of the absorption of the sun's intense radiation by the few remaining atmospheric gas particles—mainly hydrogen, helium and single oxygen atoms. (Because of the high energy input from the sun, oxygen atoms have too much energy to remain bound together as diatomic oxygen.)

Mesosphere

What's this? As you leave the stratosphere your pressure gauge is telling you that the pressure is less than 1% of the pressure at the earth's surface, but you are still in the lower atmosphere! The density of gases is highest on the ground, so the greatest mass of gases and the greatest pressure are also at the ground surface. The temperature of the atmosphere decreases throughout the mesosphere as the atmosphere grows thinner. There is less and less ozone to absorb sunlight. There is so much high energy sunlight here that the atoms begin breaking apart into energetic ions. This will continue to happen throughout the rest of the atmosphere. As you leave the mesosphere, the temperature gauge reads $-100^{\circ}C$.

Thermosphere (85-650 km)

Stratosphere

As you enter the stratosphere you are likely to happen by a jet aircraft flying above the clouds that produce most of the rain and snow. Because the atmosphere at this level is not as well protected from the sun's rays, the increasing solar energy will cause the oxygen atoms to collide with greater force producing more and more ozone. Because ozone absorbs ultraviolet radiation, the atmosphere begins to get warm again as you ascend. The temperature increases to about the same temperature as it was on the ground.

Mesosphere (55-85 km)

Troposphere

First you quickly pass through the troposphere—the part of the atmosphere that touches the earth. This part of the atmosphere contains all but a few of the highest clouds. Watch your temperature gauge as you climb; notice that the temperature drops steadily from ground temperature (perhaps $20^{\circ}C$) to about -60° as you enter the stratosphere.

Stratosphere (12-55 km)

Troposphere (0-12 km)

These are the reasons why the atmosphere is important, but they are also the reasons why we study to know and to understand our atmosphere. We want (and sometimes need) to know how it protects us, warms us, contributes to our health, provides for us, and affects our living environment. Sometimes our atmosphere can be harsh, and it becomes important to know how to protect ourselves from its fierceness.

There is an incredible balance needed to maintain life. We live approximately at sea level where the plants have just enough carbon dioxide and sunlight to live, and animals and humans breathe the air with just the right amount of oxygen. Mountain climbers face extreme temperatures and require an oxygen supply when they climb to heights where few breathing animals live.

Exercises:
1. Would we be harmed by breathing a small amount of nitrogen gas? How do you know?

2. Because oxygen is the part of air that we rely on, can we assume that we would be just as well off in an atmosphere of pure oxygen? Explain your answer.

3. True or false?

    a. The layers of the atmosphere are different kinds of gases separated by invisible lines that gases cannot cross.

    b. The layers of the atmosphere are layers of gases that simply collect in certain areas because of their properties (*e.g.*, mass, density, temperature).

    c. The layers of the atmosphere are not clearly defined, but they tend to run together at the borders because they are gases.

    d. The closer to the earth's surface you get, the more tightly the gases are packed, partly because more dense gases tend to sink.

    e. The closer to the earth's surface you get, the more tightly the gases are packed, partly because the higher layers put pressure on the lower ones.

11: *Meteorology and Climatology*

The study of our **weather** is really just a study of the atmosphere where we live. It is called **meteorology**. Your local news station has its own meteorologists who can be seen on TV talking about the weather. These people may or may not be weather experts, and are quite often actors or communicators with little training in science. Their job is to be on TV and to communicate the weather to the people watching. There are other meteorologists whom we never see on TV. These are specialists who are involved in the science of meteorology. They attempt to increase our ability to predict the weather by studying and advancing our understanding of the atmosphere. Most of the weather information that the TV meteorologists report is obtained from these scientists.

In the part of the world that includes the United States the weather is fairly unpredictable. It takes a lot of information to try to predict what the weather is going to be like, and even then we often fail to predict accurately. This is not true everywhere on Earth.

Lightning is caused by build-up of static charges in the atmosphere that meet with static charges on the surface of the Earth or elsewhere in the atmosphere. The result can be an intense release of electrical energy.

Earth climates are relatively simple to understand because they are largely controlled by a few factors. We have a pretty good understanding of those factors. They include the position of the sun in relationship to the Earth, the rotation of the Earth, and the makeup of our atmosphere. Let's begin to understand how these factors affect climate.

Flooding results when too much rain comes at once. The earth can't accept that much water at once, forcing it to run to low-lying areas until it can seep in. Those low-lying areas can fill up quickly. During floods many people die by being swept into churning currents of water. Many others die from water-borne diseases that can be spread through sewage backups and overflows. Young children and elderly people are particularly susceptible because of their poorly-equipped immune systems.

Tornadoes, a topic of study in Lesson 17, create damage from the 50 to 100 mile-per-hour winds that they generate.

In Yellow Lesson 2 we learned how fog forms from the condensation of moisture in the air. After reading through these lessons, you will be able to predict where and when fog is likely to occur.

Blizzards (below) are winter storms with hard snowfall under driving winds that can cover entire houses in white blankets and leave drivers stranded in their cars. They may also be the most beautiful of the natural disasters.

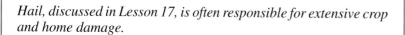

Hail, discussed in Lesson 17, is often responsible for extensive crop and home damage.

Wildfires (left) may be caused by drought conditions—the lack of sufficient rain. Plant foliage becomes dry and burns more easily. These fires are responsible for great losses of property and homes.

Exercises:

Which of the following statements describe the weather and which describe the climate?

1. Today it is raining.
2. I live in a temperate region.
3. We get 16 hours of daylight in the summertime.
4. In the Cascade Mountains of Washington State they may get 200 cm per year of rainfall.
5. The barometric pressure is dropping.

12: *Stirring the Atmospheric Pot*

Let's begin by considering the sun. Would you like to guess what effect the sun has on climate? Sunlight isn't absorbed well by the atmosphere, so most of it passes through to the Earth where it is absorbed by the Earth's surface matter. When molecules that are present on the surface of the Earth interact with the wavelengths of light given off by the sun, the Earth's surface warms up and gives infrared light back to the atmosphere. These infrared rays are absorbed by the air molecules.

Do you want to guess what part of the Earth is the warmest? It's the part that's closest to the sun. This is the first and most fantastic rule of climate. The sun makes the Earth warm, which in turn makes the atmosphere above it warm! Isn't that exciting? (Probably not.) But what effect does heat energy have on the atmosphere? Now remember (from Lesson 6 of the Red Section), the atmosphere is a fluid. What do you think will happen to it when energy is introduced? Well, I'm waiting. You can't figure it out, can you? Okay, I guess I'll have to tell you. It moves. And how do energized fluids move? In waves—ordered areas of expansion and contraction.

Imagine filling a pan with water and putting it on the stove. You've done this before. You turn the burner on high, and after a few minutes the water begins to boil. As the water turns to steam, you can see the swirling motions of the steam mixing with the air, and pushing air out of its way as it travels upward into the air. Why does it go up? While cool water is more dense than air, if you heat it up to its boiling point it expands to become less dense. The less dense gas is the one that rises.

This is the same kind of fluid motion that takes place in the atmosphere when molecules of air are warmed by energy from the sun. The heated gases expand, so they rise under the pressure of the more dense gas. This may not seem all that important, but it has a huge impact on the climate of the whole globe. Air at the equator is warmest, so it is the most energetic air on Earth. Because it is so energetic it expands and becomes less dense. Because it is less dense it rises from the Earth. When it rises, more dense air comes in behind it, so it too will be warmed and travel upward.

Exercises:
1. Peek back at Red Lesson 6. Notice that the atmosphere is a fluid, and decide what kind of motion would be expected if the atmosphere were stirred with energy.
2. Look back at Red Lesson 24. The atmosphere is made of gas molecules. What happens to gas molecules when they absorb sunlight or another form of energy?

13: *Bringing Order to Mixed Fluid*

As heated air rises, it cools, so it stops going up and instead is forced outward by the warmer air rising behind it. Cooler air that has risen above the equator is forced north and south toward the poles. The longer it stays high in the atmosphere, the cooler it gets. At some point, it becomes too cool to hold water any longer, so the water condenses and falls out as rain. This cool air then begins to sink back toward the ground.

Now it's time to introduce air pressure. As you know, fluids travel in waves because they can be compressed, or squished. When they compress in one area, that area expands into the next decompressed (unsquished) area. If you were standing on the equator where the air is decompressed and rising upward, would the air be pushing on you more or less than if it was compressed and falling on your head? Would you feel squished or unsquished? If there is less atmospheric pressure, you would feel less squished. Areas where expanded air is rising are **low-pressure zones**. Areas where dense air is falling toward the Earth are **high-pressure zones**. What happens when you place air at high pressure close to air at low pressure? Simple—the pressurized air moves to the area where the pressure is low.

So follow this: Air in the tropics travels in circular patterns. It rises near the equator and splits into two flows—one going north and the other going south. As it cools, it drops all of its moisture as rain over the tropical areas. This cool, dense, dry air sinks toward the Earth, warming as it goes. It puts pressure on the air below, so the places where the air descends are under high pressure. Because high-pressure air naturally moves toward areas of lower pressure, this air will be forced to return to that low-pressure zone at the equator where the warm, expanded air is rising. As it moves back toward the equator it continues to warm and gather moisture, starting the cycle again. In this way, two large zones of circulating air just north and south of the equator are formed. These circulating patterns of air are called **Hadley cells**.

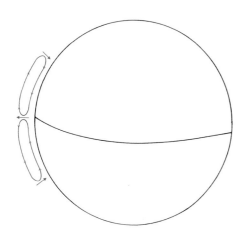

Hadley cells are circulating currents of air rising above the equator and descending at the dry latitudes. In the meantime they provide rain to the tropical rain forests.

Exercises:
1. When gases expand do they become more or less dense?
2. When gases become less dense do they rise or sink relative to more dense gases around them?
3. When dense, sinking gases fall to the earth do they create a zone of high pressure or low pressure there?

14: *Atmospheric Currents*

If it were not for other influences acting on the air, Hadley cells might extend from the equator all the way to the poles, but the situation is not that simple. In explaining patterns of atmospheric circulation, we have to throw in another factor with which we are already familiar. What happens to any mass when it gets started moving in one direction? It tries to keep going in the same direction, right? This is called inertia, and it was one of our first concepts of physics. The gases in the atmosphere have mass, so they too are subject to inertia. When they get started traveling toward the equator along the surface of the Earth, they want to keep traveling in the same direction. This presents a problem—under the influence of gravity the atmosphere rotates with the Earth. Now we have two influences affecting the flow of those gases—inertia in the north to south direction because of the circulation between the equator and the poles, and the rotation from west to east.

Earlier in our study of physics we said that masses having two forces acting in different directions tend to follow a curved path. As with a cup of water swinging in a circle at the end of a string, the cup's inertia tends to make it travel in a straight line from its position, but the perpendicular force of the string tends to hold it in; the resulting path is curved. The diagrams on these pages show how the separate influences balance each other to set up the circulation of gases in patterns around the Earth. Because of the curling motion taken on by the atmosphere, we get an area in the middle latitudes where the currents travel in the opposite direction. Cold air at the poles, on the other hand, is under high pressure, so it tends to spread out. The effect of the rotating Earth is to make these currents travel east to west, just like at the equator.

Of course, air in motion is called **wind**. These patterns of air circulation are responsible for what we call the **prevailing winds**. If something prevails, it wins out over others by its strength. There are certainly other winds that rise and fall all over the Earth, but these prevailing winds are consistently strong. Long before we had this global view of the Earth's

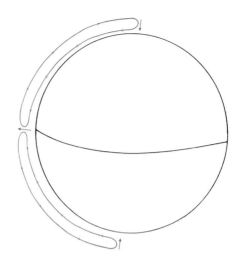

If the Earth were still, Hadley cells might extend from the equator all the way to the poles.

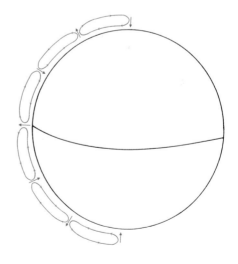

Because the earth rotates, the cells get broken up into three main sections. The middle section rotates in the direction opposite the other two.

rotation, inertia and atmospheric science, people knew the effects of the prevailing winds (or "**trade winds**" as they are sometimes called) on ships. Sailors took advantage of the prevailing winds in charting their trade routes across the oceans.

Before they understood inertia and the Earth's rotation, people also knew about the curved pathways taken by fluids. It was once thought that a force existed which drew masses in a circular path when they traveled from north to south. The **Coriolis effect**, as it is properly called in physics, is not a force, but rather, it is the effect of inertia on objects (fluids in this case) as they move across a spinning Earth. As you can image, the Coriolis effect is just as important in deciding the paths taken by solid objects such as aircraft, missiles, rockets and satellites as it is in deciding the flow patterns of fluids. It is also important in determining the flow patterns of water in the oceans.

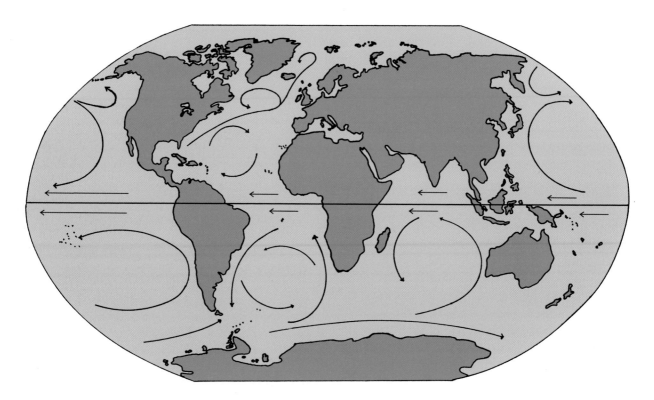

Prevailing winds are strong ever-present winds created by the inertia of water and the turning of the Earth. These winds correspond to prevailing ocean currents that navigators can count on to either help them or conflict with them on their journeys.

Exercise:

If you were standing at the north pole and fired a torpedo over the surface of the Earth toward the equator, would the torpedo continue southward along the surface or would its pathway curve to the east or west? Why?

15: *What the Currents Do to Climate*

As we said, the rising air at the equator is experienced at the surface of the Earth as **low pressure** because the air mass is traveling up from the Earth. Because the direction of air travel is vertical, no wind is experienced. This particular area of low pressure at the equator is called the **doldrums**. The word comes from an Old English word meaning "dull" or "stupid." When we say someone is "in the doldrums," we usually mean they are feeling depressed. Sailors traveling for days on end through this area used to get cranky as they drifted without any wind in the hot air of the equator.

When the air rises and cools it passes over the tropics, and the water falls out of the air. This is the rain that, along with the warming tropical sunshine, falls on the **tropical rain forests** with their lush green plant life and all of the animal life that these dense plants can support. As the dry air descends it falls back to the Earth. By the time it gets there it is quite hot again. Land where this hot, dry air continuously pours over its surface tends to be **desert**-like. The dry air then sweeps back toward the equator keeping the tropical lands warm and picking up tons of water from the ocean to support the next tropical rains.

Because tropical rain forests have such complete cover of vegetation, they provide a fantastic base for growth of plant-eating organisms. Of course, this provides a great food source for predators and organisms that eat dead matter. You could say that the tropical rain forest is the world's richest biological resource.

The tropical rain forests of South America support the greatest concentration and diversity of life on the planet. People who live in these areas of the world have recently discovered the value of their land for growing crops. In order to use the croplands they are cutting down and burning the vegetation that grows in the rain forests. This removal of rain forest has come to be known as **deforestation**. Many scientists and other citizens are concerned that we are losing much of our animal diversity that is provided by the forests because the **habitats** (homes) of these animals are being wiped out. Of course, once the animals that live in these rain forests are rendered extinct, they can never be revived. This will be a tremendous loss to the wondering eyes that have marveled at the creativity of God through the natural diversity present in these amazing places. On the other hand, these lands are the source of livelihood for a large community of people, and the land is in their possession. Convincing them to surrender their livelihood to preserve the natural diversity of the world seems unfair and unlikely. A solution to this problem does not appear to be around the corner.

Because of the lack of vegetation and organic material, this is what most people think of when they hear the word desert—sand! This photograph is from White Sands National Park in Utah.

The dry deserts of the southwestern United States are examples of the effects of descending dry air—the result of the air's loss of water to the tropical rain forests. Here, conditions of high pressure prevail most of the year.

Exercises:

1. Which will hold more water—warm air or cold air? Why? (Look back at Applications Lesson 4 if you need to.)

2. If you get warm air as moist as possible, then cool it down, what will happen?

3. Decide whether each statement is true or false.

    a. The United States has a temperate climate in most regions.

    b. Canada is somewhat temperate, but may also be tropical.

    c. Mexico has a polar climate.

    d. Our weather patterns are produced by conflict between cool tropical air from the north and warm polar air from the south.

16: *The Ever-Changing Weather*

Air pressure is measured using an instrument called a **barometer**. If you took a barometer all over the surface of the Earth, you would find that there are patterns that we identified at the equator,

This is a weather map showing a cold front and a warm front. These are zones where cold and warm masses of air sweep the surface of the globe in the war between cold polar air from the north and warm tropical air from the south. This war makes mid North America a primary battle zone, supplying us with the wonderful diversity of weather that we experience. Also shown are high-pressure and low-pressure zones. These are zones of circulating air that is either descending on our heads (high pressure) or rising upward to the sky (low pressure). Their circular motion comes from the Coriolis effect—the inertia of air affected by the spin of the earth.

the poles and at the 30° latitudes, but the **barometric pressures** (atmospheric pressures measured with a barometer) across the surface of the Earth change from place to place and time to time. Each high- and low-pressure area is associated with rotating air currents called **cyclones** (at low-pressure

A hurricane—a cyclone at sea—generates violent winds in excess of 200 miles per hour. These winds may be destructive if they come ashore. Conditions are often right for the formation of hurricanes in warm tropical waters. The small circular area in the center of the hurricane, called the "eye," is deceitfully calm.

centers) and **anticyclones** (at high-pressure centers). Air is continuously exiting an area of high pressure. Because of the Coriolis effect, the rotation of air is clockwise in the northern hemisphere and counterclockwise in the southern hemisphere. When low-pressure zones occur, air enters from all directions, so the rotation is opposite. As we said earlier, air in a high-pressure system is generally dry, sinking toward the Earth, and warming. These conditions are not consistent with rain. Air that is rising in a low-pressure zone is cooling and laden with moisture. Low-pressure zones are associated with strong thunderstorm activities. Places where these **weather systems** come together are characterized by intense changes in weather.

The middle latitudes or **temperate** zones include most of North America in the northern hemisphere, and Australia and the southern parts of South America in the southern hemisphere. Temperate zones are on the battleground between the cold polar air and the warm air from the tropics. Air from either of these zones can control the temperate zones at a given time, and the clash between the two can quickly spawn a storm. This makes the weather difficult to predict. Small high-pressure zones and low-pressure zones can spin off from the major atmospheric patterns and cross our land masses. Air masses come in from the poles, from over the oceans, or up from the tropics, each having its own impact on our weather. When these zones go to war above land they can bring great variety in the weather patterns.

Nowhere in the world is the weather any more variable than right here in North America. Because the general air direction is from west to east, and land has an impact on weather as well, the weather on the east coast is more variable than that on the west coast. The national weather service uses complex computer models to try to predict what will happen across the country. Although these models are detailed, they occasionally fail to predict accurately what will happen in a given location.

Another feature of our atmosphere that you hear about on the weather report from time to time is the **jet stream**. There are actually four permanent jet streams surrounding the Earth, two in each hemisphere. The **polar jet streams** are composed of warm air that rides along the top of the battle zone between the warm tropical air and the cold polar air at the top of the troposphere. They swing wildly around the surface of the globe in the temperate regions. In the northern hemisphere the polar jet stream (the one we hear about in the United States) is found at altitudes between 12,000 and 14,000 kilometers (or approximately 8 miles) above the Earth. It is a westerly wind (traveling from west to east) that may exceed 400 kilometers per hour (250 miles per hour). It is several miles thick and hundreds of miles wide. Like all jet streams it can be thought of as a flat tube of air with faster-moving air in the center, surrounded by slower-moving air. Typical air speeds in the center are in the 50 to 100 mile per hour range. These wind speeds are close to those measured near tornadoes.

Exercises:
Why should the meeting of warm, water-laden air from the south and cool, polar air from the north cause any disturbance? In your answer mention something about a transfer of energy.

17: *Clouding the Issue*

The last features of weather for your consideration are **clouds**. These structures are made up of water or ice particles that are a few micrometers (thousandths of a millimeter) to under 100 micrometers in diameter, so they are microscopic in size, and small enough to remain in suspension in the air for a long time. Clouds have a cooling effect on the Earth during the daytime because they reflect more of the sun's radiation back up into space. At night, cloud cover acts as a blanket, holding in the heat that the Earth gathered in the daytime. So, under heavy cloud cover, there may not be much difference between the daytime high and the nighttime low temperatures. Clouds also hold the water that condenses into rain or crystallizes into snow.

Clouds are divided into four main groups: low, middle, high and vertical. Low clouds, composed mainly of water droplets, include the **stratus** clouds which are flat, white blankets hanging close to the ground. **Stratocumulus** clouds are large, billowy, gray-looking sheets that may cover the entire visible range of the sky. Blue sky may appear through breaks in the sheets. **Nimbostratus** clouds are dark, thick and shapeless clouds that bring snow or rain.

The middle altitudes are the domain of the **altostratus** and **altocumulus** clouds. Altostratus clouds are the large, thick, sheet-like clouds that may take on a bluish or gray appearance as they partially block the sun. Altocumulus clouds look like balls or puffs of fleece or cotton and are also dense enough to partially block sunlight, giving them a somewhat gray appearance.

High clouds are usually **cirrus** clouds, located five miles or more above the Earth where passenger jets fly. These are wispy, feathery-looking clouds made of tiny ice crystals. When cirrus clouds take on a layered appearance looking like large sheets, they are called **cirrostratus**. They may also gather in clusters called **cirrocumulus** clouds.

The vertical clouds form when a hot spot on the Earth generates enough heat in a column of air to break through into the colder air above. When this **thermal air column** rises high enough, the moisture from the thermal column cools and condenses into clouds. The conditions are often best for this process in the middle to late afternoon. Sometimes the condensed water forms ice crystals. The size of the cloud depends on the heat intensity and amount of moisture contained in the thermal column that formed it. Clouds of this group may extend from less than a mile to eight miles above the Earth. They are usually flat on bottom and billowy on top. The large, heavy **cumulonimbus** clouds, often called **thunderheads**, are among these vertical-forming clouds.

Stratocumulus

Cirrostratus

Wall cloud

Altocumulus

Cirrus

Cumulonimbus

Within these clouds air may circulate, carrying water up to heights where it can freeze. The ice then falls back down where water can condense on its cold surface. If the wind within the cloud is strong enough to carry the ice back up several times, it may get large enough to fall to the ground as **hail**, which is ice balls made from several layers of ice. It takes strong updraft winds to form large hailstones, so they tend to be small; but they can reach several centimeters, or even more than a decimeter in diameter in some cases! As you can imagine, large chunks of ice falling out of the sky may be quite damaging to crops, houses and cars, and dangerous to people and animals.

Jet airplanes flying high in the atmosphere may leave a type of artificial cloud called a **contrail**. As we discussed in our chemistry section, combustion of fuel produces water. This water is ejected from the engine and freezes into ice crystals in a path where the plane has flown. Because these clouds are high and made of ice crystals, they have the same wispy appearance of cirrus clouds.

Tornado

Funnel cloud

When warm, moist air, such as from the Gulf of Mexico, meets cool dry air, such as from Canada, conditions are right for the formation of a **tornado**. The barometric pressure is low, so the air has a natural rotation as the two air masses accelerate toward the center of the weather system. While all of the details of how tornadoes are formed are not fully understood, we know some signs that a tornado is likely. A wall cloud—a tall formidable-looking thunderhead—will display a characteristic rotation along the cloud bottom, which is low to the ground. A funnel will form, looking like a small point on the underside of the cloud. As the rotation gathers speed and strength it may remain above the ground or descend to touch the ground, picking up soil and debris, and darkening as it ages. The sound is the low hum of a freight train rumbling along a railroad track. Tornadoes are known for producing winds upwards of 100 miles per hour, destroying buildings, uprooting massive trees, overturning cars and claiming lives. The best shelter is beneath the surface of the Earth under heavy cover away from windows, such as the center of a basement.

Exercises:
True or false? The naming of clouds is always clear-cut because they fall into nice neat groups and appear only where they are supposed to. (Do you detect a hint of sarcasm?)

18: *Leaving Earth—Our Solar System*

Ever since there have been people, I suppose they have been staring out into space at night in amazement at the endless number of heavenly lights. We can see these lights rising and falling in the sky from east to west. People who cared about these sorts of things once thought that Earth was at the center of all of these lights and that they all moved about us. This school of thought was called **geocentric**, or "Earth-centered," thinking. But from the mid 1500's those thoughts were changed to **heliocentric**, or "sun-centered," thinking, led by a Polish astronomer named Copernicus. He showed through his studies that the sun is at the center of our solar system, and that the Earth and the other planets revolve around it.

The religious people in the day of Copernicus had made a huge mistake. Many of them believed that if God made the Earth for His special purposes, and if the rest of the universe was here for the pleasure of man, then God must have put the Earth right smack in the middle of it. As you can imagine, Copernicus (as well as others who studied the "heavens") upset a lot of people with his observations. From this, we learn an important lesson. We mustn't let our personal beliefs and opinions take the place of the truth. Even today, atheists point to this example of the error of religious people who deny "the truth" in favor of religion. No person was ever made to feel ashamed for accepting God's words, but people are often proven wrong and made to feel ashamed for using the words of God to support their own opinions.

Now it is known (as well as man can know) that the sun has a system of at least nine planets that **revolve** around it. They are, in order of their distances from the sun, Mercury, Venus, Earth, Mars, Jupiter, Saturn, Uranus, Neptune and Pluto. The first four are called the **terrestrial planets** because they are made up of mostly solid materials. They are relatively small and close to the sun. Except for Pluto, the other planets are thought to be made up of mostly hydrogen, helium, methane and ammonia. Pluto is so small and distant, we don't know a lot about it, but it is thought to be more solid than its larger neighbors. While all other planets revolve around the sun on the same plane, Pluto has a path around the sun that is tilted with respect to the others. It also has a moon that is half its own size. You could think of Pluto as two planets revolving around each other as they both revolve around the sun.

The moon is the only celestial body besides the sun close enough to see as a planet with the naked eye rather than a point of light. We can also visibly see the impact this closest neighbor has on Earth by the rising and falling tides of the oceans that are in large part caused by the gravitational attraction of the moon for the earth.

Earth

The Earth's moon

The terrestrial planets are close in size to the Earth yet nothing is believed to live on them. Is it chance that among these terrestrial planets so similar in vicinity to the sun that only one has the incredible necessities to sustain life? Although Mars is referred to as the "red planet," Venus appears reddish in the photo below due to the photography techniques used.

Mercury

Venus

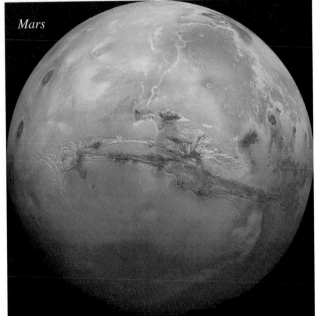

Mars

Jupiter

Between the terrestrial planets and the outer planets there is a ring of rock-like objects that also orbit the sun. These are called **asteroids**, and the group that they form is called the **asteroid belt**. **Meteoroids** are rocks that have different orbits from the asteroid belt and are believed to have resulted from asteroid collisions. **Meteors** are rock fragments that enter the atmosphere of a planet, especially Earth. We see them at night burning up as they enter the outer atmosphere because of friction between the atmospheric gases and the solid meteor. We call them "shooting stars" because to us they look like stars shooting across the sky. Occasionally one of these objects is massive enough to survive the intense heat of the friction and hits the Earth. Such objects are called **meteorites**. The Earth shows signs of having been hit by some pretty big meteorites. Some scientists even suggest that global changes in temperature following a large meteorite were responsible for the extinction of the dinosaurs.

Uranus

It's fun to listen to scientists speculate; and it's harmless as long as we realize that it is just that—*speculation*. Scientists are just people. Occasionally people get passionate about their speculations and try to convince others that these speculations are true. Just because someone is passionate about something doesn't make it true. Be sure you test everything on the basis of its evidence and not on the basis of the beliefs or passions of others.

Comets are other objects that revolve around the sun. These are collections of dust, ice, liquids and gases. They are made up of a disk-shaped **coma** and a long **tail** of ionized gases. A comet

Saturn

Neptune

The outer planets are also called the Jovian planets, *named after the Roman emperor Flavius Claudius Jovianus. The temperatures on these planets' surfaces are believed to be below -100°F.*

Table: Characteristics of Planets

Planet	Diameter (km)	Relative Mass (Earth = 1)	Distance from Sun (km)	Length of Day (Earth time)	Length of Year (Earth time)	Number of Satellites
Mercury	4880	0.055	57,900,000	59 d	88 d	0
Venus	12,100	0.815	108,200,000	243 d	117 d	0
Earth	12,756	1	149,600,000	23 hr, 56 min	365 d	1
Mars	6,794	0.107	227,900,000	24 hr, 37 min	687 d	2
Jupiter	142,984	318	778,300,000	9 hr, 55 min	11.86 yr	16
Saturn	120,536	95.2	1,429,000,000	12 hr, 39 min	29.46 yr	18
Uranus	51,100	14.5	2,875,000,000	17 hr, 18 min	84 yr	15
Neptune	49,500	17.2	4,504,000,000	16 hr, 06 min	165 yr	8
Pluto	2,300	0.002	5,900,000,000	6 d, 9 hr, 18 min	248 yr	1

Planet	Composition	Features
Mercury	Silicates, nickel, iron	Swiftest planet; daytime 400°C, nighttime 180°C
Venus	Silicates, nickel, iron	Days longer than Earth years
Earth	Silicates, nickel, iron	Life
Mars	Silicates, iron sulfide	Red surface
Jupiter	Liquid hydrogen, molten rock	Largest planet
Saturn	Liquid hydrogen, water, ammonia, molten rock	Rings
Uranus	Liquid hydrogen, helium, ammonia, water, molten rock	Tilt is 82.1° from vertical (Earth's tilt is 23.5°)
Neptune	Liquid hydrogen, helium, ammonia, water, molten rock	Orbit's path crosses with Pluto's
Pluto	Unknown	Smallest planet; moon of comparable size

shines brightly as it approaches the sun, and the **solar wind** blows the tail away as the comet circles nearby. The comets travel long, narrow, elliptical orbits (that is, orbits that look like circles stretched out of shape). These orbits extend far beyond the planets into the galaxy. A few visit the Earth often, but most of them are on paths that will bring them back only over periods of thousands of years.

We have a **moon** that revolves around our Earth, but we are not the only planet to have one. In fact, the planet Jupiter has at least 16 moons, each of them being its own fascinating place. Two of those moons are big enough to be considered planets if they revolved around the sun instead of Jupiter. Another word for moon is **satellite**. A satellite is any object that circles (**orbits**) a planet. Humans have put artificial satellites around the Earth and other planets to help us "view" these bodies from high above their surfaces.

The **sun** is an enormous ball of hydrogen that is burning under force of a nuclear reaction where hydrogen is being fused together to form helium while giving off a tremendous amount of energy. Approximately one million Earths would fit inside the sun. The sun shines its rays on us from 93 million miles away. At the speed of light, it requires approximately eight minutes for light leaving the sun to get here.

This photo taken on the Galileo mission shows asteroid 243 Ida and its small satellite Dactyl (right). Ida is 58 KM along its long axis.

This image of Pluto and its satellite Charon were taken by the NASA Hubble Space Telescope with the Faint Object Camera.

Exercises:
1. What force keeps planets from flying out into space? (Review Red Lesson 5 if necessary.)
2. What influence keeps planets from falling into the sun under gravitation?

19: *Sun and Earth*

Any orbiting object, whether it orbits the sun or a planet, also **rotates** around an **axis**. The axis is an imaginary line that extends through the planet at its imaginary north and south **poles**. Since this rotation decides the position of the planet's surface in relationship to the sun, it also determines the length of day and night on the planet. There is also a third type of motion in each planet. If you have ever watched a top as it spins, you will notice that the top tip (or the tip top, that is, the tip of the top) also makes a circle. This motion is called **precession**. It is the tilt of the Earth due to this precession that brings about the seasons.

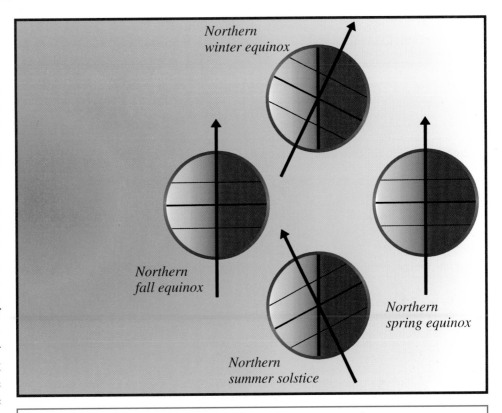

As any spinning object spins, its axis wobbles. This wobbling of the Earth's axis gives it a tilt in relationship with the sun. This tilt is responsible for the seasons. As the Earth completes its yearly revolution around the sun, consider how the position of the north pole can be either nearer or farther away from the sun. When the north pole is nearest the sun, it's summertime in the northern hemisphere. When the north pole is farthest from the sun, it's winter. The season in the southern hemisphere is opposite that in the northern.

The Earth's axis is tilted approximately 23.5° from vertical. As the Earth orbits the sun, this tilt makes one pole or the other closer to the sun. If you live in the northern half of the planet (called the **northern hemisphere**) as we do in the United States, summer comes when the Earth is angled so that the northern half of the planet is closer to the sun. When the **southern hemisphere** is closer to the sun, it's winter in the northern. Here, the longest day of the year occurs when the northern tip of the Earth is as close to the sun as it ever gets. That is the day of the summer solstice which marks the first day of summer and is around June 21ˢᵗ every year. There is a winter solstice that falls around December 21ˢᵗ when the tip is at its greatest distance from the sun, marking the first day of winter.

There are two times in a year when the two poles of the planet are the same distance from the sun. These two times are the spring and fall **equinoxes** that take place around March 22ⁿᵈ and September 22ⁿᵈ. These dates mark the beginnings of **spring** and **fall**. At these times you could say that the sun is directly "above" the equator. The sun's rays hit the equator most directly at these times.

If you don't like the time of year the seasons come about, just hang around. Because of precession, the Earth's axis wobbles. In several thousand years, winter will have moved to summertime and summer to wintertime. The period of one complete "wobble" is estimated (pretty accurately we think) at about 26,000 years! I hope you have something else to do while you're waiting.

See how this gyroscope wobbles on its axis? This is the secondary motion called precession.

Exercises:

1. When it's winter in the northern hemisphere, what is it in the southern hemisphere?
2. When it's daytime in the northern hemisphere, what is it in the southern hemisphere?
3. Sorry about that last one. I couldn't resist.

20: *Far Away from Home*

In order to look any farther out of our universe, we have to begin to think of really large numbers. You know how much a hundred is because you have seen 100 (1×10^2) apples on the grocer's shelves. You have even seen 1000 (1×10^3) grapes on those shelves. Maybe you have seen 50,000 (5×10^4) people get together in a large stadium to watch the World Series. You may have seen 100,000 (1×10^5) letters, spaces and other characters that make up a book, or even a few million (a few $\times 10^6$) if the book is as big as the Bible. But how many is a billion (1×10^9) or a trillion (1×10^{12}) or a quadrillion (1×10^{15})? These numbers are easy to write, but they become harder and harder to imagine. But these are the numbers that we have to get used to discussing when we talk about the universe.

We have worked our way only to the sun and to Pluto, the most distant planet. But what lies outside our solar system? We can see the light given off by stars. Many stars are out there, but how many? We live in a huge galaxy called the Milky Way; and beyond the Milky Way lie perhaps 10^{11} other galaxies. Each of those galaxies is made up of perhaps 10^{11} stars. So the total number of stars may be something like $10^{11} \times 10^{11} = 10^{22}$ stars. If we wrote this number out it would be 10,000,000,000,000,000,000,000; ten thousand million million million.

But it gets worse. The universe is mostly empty space. Measuring this space in miles would be like measuring the Earth in Angstroms (the units used to measure atoms). We need a larger measuring device. The common measuring device for such large distances is the light year. This is the distance light travels in one year. Because light travels at a speed of 3×10^8 meters per second (that's roughly 186,000 miles per second or eight times around the Earth per second), in one year it travels 9.5×10^{15} meters.

It's a crazy thing, this measuring of the universe. What happens when we get to the end? What do we find? Only God knows. Perhaps we find nothing, but then, what *is* nothing? We are not sure how big the universe is, but it is estimated at some tens of billions of light years across. Our average-sized galaxy, the Milky Way, has been estimated at *only* 100,000 light years in diameter.

This is the Orion nebula—a cloud of gases and stars too distant to be distinguished without a telescope. Beyond our view lie many wonders of the universe yet to be explored.

Exercise:

Give thanks to God for the marvels in the universe. As we see our smallness before Him, thank Him for caring enough about us to give us guidance through the unknowns that remain before us. Ask Him for wisdom to learn—first from Him, then from our own ponderings of things too great for us. Give Him thanks in the name of One who became small that we may be glorified with Him. To His name be honor and glory and majesty forever.

Bibliography

Anthony, C.P. and G.A. Thibodeau, 1979. *Textbook of Anatomy and Physiology*, 10th Ed., C.V. Mosby Co., St. Louis.

Bevelander, G. and J.A. Ramaley, 1979. *Essentials of Histology*, 8th Ed., C.V. Mosby Co., St. Louis.

Curtis, H., 1975. *Biology*, 2nd Ed., Worth Publishers, Inc., NY.

Edwards, G.M., Ed., 1998. *The Encyclopedia Americana International Edition*, Grolier Incorporated, Danbury, CT.

Gallant, R.A., 1994. *National Geographic Picture Atlas of Our Universe*, Revised Edition, National Geographic Society, Washington, DC.

Goetz, P.W., Ed., 1986. *The New Encyclopedia Brittanica*. Encyclopedia Brittanica, Inc., Chicago.

Hickman, C.P., 1973. *Biology of the Invertebrates*, 2nd Ed., C.V. Mosby Co., St. Louis.

Landau, S.I. *et al.*, Eds., 1975. *The Reader's Digest Great Encyclopedic Dictionary*, The Reader's Digest Association, Inc., Pleasantville, NY.

Lehrman, R.L., and C. Swartz. 1965. *Foundations of Physics*, Holt, Rinehart and Winston, Inc., NY.

Lorimer, L.T., Ed., 1996. *Academic American Encyclopedia*, Grolier Incorporated, Danbury, CT.

Masterton, W.L., and E.J. Slowinski, 1977. *Chemical Principles*, 4th Ed., W.B. Saunders Co., Philadelphia.

Microsoft Corp., 1996. *Microsoft Encarta 96 Encyclopedia for MacIntosh and Windows*, Microsoft Corp., Redmond, WA.

McKechnie, J.L. *et al.*, Eds., 1983. *Webster's New Twentieth Century Dictionary Unabridged*, 2nd Ed., Simon and Schuster, NY.

Morris, C.G., Ed., 1992. *Academic Press Dictionary of Science and Technology*. Academic Press, San Diego.

Morrison, R.T., and R.N. Boyd, 1973. *Organic Chemistry*. 3rd Ed., Allyn and Bacon, Inc., Boston.

Orr, R.T., 1976. *Vertebrate Biology*, 4th Ed., W.B. Saunders Co., Philadelphia.

Reynolds, C.S., 1984. *The Ecology of Freshwater Phytoplankton*, Cambridge University Press, Cambridge.

Streyer, L. 1981. *Biochemistry*, 2nd Ed., W.H. Freeman and Co., San Francisco.

Thaxton, C.B. *et al.*, 1984. *The Mystery of Life's Origin: Reassessing Current Theories*, Philosophical Library, Inc., NY.

Villee, C.A., *et al.*, 1973. *General Zoology*. 4th Ed., W.B. Saunders Co., Philadelphia.

Weast, R.C., *et al.* Eds., 1986. *CRC Handbook of Chemistry and Physics*. 67th Ed., CRC Press, Inc., Boca Raton, FL.

Wetzel, R.G., 1983. *Limnology*, 2nd Ed., Saunders College Publishing, Philadelphia.

Wilson, J.D., 1977. *Physics: Concepts and Applications*. D.C. Heath and Co., Lexington, MA.

Windholz, M. *et al.*, Eds., 1983. *The Merck Index*, 10th Ed., Merck & Co., Inc., Rahway, NJ.

Applications Lessons 11, 16 and 17 images © 1982-1993 Weatherstock Photo Agency, Tucson
Red Lesson 16 images courtesy of Northern States Power, Minneapolis
Chemistry Lesson 11 and Applications Lesson 9 images courtesy of BioTrol® Eden Prairie, MN
Applications Lessons 2 and 18 images courtesy of NASA
Red Lessons 11, 18, 20, and 23 images courtesy of the U.S. Department of Energy, Nevada Test Site

Images © Corel Corporation:
Physics Lessons: 2, 3, 6, 8, 10, 11, 12, 13, 14, 21, 22, 25, 26, 27 and 29
Chemistry Lessons: 1, 2, 3, 7, 17, 20, 22, 23, 24 and 27
Biology Lessons: Introduction, 1, 9, 10, 14-30 and 39
Applications Lessons: 2, 3, 4, 15, 17 and 20

All original photographs © Bio Enterprises, Inc. dba Beginnings Publishing House by Dr. Durell Dobbins
Original illustrations produced by Robert Kingsley Elder or co-produced by Mr. Elder with the author.
Physics Lessons: 5, 6, 12, 18, 24, 25, 27
Biology Lessons: 12, 13, 15, 16, 17-30
All other original illustrations produced by the author with technical assistance from Mr. Elder.
Page layout by Robert Kingsley Elder.
Text editing by Dr. Mark E. Bingham.
Cover layout by Kim Weeks & Robert Kingsley Elder, Sexton Printing, W. St. Paul, MN
Printing by Sexton Printing, Inc., W. St. Paul, MN

Glossary of Terms

abdomen - lower body containing the stomach, intestinal tract and reproductive organs

abiogenesis - doctrine, belief or principle of life forming from non-living matter

absorb - "soak up"; with reference to light, the acceptance of light energy by matter resulting in its transformation to other forms of energy, especially heat and kinetic energy in the particles of the matter

acceleration - increase in velocity over time

acid - molecule that releases a hydronium (H^+) ion when dissolved in water

acid, amino - one of a group of compounds that are bonded together in a series to form proteins; called "the building blocks of proteins"

acid, deoxyribose nucleic - large molecules made of nucleic acid "bases" held together by a chain of deoxyribose sugar phosphates. These molecules form complex codes storing information which is used by the cell to direct its activities

acid, fatty - long-chain hydrocarbons that are linked together to form lipids (fats)

acid, nucleic - large molecules made of nucleic acid bases held together by a chain of sugar phosphates; see **acid, deoxyribose nucleic** and **acid, ribose nucleic**

acid, ribose nucleic - large molecules made of nucleic acid "bases" held together by a chain of ribose sugar phosphates. These molecules form complex codes storing information which is used by the cell to decode the information stored in DNA

acquired immune deficiency syndrome (AIDS) - a deadly viral infection characterized by loss of the body's immune system resulting in death from infection by pathogens

actinoid series - see **series, actinoid**

adaptation - genetically directed change in an organism making it more fit for its environment

adaptive evolution - beneficial changes to an organism making it more fit for the survival of its kind

adrenal gland - organ that rests on the kidneys and produce adrenaline—a substance that boosts the body's ability to respond quickly to threat

aerobic - relating to a process that takes place or an organism that lives in the presence of oxygen

agronomy - soil science, especially as it relates to agricultural uses

AIDS -see **acquired immune deficiency syndrome**

alga, green (pl. green algae) - simple aquatic plants often growing in colonies or in long, single-cell-width strands

aliphatic hydrocarbon - see **hydrocarbon, aliphatic**

alkali metal - see **metal, alkali**

alkaline earth metal - see **metal, alkaline earth**

alkane - hydrocarbon having only single bonds in its structure

alkane, linear - alkane, the structure of which consists of a straight chain of carbon atoms

alkene - hydrocarbon having one or more double bonds between carbon atoms in its structure

alkynes - hydrocarbon having one or more triple bonds between carbon atoms in its structure

altocumulus - see **cloud, altocumulus**

altostratus - see **cloud, altostratus**

alveolus (pl. alveoli) - tiny sac-like structure in lung tissue within which gases (oxygen and carbon dioxide) are exchanged between the atmosphere and the organism's blood

amensalism - relationship among organisms from which one or more organisms benefit but others are harmed

amino acid - see **acid, amino**

amphibian - any of a class of vertebrate organisms having moist skin and living part its life in water and part of its life on land in moist environments

amphipod - any of an order of crustacean arthropods typically a few millimeters in length and flattened from side to side; includes sand fleas

AMU - see **atomic mass units**

anatomy - science of the body plans and structures of organisms

ancestor - organism, either living or dead, that has made a genetic contribution to a subject organism at some point in its family history

angiosperm - "higher plant" that reproduces sexually through the use of a flower

animal - eukaryotic organism, either unicellular or multicellular at any of several levels of organization whose cells lack cell walls

anion - chemical that is negatively charged because of an overabundance of electrons

Annelida - a phylum of segmented invertebrates including earthworms and leeches

antenna (pl. antennae) - long, slender sensory organ on the head of many arthropods generally providing a tactile sense (sense of "touch")

anther - bulb

antibiotic - substance (either natural or synthetic) that kills bacteria

antibiotic-resistant bacteria - see **bacteria, antibiotic-resistant**

anticyclone - high-pressure area characterized by outward-flowing air currents spiraling clockwise in the northern hemisphere and counterclockwise in the southern hemisphere due to the **Coriolis effect**

antiviral - describing a substance having an inactivating effect on one or more groups of viruses

anus - external, terminal opening of the digestive tract from which solid waste (feces) exits the body

appendage, lower - in humans, any portion of the pelvic girdle, legs or feet

appendage, upper - in humans, any portion of the shoulder girdle, arms or hands

aquatic - having to do with water (either fresh water or saline), especially as it relates to the habitat of organisms

arachnid - any of a class of chelicerate arthropods having four pairs of legs and two body segments; includes spiders, mites, ticks, daddy-longlegs and scorpions

archaeon (pl. archaea) - prokaryotic microorganism, often occupying extreme environments, similar to a bacterium in size but genetically and biochemically distinct

arteriole - blood vessel not among the major blood vessels being of lesser size and carrying a lesser volume of blood

artery - major blood vessel carrying oxygen and nutrients from the heart and lungs throughout the body

Arthropoda - most numerous and widespread of all animal phyla including many marine animals and the insects characterized by their many jointed legs

asexual - referring to reproduction without sexual involvement

asexual spore - see **spore, asexual**

ash - non-combustible materials that remain after combustion

asphalt - non-boiling tar remaining after the boiling fractions of petroleum have been distilled away

assumption of uniformity - an assumption made to simplify theory that processes continue at the same rate and in the same way unless there is some reason to suspect a change has occurred

asteroid - large fragment of rock among the planets held in orbit around the sun

asteroid belt - high concentration of asteroids having approximately the same orbit

atmosphere - gases held to a large mass by the force of gravitation

atom - smallest stable form of matter consisting of some number of protons and neutrons in a central solid nucleus and a series of electrons held in orbit about the nucleus

atomic bomb - explosive device that makes use of nuclear energy

atomic mass - see **atomic mass unit**

atomic mass unit (AMU) - unit of measure of atomic mass measured in relationship to pure carbon having six protons and six neutrons (and six electrons having little mass)

atomic symbol - one- or two-letter designation given to the atom of a particular element and widely recognized as its symbol

axis - the imaginary line that passes through both poles of a planet around which the planet revolves to provide its day/night cycle with reference to sunlight

bacteria, antibiotic-resistant - bacteria that possess a resistance to the effects of one or more antibiotics

bacteriophage - virus infecting bacteria

bacterium (pl. bacteria) - prokaryotic organism on the order of 1 micrometer in diameter having a cell wall and reproducing by asexual means

ball and socket joint - see **joint, ball and socket**

barometer - device for measuring atmospheric pressure

barometric pressure - see **pressure, barometric**

base - molecule that releases a hydroxide (OH⁻) ion when dissolved in water

base, nucleic acid- one of five compounds that are found repeatedly in the structure of RNA and/or DNA that are used in creating the genetic code of a cell

base pair - see **pair, base**

basin - geological structure in which water collects under the influence of gravity to form a lake or other body of water

biconcave - lens which is thicker at the outer edges and increasingly thinner toward its center due to the concavity of each of the two opposing surfaces

biconvex - lens which is thinner at the outer edges and increasingly thicker toward its center due to the bulging of each of the two opposing surfaces

big bang theory - see **theory, big bang**

bilateral symmetry - similarity of an organism in its right and left halves, each a mirror image of the other; body plan of many higher organisms

bile - liquid produced in the gall bladder and introduced into the stomach to aid in digestion, especially of fats

binomial system - system based on two names; term used to describe the scientific system of giving a pair of names—a genus and a species name—to each organism

biochemistry - chemistry of the molecules produced in and making up organisms

biology, molecular - study and applications of biomolecules, especially DNA and RNA

biomass - matter, living or dead, produced by or making up any part of an organism

biomolecule - molecule, produced by or making up part of an organism, typically having a high molecular weight and consisting of an ordered arrangement of smaller molecules; includes nucleic acids, proteins, polysaccharides and lipids

biosphere - portion of the earth populated by organisms, thus far known to include most of the upper 400 meters of the earth's crust and the atmosphere as high as the stratosphere

bird - any of the warm-blooded, egg-laying feathered vertebrate animals of the class Aves having forelimbs in the form of wings

birth rate - see **rate, birth**

bladder, urinary - sac-like organ that receives urine from the kidneys through the ureters and holds it until urination; urine passes from the urinary bladder through the urethra

blood - medium for carrying nutrients and oxygen to cells and for carrying waste materials from cells for elimination; whole blood consists of red and white blood cells, platelets, immune complexes, chemical waste compounds, inorganic ions and innumerable organic chemicals that serve as communication links among various body systems

blood plasma -see **plasma, blood**

body cavity - see **cavity, body**

boiling point - the point at which a liquid boils during its conversion from liquid to gas at a given pressure (usually 1 atmosphere)

bomb, atomic - bomb acting on atomic energy that is released by the splitting (fission) of atomic nucleus

bond, chemical - collective forces of attraction and repulsion that tend to hold the atoms of a molecule at a more-or-less constant distance from one another

bond, covalent - chemical bond resulting from the sharing of electrons among atoms

bond, ionic - chemical bond resulting from electrical attraction between opposite-charged ions

bone - organs of the skeletal system or the rigid living cellular tissue making up such an organ; bones are hard due to deposition of calcium salts around the bone cells

bony fish - fish having true bones in their skeleton as opposed to cartilaginous fish having only cartilage

brachiopod - any of a phylum of common but poorly known shellfish called "lamp shells," usually having a long pedicle (stalk) by which they attach to submerged objects

brain - portion of the central nervous system located in the head of an organism responsible in large part for processing of sensory and response signals to and from the rest of the body

branched aliphatic compound - see **compound, branched aliphatic**

breeding, selective - mating of organisms having a desired characteristic for the purpose of generating offspring that show greater strength of expression in that feature

bronchiole - subbranch of a bronchus serving as an air passage to a portion of a lung

bronchus (pl. bronchi) - one of a pair of main branches of the trachea serving as an air passage and connecting the trachea to a lung

calyx - cup-like support at the base of a flower composed of sepals

canine - "dog-like"; referring to the pointed teeth, third from the center in humans and greatly emphasized in dogs, that are most useful for holding and tearing food

capillary - the smallest of the blood vessels through which nutrients and oxygen diffuse from blood cells to other cells of the body and which link the vessels leading away from the heart to those leading toward it

carnivore - meat eater

carpel - in zoology and human biology, the bones of the fingers; in botany, the female reproductive organs in flowering plants

cartilage - connective tissue lacking the mineral calcium deposits of bone but providing flexible support as, for example, to the tip of the nose or the external ears of humans

catalytic converter - see **converter, catalytic**

catastrophic - of or relating to a major disaster

cation - positively charged ion resulting from the loss by an element of an electron

cavity, body - space within the body of an organism that separates the outer lining of its organs from the inner lining of its outer wall

cell - basic unit of a living organism consisting of membrane-bound cytoplasm containing a genome of DNA

cell membrane - see **membrane, cell**

cell wall - rigid covering surrounding the cell membranes of archaea, bacteria, fungi and plant cells having characteristics that differ with the type of cell

cellulose - polysaccharide of glucose units making up the wood and woody components of plants

centrifuge - device for separating suspended particles based on their densities by spinning containers of the suspension around a central axis at high velocity

cephalopod - any of a class of mollusks including squids, octopuses, cuttlefish and nautiluses having complex nervous and motor (muscular) response systems

chaetognath - any of a phylum of widespread, planktonic (suspended), small marine worms commonly called arrow worms

charge - basic characteristic of a particle that displays a force of electrical attraction to an opposite-charged particle

chelicerate - any of a subphylum of arthropods having claw-like appendages for grasping and crushing; includes horseshoe crabs and arachnids (scorpions, spiders, daddy-longlegs, ticks and others)

chemical - specific type of matter distinguished from other types based on the specific elements making it up and how they are bound one to another

chemical bond - see **bond, chemical**

chemical evolution - see **evolution, chemical**

chemical reaction - interactions of chemical compounds to form new combinations of elements drawn to these changes by the forces that exist between their atoms

chemistry, organic - study of the interactions of carbon atoms with other atoms of carbon and of other elements

chitin - protective substance made of nitrogen-containing polysaccharides (multiple sugars) found in the exoskeletons of arthropods and mollusks

chiton - an oval dome-shaped organism dwelling on the ocean floor and having eight protective, overlapping plates on its back

chlorophyll *a* - most abundant pigment in green plants that absorbs light to participate in photosynthesis

chordate - animal, including the vertebrate animals and humans, having a hollow nerve cord running the length of the trunk of its body

chromosome - individual molecule of DNA which in higher animals is part of the genome

cirrocumulus cloud - see **cloud, cirrocumulus**

cirrostratus cloud - see **cloud, cirrostratus**

cirrus cloud - see **cloud, cirrus**

class - taxonomic group of organisms which, along with other classes, make up a phylum and which may be subdivided into one or more orders

climate - patterns of weather that characterize an area of the globe due to the major influencing factors such as position on the planet relative to the sun and the spin of the earth

cloud - visible concentration of water vapor in the troposphere or stratosphere

cloud, altocumulus - mid-altitude clouds appearing as tufts arranged in parallel rolls or bands or as adjacent tufts with spaces between them

cloud, altostratus - mid-altitude clouds appearing as gray or blue-gray layers; sun may be vaguely visible through the cloud

cloud, cirrocumulus - high-altitude, rippled patch of cirrus more opaque that cirrostratus

cloud, cirrostratus - thin veneer of high-altitude white haze producing a halo when the sun shines through

cloud, cirrus - high-altitude cloud appearing as fibrous wisp

cloud, cumulonimbus - vertical-forming cloud that reaches from low in the atmosphere to great heights, often containing anvil-shaped portion that reaches into the higher altitudes; called "thunderhead" because it often produces severe weather

cloud, nimbostratus - low- to middle-altitude, formless, dark-gray cloud layer, often producing continuous rain or snow

cloud, stratocumulus - low-altitude, extensive, opaque, gray sheet of cloud with rounded masses protruding

cloud, stratus - low-altitude, gray, ragged, patchy, layered cloud

cloud, thunderhead - see **cloud, cumulonimbus**

club moss - see **moss, club**

code, genetic - code stored in the sequence of nucleic acid bases making up a DNA molecule that directs a cell's activities

coelenterate - any of a phylum of freshwater or marine animals having a mouth surrounded by tentacles and possessing stinging cells for capture and paralyzation of prey; includes hydra, jellyfish, sea anemones and corals; also called a cnidarian

cold (viral) - contagious viral sickness accompanied by any combination of itchy watery eyes, stuffy, runny nose, sneezing, itchy/sore throat, coughing and general feeling of tiredness, typically intense for 3-5 days with noticeable symptoms lasting up to 14 days

collagen - stretchy fibrous connective tissue found throughout the human body

colony - group of similar organisms living together, each living independently and having the same function within the colony

color - perception and interpretation by the brain of different energies (or wavelengths) of electromagnetic energy (light)

column, thermal air - vertical stream of warm air rising from the surface of the earth and breaking through into a layer of cooler, denser air lying above it

coma - main body of a comet composed of a variety of minerals and frozen fluids

comet - body composed of ice solid mineral matter and various gases having oblong orbits around the sun

commensalism - relationship among organisms from which one organism benefits but the other does not

competition - conflict of organism against organism for a limited resource

compound - molecule or group of identical molecules consisting of bound atoms of more than one element

compound, branched aliphatic - chemical compound involving a straight hydrocarbon chain without double or triple bonds with one or more side chains branching from the main chain

compound, cycloaliphatic - chemical compound involving a straight hydrocarbon chain having no double or triple bonds and having ends that are joined to form a loop

compound eye - see **eye, compound**

compress - squeeze together as gas under pressure

concave - any flattened object, especially a lens, that is thicker at the edges than in the center

condense - change from gas to liquid by cooling or by increase in pressure

conductor - substance that readily transfers heat (heat conductor) or electrons (electric conductor) from a source to a destination

conifers - trees bearing seeds in cones, including pines, firs, hemlocks, and cedars

connective tissue - tissue located throughout the bodies of animals that serves as a bonding material adding strength and flexibility to tissues; especially concentrated in ligaments and tendons that support joints between bones

conservation of energy, law of - see **energy, law of conservation of**

constant - not changing, the same under all circumstances; in mathematics, a value that does not vary as the gravitational acceleration constant in a vacuum is constant for all masses

consumer, primary - organism that consumes a (photosynthetic) primary producer

consumers, ultimate - concept that certain organisms consume organic matter to produce carbon dioxide which is then no longer organic and so no longer available for consumption by other consumers

continental drift - see **drift, continental**

continental rise - see **rise, continental**

continental shelf - shallow, gently-sloping shelf beneath the ocean surface at the outer margin of the continents

continental slope - see **slope, continental**

contract - pull together, as of molecules when they cool, having less vibrational energy; opposite of expand

contrail - trail of ice crystals from water vapor arising from combustion of jet fuel marking the path of a jet as it flies at high altitude

control (experimental) - experimental subject that is intended to remain unaffected by experimental manipulation

control group - group of experimental control subjects

convergent evolution - see **evolution, convergent**

converter, catalytic - device used in the exhaust passage of a combustion chamber to complete the combustion of reaction products, especially the conversion of carbon monoxide to carbon dioxide

convex - - any flattened object, especially a lens, that is thicker at the center than around the edges

cord, nerve - cord in higher animals that receives signals from various locations throughout the body and transfers them to the brain and *vice versa*

cord, spinal - the nerve cord of vertebrates that extends from the brain and serves as the primary route of passage for nerve signals from the brain to remote parts of the body

core - innermost layer of the earth believed to be made of solid iron mineral matter surrounded by molten iron mineral matter

Coriolis effect - effect of inertia on objects moving over the surface of the earth causing them to assume a curved path

coulomb - unit of electrical charge of 6.3×10^{18} electrons, equivalent to the amount of electricity transmitted in one second when the current is one ampere; named after the French physicist C.A. de Coulomb (1736-1806)

covalent bond - see **bond, covalent**

crust - surface layer of the Earth comprised largely of rock, water, minerals, organic matter and soil and varying from approximately 20 to 40 miles in depth

crustacean - any of a class of (mostly aquatic) arthropods having two pairs of antennae, one pair of mandibles, two pairs of maxillae and appendages on their thorax; includes lobsters, crabs, crayfish and shrimps

ctenophoran - any of a phylum of marine organisms commonly called comb jellies and having a set of ciliated "comb plates" for locomotion

cumulonimbus cloud - see **cloud, cumulonimubus**

current - main path of travel of a fluid

cuticle - outer layer, as of skin, the waxy coating of a leaf, or the outer margin of skin where it meets the fingernails and toenails

cyanobacteria - prokaryotic organisms having the appearance of bacteria but containing chlorophyll and obtaining energy from sunlight for photosynthesis; formerly known as "blue-green algae"

cycle, life - series of major changes undergone by organisms as they develop throughout their life as from sporophyte to gametophyte in ferns or from larva to nymph to naiad to adult in insects

cycle, menstrual - woman's 28-day cycle that begins with preparation of the uterine lining for receipt of a fertilized egg and ends with ridding of the unused lining at the time of menstruation

cycloaliphatic compound - see **compound, cycloaliphatic**

cyclone - low pressure characterized by inward-flowing air currents spiraling counterclockwise in the northern hemisphere and clockwise in the southern hemisphere due to the **Coriolis effect**

cytoplasm - the fluid contents of a cell that serve as a medium in which all of the cell's processes take place

dam - natural or man-made wall across a stream of water to collect ("impound") a pool of water on one side of the upstream side

Darwinian evolution - see **Darwinism**

Darwinism - doctrine proposed by Charles Darwin that all living species evolved from a common ancestor by a process he termed *natural selection*

death rate - see **rate, death**

decapod - group of crustaceans having the most species, mostly marine, generally having nineteen pairs of legs; includes shrimps, prawns, crayfish, crabs and lobsters

deforestation - aggressive removal of tropical rain forest by clear cutting to use the land for other purposes

density - property of matter that indicates the amount of matter (mass) that occupies a given amount of space (volume) and is expressed mathematically as mass/volume

deoxyribose nucleic acid (DNA) - see **acid, deoxyribose nucleic**

desalinize - remove salt from water, especially sea water

desert - area characterized by relatively few forms of life generally due to a lack of water, especially the hot, dry, high-pressure regions beneath the descending air of Hadley cells

detritus feeder - organism that feeds on organic material from dead organisms

diatomic molecule - see **molecule, diatomic**

dicotyledon - group of higher plants characterized by two leaves (cotyledons) that first emerge from the seed

diesel fuel - see **fuel, diesel**

digestion - process by which food is broken down into particles small enough to be transferred to blood to be transported to and utilized by cells

disease - sickness

dissolve - completely disperse one compound within another at the molecular level such that individual molecules of the two substances are randomly distributed within the resulting solution

distribution, nutrient - arrangement in given space or area of materials that can be used for food

diurnal - relating to a day; opposite of nocturnal

diverse - showing marked variability within a group

DNA - deoxyribose nucleic acid; a polymer of deoxyribose sugar phosphates with attached nucleic acid bases that form a genetic code

doldrums - dull; in particular, the hot, low-pressure, windless area near the equator

dormant - not active; opposite of vegetative; especially refers to inactive forms of living organisms such as seeds of plants and the spores of bacteria and microeukaryotes

drift, continental - principle that the continents continue to move about the surface of the Earth by shifting of the large plates of the Earth's crust upon which they ride

ductility - property of a substance that allows it to be stretched into long strands

earthquake - often violent tremor of the Earth thought to be caused by the movement of plates of the Earth's crust (tectonic plates) against one another

echinoderm - any of a phylum of radially-symmetrical animals having appendages that occur in a five-pronged pattern; these organisms are highly ordered having a series of complex internal systems; they include starfish, brittle stars, sea urchins and sand dollars

edentate - without teeth; referring to a group of mammals having greatly enlarged front claws used for digging or hanging from the limbs of trees; includes anteaters, tree sloths and armadillo-like animals

egg - female gamete containing half a complete genome which upon combining with a male sperm cell forms a new individual

electric force - see **force, electric**

electromagnetic force - see **force, electromagnetic**

electromagnetic radiation - see **radiation, electromagnetic**

electromagnetism - see **force, electromagnetic**

electron - as viewed by most theorists, one of the three fundamental particles making up atoms having a negative charge

element - a single atom or pure substance having a certain characteristic number of protons

elements, periodic table of the - systematic arrangement of symbols of all of the elements by their numbers of protons into rows (called "periods") and columns (called "groups") that relate to their reactivities

element, post-transition - elements on the right hand side of the periodic table after the transition metals constituting groups 4A, 5A, 6A, 7A and 8A

embryo - developing organism soon after fertilization

emulsification - making of an **emulsion** often by addition of a third liquid to two insoluble liquids

emulsion - mixture of two liquids, especially at the boundary between two insoluble liquids

endangered - referring to an organism that is in danger of extinction

ending, sensory - specialized cell capable of receiving inputs from the environment (such as heat, the lack of heat, pressure, or relative position) and translating them to electric impulses that are sent to the brain

endoplasmic reticulum - see **reticulum, endoplasmic**

endoskeleton - internal skeleton such as that found in mammals; opposite of exoskeleton

endothermic - describing chemical reactions that absorb heat from their surroundings

energy, kinetic - energy of motion; opposite of potential (resting) energy

energy, law of conservation of - universal principle that energy is neither created nor destroyed but is transferable from one form to another

energy, mass - expression of mass as a form of energy or the quantity of energy present in the form of mass

energy, potential - energy stored in an object by doing work against a force

engineering, genetic - manipulation of the genes of an organism using molecular biochemistry

enzyme - proteins that encourage chemical reactions by bringing the reactants in position to one another

enzyme, oxidative - enzyme that carries out an oxidation reaction

equinox - position of the sun directly above the equator marking the beginning of spring (vernal equinox) or fall (autumnal equinox)

erosion - wearing away over time of mineral surfaces due to abrasion caused by wind, rain or other natural abrasives

esophagus - tube of soft tissue in animals connecting mouth to stomach

eukaryote - organism, the cells of which have membrane-bound nuclei

eutherian - any of the subclass of mammals whose young survive in the uterus of the mother via a placenta—a mass of tissue that allows passage of nutrients and oxygen from the mother to the developing fetus

evaporate - change from liquid to vapor

evolution, adaptive - natural change in an organism making it better suited to its environment

evolution, chemical - thought of chemicals increasing in complexity over time with input of energy to eventually become capable of reproducing and thus become "living"; also called "abiogenesis"

evolution, convergent - presumption that similar traits have developed in organisms that are quite different from one another in response to similar environmental pressures such as the eyes of octopuses and humans

evolution, Darwinian - see **Darwinism**

evolution, general theory of - see **Darwinism**

evolve - change over time, especially according to the theory proposed by Charles Darwin (see **Darwinism**)

exoskeleton - external supporting and protective structure, as in insects, composed of a hardened case

exothermic - chemical reactions that give up energy to their environment

expansion - spreading out of the molecules in a substance due to absorption of heat energy by the atoms and an increase in their vibration

experiment - comparison of an experimental treatment subject (or group) with a control subject (or group) to determine whether a hypothesis is true or false

explosion, population - thought of a dramatic increase in population causing the world to become overpopulated; this thought was common in the 1960's and 70's

extremity, lower - the arms and hands or parts of these in humans

extremity, upper - the legs and feet or parts of these in humans

eyes, compound - organ in insects consisting of many light sensitive eye spots clustered together providing excellent detection of motion

fall - time of year between the autumnal equinox and winter solstice

family - taxonomic group of organisms which, along with other families, make up an order and which may be subdivided into one or more genera

fat - chemical compounds used by animals to store energy; also called "lipids"

fatty acid - hydrocarbon chain, typically 14 to 24 carbon atoms in length ending in an acid group (-COOH) that are linked together in parallel to make lipids

female - sex of a species that produces an egg to be fertilized by the male of the species

fern - low-growing plants characterized by feather-like leaves and simple veins typically growing at the edge of shade

fertilize - introduction into an egg cell of genetic material by a sperm cell (animal) or pollen (plant)

filament, light bulb - narrow piece of wire, usually tungsten, which glows when an electric current is passed through it

filament, stamen - in a male flower, stalk of a stamen to which the anther is attached

filamentous - long and narrow; typical form taken by a filamentous fungus which grows in long strands a single cell wide

filter - sheet of porous material most commonly used for separating solids from liquids by allowing passage of the liquid while preventing passage of solid particles

first law of motion - see **motion, first law of**

fish - cold-blooded water animal that obtains oxygen directly from water using gills

fish, bony - fish having a bony skeleton as compared to the cartilaginous fish (sharks, skates and rays) which lack true bones

flagellum - whip-like member on many microorganisms used for locomotion

flower, pistillate - female flower containing a pistil and producing egg cells (ova) which are fertilized by pollen

flower, staminate - male flower containing the stamen and producing pollen

fluid - non-solid matter (liquids or gases) that are characterized by their tendency to flow when acted upon by forces

fluid, tissue - fluid within tissues which continuously bathes the cells with nutrients and oxygen and serves as a medium through which waste products can leave the cells

fluorescent - type of light bulb filled with a gas or vapor that "fluoresces" (gives off light energy) when an electric charge is placed across it; more generally, fluorescence relates to the giving off of light by a substance that is excited by energy input

food chain - progression of plants and animals in an order of production and consumption of organic material beginning with plants (primary producers) and ending with animals that digest matter to produce carbon dioxide (ultimate consumers)

foot, tube - structure located on the underside of echinoderms used for locomotion by hydrostatic pressure

force, electric - force of attraction or repulsion existing between two fundamental particles (protons or electrons); one aspect of the electromagnetic force

force, electromagnetic - either of two related natural attractions (electric or magnetic) between two objects having either opposite charges or opposite magnetic poles

force, nuclear - natural force of attraction between protons within the nucleus of an atom that prevents them from repelling one another from the nucleus

fossil - mineralized body or body part of a dead organism leaving a lasting record of that organism in the earth

fossil fuel - see **fuel, fossil**

fraction, petroleum - portion of petroleum that boils within a given temperature range allowing it to be separated from other fractions

fuel, diesel - hydrocarbon fuel fraction of petroleum that is used in diesel engines including compounds of higher molecular weight than those of gasoline and lower than those of lubricating oils, generally in a range from 15 to 25 carbon atoms in length

fuel, fossil - fuel thought to have arisen over time from the decay of biomass beneath the surface of the earth

fulcrum - pivot point of a lever where the direction of motion changes

function - in chemistry, the role played by a certain chemical in a living system

fungus (pl. fungi) - any of a wide variety of aquatic plants mostly organized at the cellular or colonial level, many of which occur in filaments

gall bladder - gland producing bile that enters the stomach participating in the digestion of fats

gamete - sex cells, male (sperm or pollen) or female (eggs) that come together with cells from the opposite sex of the species to form a zygote or new, single-celled individual

gametophyte generation - see **generation, gametophyte**

gas - substance having a loose arrangement of molecules such that the substance spreads out to fill the volume of any container

gas, greenhouse - gaseous molecules in the atmosphere that tend to absorb infrared radiation slowing the escape of the sun's energy from the atmosphere and thus increasing the temperature at the earth's surface

gas, natural - a mixture of hydrocarbon gases, largely methane, found primarily in petroleum deposits beneath the Earth's surface

gas, noble - any of the group 8A elements having a full complement of electrons making them nonreactive

gaseous - having the properties of a gas

gasoline - petroleum fraction generally consisting of low-boiling compounds in a range from approximately five to ten carbon atoms

gastropod - any of the largest class of mollusks having a distinct head and a single (usually coiled) shell; includes snails, whelks, cowries, periwinkles and slugs

general theory of evolution - see **evolution, general theory of**

generation, gametophyte - portion of a life cycle of many plants in which reproduction is sexual (by fertilization of an ovum with a sperm nucleus from a pollen grain)

generation, sporophyte - portion of a life cycle of many lower plants producing asexual spores for reproduction

generator - device for generating electricity by moving a magnetic field in the vicinity of an electrical conductor

genetic code - see **code, genetic**

genetic engineering - see **engineering, genetic**

genetics - science of inheritance; the study of genomes of any organisms

genome - any organism's full complement (entire set) of DNA

genus (pl. genera) - taxonomic group of organisms which, along with other genera, make up a family and which may be subdivided into one or more species

geocentric - describing the belief system existing prior to Copernicus (A.D. 1500's) that the earth is at the center of the universe

geochronology - study of the age of the earth and

the timing of events since its formation mainly based on radioisotope studies of minerals and on study of the occurrence of fossils and the strata (layers) of the earth crust in which they appear

geology - study of the earth, especially with regard to its structure

germinate - leave a state of dormancy to become vegetative

girdle, pelvic - series of bones making up the support structure to which the legs are attached and which support the body as it rests upon the lower extremities

girdle, shoulder - series of bones making up the support structure from which the arms are suspended

gland, adrenal - glands resting on the kidneys responsible for producing hormones, most notably insulin

gland, mammary - glands in females of mammals that produce milk to feed the young

glare - reflected light from a surface that interferes with clear vision

gliding joint - see **joint, gliding**

glucose - simple sugar having the chemical formula $C_6H_{12}O_6$ that occurs in both plants and animals as a source of carbon and energy and that is used in the synthesis of many important polysaccharides including cellulose, starch and glycogen

glycogen - plant storage polysaccharide made mainly of glucose

glycolipid - lipid made from three fatty acid units attached to a glycerol backbone

gram - basic unit of mass in the metric system; 453.6 grams are equivalent to one pound

gravitation - basic natural force of attraction existing among all masses in the universe but noticeable only in the large masses, such as planets, stars and natural satellites

gravitational field - gravitation of a particular mass over its entire extent of influence

gravity - gravitation displayed by the earth

green alga (pl. algae) - see **alga, green**

greenhouse - enclosure for growing plants consisting of a structure that allows light to pass through the walls while holding in its warmth

greenhouse gas - see **gas, greenhouse**

ground water - see **water, ground**

growth rate - see **rate, growth**

guard cell - either of a pair of cells surrounding a stoma on the surface of a leaf of a higher plant that is involved in the control of the plant's water balance

gymnosperm - any of three classes of vascular plants whose ovules and seeds are not encased in an ovary or case; includes conifers, cycads and ginkgoes

habitat - dwelling place of a particular organism or group of organisms

Hadley cell - circulating air masses extending north and south from the equator resulting in ascending air at the equator and descending air in the middle latitudes in each hemisphere

hail - ice resulting from freezing water in the atmosphere repeatedly falling and ascending, adding additional layers of ice with each cycle, then falling to the earth under the mass of the accumulation

halogen - any of the reactive, group 7A elements having seven valence electrons

head - body segment at the mouth end of higher animals housing the brain or other main processing center of the central nervous system

heavy metal - see **metal, heavy**

heliocentric - describing the belief system existing since Copernicus (A.D. 1500's) that the sun is at the center of the earth's solar system

hemichordate - any of a phylum of gilled, shallowmarine worms having short nerve cords; includes acorn worms and tongue worms

hemisphere, northern - half of the Earth north of the equator

hemisphere, southern - half of the Earth south of the equator

hemoglobin - red pigment in blood containing iron that carries oxygen throughout the bodies of many higher animals

herbivore - plant eater

hexapod - class of arthropods including the insects having three body parts, six legs and typically two pairs of wings

higher organism - see **organism, higher**

higher plant - see **plant, higher**

high-pressure zone - area on the surface of the Earth where cool, dense, typically dry air descends upon the Earth creating an increased air pressure at the surface

hinge joint - see **joint, hinge**

histone - protein frame about which the DNA of higher organisms is structured

hoof - hard foot-covering of the Artiodactylan and Perissodactylan mammals

hornwort - small, non-vascular plant growing in the moist environments of ponds and slow streams

horsetail - plant of the subphylum Spenophytina (in a single genus) having a jointed, hollow stem and small, close, scale-like leaves at the joints

human - highest of all organisms having advanced language and thought and the ability to extensively manipulate his environment; *Homo sapiens*

hydrocarbon, aliphatic - chemical compound consisting of a chain of carbon atoms having their available bonds taken up by either other carbon atoms or hydrogen atoms

hypothesis (pl. hypotheses) - educated guess that serves as the basis for a test (experiment) to show it to be either true or false

hyrax - any of an order of small, hoofed herbivores of Africa and Asia having a reduced tail, short legs and suction pads for climbing

immune - not subject to the effects of; relating to the system in higher animals that protects the body from infection

impoundment - pool of water created by damming a river

incandescent - type of light bulb consisting of a narrow wire, usually of tungsten alloy, called a "filament," that glows brightly when an electric current is applied across it

incisor - in mammals, a front, knife-like tooth typically used for piercing and cutting food as it enters the mouth

inefficient - not making the best or most complete use of resources; inefficient burning of fuel sug-gests that the products could be further used for energy

inertia - tendency of moving objects (masses) to keep moving and of stationary objects to remain stationary unless they are acted upon by forces

infect - invasion of an organism by a microorganism

inflammation - swelling that occurs at the site of infection or irritation due to the body's responses to the problem; externally, inflammation may include reddening, whitening, swelling or warming of the affected area; internally, inflammation may be accompanied by accumulation of blood, tissue fluid, lymph cells and immune factors (chemicals)

infrared - electromagnetic radiation (light) having energies lower than those of the red end of the visible spectrum

insect - see **hexapod**

insectivore - literally, any organism that feeds on insects; specifically a group of insect-eating mammals that includes shrews, hedgehogs and moles

integument - outer covering of an organism; the skin, hair and nails of mammals

interaction - any result of an encounter among objects

intestine, large - 1.5 meter-long tubular structure near the ends of the digestive systems of higher animals, approximately 6 cm in diameter in which moisture is absorbed into the body and mucus is produced for helping in eliminating waste matter from the body; also called "colon" or the "large bowel"

intestine, small - 6 meter-long tubular structure in the digestive systems of higher animals, 2-3 cm in diameter, having high surface area for absorption of nutrients from digested food

invertebrate - describing lower macroscopic animals having no spinal cord

ion, polyatomic - set of atoms commonly found in a group having a net charge, and not being broken apart during most chemical reactions

ionic bonding - formation of a compound by the electric attraction of opposite-charged ions

isopod - any of a large order of wide-ranging crustaceans having flattened, segmented bodies; includes sow bugs and pill bugs

jelly, petroleum - semisolid made from high-molecular-weight distillates of petroleum and used in medicine and personal care as a moisture barrier

jet stream - any of four, wide, flat tubes of fast-moving air over northern and southern hemispheres that affect weather patterns and can serve as pathways for jets to travel more efficiently in their direction

jet stream, polar - westerly jet stream in each of the northern and southern hemispheres above the edge of the polar front

joint - point of attachment and movement of bones

joint, ball and socket - joint, such as the shoulder and hip joints in humans, that resembles a ball that rotates within a socket providing for complete circular motion of the appendage

joint, gliding - joint, such as the wrist and ankle joints in humans, that is composed of a series of small bones providing for a full range of rotation and some degree of cushioning from shock due to their unique arrangements of small bones cushioned by connective tissue

joint, hinge - joint, such as the knee and elbow joints in humans, that resembles a hinge of a door providing for directional movement in an imaginary plane

joint, pivot - joint, such as the forearm and lower leg joints in humans, which allows the appendage to twist about a central axis

joint, saddle - classification of the human thumb joint which allows the thumb to cross the palm of the hand (process called "opposability")

kerosene - mid-range (200-300ºC) boiling fraction of petroleum having approximately 11- to 18-carbon-length hydrocarbons and often used for fuel, especially in oil-burning lamps and in heaters

kidney - organ for eliminating unneeded ions and cell waste products from blood, producing waste that varies from organism to organism (urine in humans)

kinetic - concerning the rate at which reactants are converted to products during a chemical reaction

kinetic energy - see **energy, kinetic**

kinetically stable - see **stable, kinetically**

kingdom - any of the broadest categories of living organisms, by most authors including monera (prokaryotes), protozoa (microeukaryotes), fungi (yeasts and molds), plants and animals, but most recently including a newly-recognized group of prokaryotes called "archaea"; kingdoms are subdivided into phyla

lagomorph - any of an order of small mammals having a short tail and medium to large outer ears; includes rabbits, hares and pikas

lamp shell - group of mainly single-shelled ("monovalve") brachiopods represented by few living and many extinct species

lanthanoid series - see **series, lanthanoid**

large intestine - see **intestine, large**

larynx - case of cartilage and connective tissue enclosing the vocal folds ("cords"); also called "voice box"

lava - molten rock having emerged from beneath the Earth's surface due to volcanic activity

law of conservation of energy - see **conservation of energy, law of**

lens - piece of curved glass specially shaped for bending light as in scientific instruments and optical devices (*e.g.* binoculars, reading glasses)

lever - simple machine used to change the direction of motion and/or to increase either force or distance of a motion at the expense of the other

life - variously defined by science, theology and philosophy, but, in science, generally a combination of characteristics held in common by all living things (see Blue Lesson 1)

life cycle - see **cycle, life**

ligament - band of soft, stretchy connective tissue connecting muscle to bone and providing flexible support to joints

light - electromagnetic radiation, especially in the visible band of wavelengths

limitation, nutrient - either global or local lack of availability of materials needed by living organisms for growth and reproduction

limnology - study of fresh surface water, especially as a habitat

linear alkane - see **alkane, linear**

lipids - chemicals composed of fatty acids connected by one of a number of linking structures such as phosphate or glycerol; also called "fats"

liquid - cohesive fluid (a fluid that stays together)

liver - large glandular organ that produces enzymes and fluids used in digesting food

liverwort - any of a class (Hepaticae) of small, non-vascular plants inhabiting rocks and other surfaces in high-moisture environments

locomotion - movement from place to place

logarithmic - increasing or decreasing by a factor, especially by factors of ten

low-pressure zone - area on the surface of the Earth where warm, sparse, typically moist air ascends from the face of the Earth creating a decreased air pressure at the surface

lower appendage - see **appendage, lower**

lower extremity - see **extremity, lower**

lower organism - see **organism, lower**

lymph - fluid similar in composition to blood—but containing no red blood cells—that fills the spaces between cells in animal tissues

lymphatic (n.) - vessels similar to veins that end in the spaces between clusters of cells in tissues that collect and transport tissue fluid

machine - device used in applying work for the completion of a task

macroscopic - large enough to see without the use of a device for magnification

magma - molten rock, presumably originating deep within the earth but occurring anywhere beneath its surface

magnification - increase in apparent size due to passage of light through one or more lenses

male - sex of a species producing sperm cells with which the female's egg is fertilized to produce offspring

malleability - property of a substance relating to its ability to be shaped without breaking

maltose - malt sugar; disaccharide of glucose ($C_{12}H_{22}O_{11}$), about one third as sweet as sucrose

mammal - any of a large class of vertebrate animals having hair, with females that give live birth to young and nurse the young with milk from special glands called "mammary glands"

mammary gland - milk-producing gland of mammals used to sustain the young offspring; in humans, called a "breast"

mandibulate - any of a large subphylum of arthropods having paired jaws called mandibles; includes crustaceans, centipedes, millipedes, pauropods, symphyla and insects

mantle - thick layer of dense, mostly solid rock comprising the majority of the Earth's subsurface that extends from the lower margin of the crust to the core

marine - of or relating to salt water of the oceans or seas

mass - quantity (amount) of matter

mass, atomic - mass of an atom, usually measured in atomic mass units (AMU)

mass energy - see **energy, mass**

mass unit, atomic (AMU) - unit of measure of mass of atoms based on a standard of pure carbon having six protons and six neutrons and having an atomic mass of twelve

materialism - doctrine that all in existence can be explained by observable phenomena within the physical universe

maxilla (pl. maxillae) - in humans, the upper jawbone; in insects, appendage around the mouth, also called "mouth part"

melting point - temperature at which a particular solid becomes a liquid

membrane, cell - outer boundary of a cell that controls the cell's contents by its selectivity in admitting or rejecting substances that are present at the cell surface

membrane, nuclear - thin sheet-like membrane encapsulating the nucleus of a cell

menstrual cycle - see **cycle, menstrual**

menstruation - shedding of the inner lining of the uterus characterized by ridding of blood and soft tissue by a female on an approximate 28-day cycle when fertilization of an egg does not occur; also commonly called "period"

mesosphere - layer of the atmosphere extending from approximately 50 to 85 kilometers above sea level in which the temperature decreases from approximately 0 to -100 °C

metal, alkali - any of the soft, whitish, reactive elements appearing in group 1A of the periodic table

metal, alkaline earth - any of the elements appearing in group 2A of the periodic table

metal, heavy - metal, typically in the transition metal series, having high atomic weight and often toxic to humans at low concentrations

metal, rare earth - see **series, lanthanoid**

metal, transition - any of the metallic elements in B groups of the periodic table having complex reactivities and tending to form colored compounds

metallic - describing an element having properties consistent with description as a metal (see Yellow Lesson 8 for a list of properties)

metalloid - describing an element having properties that are fully consistent with neither those of a metal nor those of a non-metal

metazoan - organism having a variety of different kinds of cells having different functions; considered "higher organisms" as compared to protozoans and mesozoans

meteor - a solid, natural body traveling through the Earth's atmosphere

meteorite - a meteor having survived the heat and friction of the Earth's atmosphere to strike the Earth

meteoroid - a solid, natural body traveling through outer space

meteorology - study of weather and weather patterns

method, scientific - series of conventions adopted by the scientific community as accepted practice for conducting scientific explorations, involving forming hypotheses by comparing experimental treatment subjects to control subjects and forming and reporting objective findings

microorganism - organism too small to be seen with the unaided eye but may be seen using a microscope

microphyta - microscopic plants

microscopic - that may be observed using a microscope

microzoa - microscopic organisms, many of which resemble free-living animal cells but some of which have plant characteristics as well

mid-ocean ridge - see **ridge, mid-ocean**

mineralogy - study of minerals that occur within the earth

mitochondrion (pl. mitochondria) - cell organelle containing chemicals for transporting electrons responsible for energy generation; called "the powerhouse of the cell"

model - representation of an object or idea; in science, a theory is a model for thinking

molar - broad teeth with large, flat surfaces used for grinding food

molecular biology - see **biology, molecular**

molecular weight - see **weight, molecular**

molecule - combination of atoms bonded together by electromagnetic forces

molecule, diatomic - molecule formed from two atoms of the same element such as molecular oxygen or hydrogen

Mollusca - phylum of eucoelomate animals having two-piece shells, including snails, slugs, mussels and clams

monocotyledon - group of higher plants characterized by a single leaf (cotyledon) that first emerges from the seed

monotreme - either of two remaining species of the mammalian subclass Prototheria of egg-laying mammals: the duckbilled platypus and the spiny anteater of Australia and New Guinea

moon - large celestial body in orbit around a planet; also called a "natural satellite"

moss - lower macroscopic plant lacking vessels to distribute water and largely restricted to growth in moist environments

moss, club - any plant of the phylum Lycophytina of moss-like, vascular, "lower plants," diverse in appearance; also called lycophyte

motion, first law of - Newton's observation that resting objects remain at rest and moving objects remain in motion unless acted upon by a force

motion, second law of - Newton's observation that a force applied to an object is proportional to the product of the mass of that object and its rate of acceleration; $F = m \cdot a$

motion, third law of - Newton's observation that every applied force is met with an equal force in the opposite direction

motor oil - see **oil, motor**

mouth - entrance to the digestive system

multicellular organism - see **organism, multicellular**

muscle - tissue that functions as a machine, using energy to provide motion to animals or their body parts; organ composed mostly of muscle tissue

muscle, skeletal - muscle tissue having a striped appearance under the microscope that is under conscious control of the brain

muscle, smooth - muscle tissue having a smooth appearance under the microscope that is not under conscious control but controls vital functions such as blood flow and digestive motions

mutate - genetically alter

mutualism - relationship among organisms from which all organisms benefit and upon which at least one of the organisms is dependent

myriapod - any of a group of terrestrial mandibulate classes including centipedes, millipedes, pauropods and symphyla

nasal passage - see **passage, nasal**

natural gas - gaseous hydrocarbons existing in petroleum deposits primarily composed of methane but containing other short-chain hydrocarbons (ethane, propane and butane)

nausea - feeling a need to vomit

nectar - sweet, nutrient-rich liquid contained beneath the reproductive parts of flowers that serves to entice insects, birds and other animals responsible for pollinating the plant

neodarwinism - Darwinism as recently modified in attempt to explain the lack of evolutionary connection displayed in the fossil record

nerve cell - cell of the nervous system responsible for transmitting or processing nerve impulses

nerve cord - cord extending the length of the back (dorsum) of the body of higher animals that serves as the main trunk of nerves leading to and from the brain from the various parts of the body; the spinal cord in humans and other true vertebrates

nervous system - see **system, nervous**

neutral - in chemistry, relating to a water solution that is neither acid nor basic; pH 7

neutralism - relationship between two organisms wherein neither organism is significantly affected by the other for the better or for the worse

neutron - subatomic particle occurring in the nuclei of atoms, having a mass of 1 AMU but no charge

Newton, Sir Isaac - 17th century physicist and mathematician considered the founder of Newtonian physics (the physics of motion) and of integral calculus among many other important observations, inventions and discoveries

nimbostratus cloud - see **cloud, nimbostratus**

noble gas - any of the elements in group 8A of the periodic table of the elements being essentially non-reactive

nocturnal - describing an animal that is active mainly at night

non-metal - not having the properties of a metal (see Yellow Lesson 8)

northern hemisphere - see **hemisphere, northern**

nuclear force - see **force, nuclear**

nuclear membrane - see **membrane, nuclear**

nucleic acid - see **acid, nucleic**

nucleoplasm - fluid contents of the nucleus of the cell that serves as a medium in which all of the activities of the nucleus take place

nucleus, atomic - central portion of an atom containing protons and neutrons held together by nuclear forces and around which electrons orbit

nucleus, cell - portion of a eukaryotic cell containing DNA and responsible for directing the cell's activities

nutrient distribution - see **distribution, nutrient**

nutrient limitation - see **limitation, nutrient**

objective - that can be determined with certainty as by comparison to a clear standard; opposite of subjective

oceanography - study of the ocean

ocellus (pl. ocelli) - light-sensitive organ in invertebrates with a lens-like body enclosed in pigment

offspring - organisms coming forth from a parent or parents; children in humans; also called "progeny"

oil, motor - petroleum compounds having boiling points greater than 400°C used as a lubricant, especially in the engines of automobiles

olfactory - describing the sense of smell

oligochaete - any of an order of annelid worms, including earthworms, having sparse tufts of bristles

opposable thumb - see **thumb, opposable**

orbit - circular motion of an object around a central point as the result of a centripetal force and its own inertia; especially the movement of a planet around the sun or a satellite around a planet

order - taxonomic group of organisms which, along with other orders, make up a class and which may be subdivided into one or more families

organ - orderly arrangement of tissues having a distinct function in the body of an organism

organelle - orderly arrangement of molecules having a distinct function in a living cell

organic chemistry - see **chemistry, organic**

organism - free-living body displaying the characteristics of life

organism, higher - organism displaying a higher degree of orderliness; in an evolutionary sense, an organism that is more evolved

organism, lower - organism displaying a lesser degree of orderliness; in an evolutionary sense, an organism that is less evolved

organism, macroscopic - organism that is large enough to see with the unaided eye

organism, microscopic - see **microorganism**

organism, multicellular - organism consisting of many cells

ovary, flower - female reproductive part of a flowering plant containing the eggs or ova

oviduct - narrow tube for passage of an egg from the ovary of an animal to the uterus

ovulation - development and release by the ovary of an egg cell by a human or higher animal

ovule, flower - segment of an ovary containing a single ovum

oxidative enzyme - see **enzyme, oxidative**

oxygen - element characterized by eight protons per atom and having an atomic weight of approximately 16 AMU; molecular oxygen is diatomic

pair, base - a pair of nucleic acid bases loosely bonded by attraction of hydrogen atoms across a double stranded nucleic acid molecule

paleontology - study of fossils

pancreas - organ located above the stomach of higher animals producing fluids that aid in digestion of food; produces insulin which plays a critical role in metabolism of sugars

pangolin - armadillo-like armored mammal of Africa lacking teeth

paraffin - high molecular weight fraction of petroleum that is solid at room temperature, and having waxy character

parallel - running alongside

parasite - organism which lives in or on another (the "host") to its own benefit but to the detriment (harm) of the host

parasitism - living as a parasite

passage, nasal - air passage through the face and head bones allowing passage of air across the sense organ for smell and serving to filter, moisten and warm air before it enters the lungs

pathogen - disease-causing organism

pathogenesis - origination of disease from a pathogen

pelvic girdle - see **girdle, pelvic**

peptide - short chain of amino acids; portion of a protein

periodic table of the elements - see **elements, periodic table of**

permafrost - water existing at high altitude where the temperature never drops below the freezing point of water

petal - leaf of a flower that reflects light of wavelengths that are attractive to insects

petroleum jelly - see **jelly, petroleum**

petroleum refinery - see **refinery, petroleum**

pH - property of water solutions describing the concentration of free hydrogen cations in solution

phage - virus that infects bacteria

phase - form taken on by a substance, either solid, liquid or gas

photosynthesis - process carried out by plants of synthesizing sugar molecules using light energy from the sun

phylum (pl. phyla) - taxonomic group of organisms

which, along with other phyla, make up a kingdom and which may be subdivided into one or more classes

physician - medical doctor; one responsible for the physical well-being of patients

phytoplankton - tiny plants that spend at least a portion of their life suspended in natural waters

pigment, biological - chemical used by photosynthetic organisms to trap light energy from the sun for use in photosynthesis; *e.g.* chlorophyll

pigment, chemical - chemical that absorbs light, giving it a characteristic color; any such chemical used as a coloring agent in products such as paints, dyes or plastics

pinnipedia - any of an order of medium- to large-sized aquatic mammals having flippers as limbs, large eyes and external ears small or lacking; includes sea lions, walruses and seals

pistillate flower - see **flower, pistillate**

pivot joint - see **joint, pivot**

planet, terrestrial - one of the innermost four planets of our solar system composed mainly of solid minerals as opposed to next four which appear to be largely liquid

planktonic - of an organism that lives suspended in a body of natural water

plant - eukaryotic organism of the plant kingdom characterized by rigid cell walls and photosynthetic metabolism

plant, higher - plant considered by evolutionists to be more evolved; relatively complex plant, especially of vascular plants

plant, vascular - plant having a system of vessels for collecting and distributing water and nutrients from roots to leaves and for distributing food produced in leaves back to the roots

plasma, blood - liquid portion of blood (without the cells)

plastid - organelle within a photosynthetic cell containing pigment and responsible for collection of light

pogonophor - any of a phylum of tube-building, deep-bottom-dwelling marine worms, also called beard worms

point, boiling - temperature that will not be exceeded by a liquid at standard pressure until it has been converted to gas

point, melting - temperature that will not be exceeded by a solid at standard pressure until it has been converted to liquid

polar - displaying an opposition of forces within a body; in chemistry, description of a molecule having a net negative charge in one area and a net positive charge in another

pole, geographical (earth) - north and south aspects of an imaginary axis through the center of the Earth about which it rotates

pole, magnetic (earth) - magnetic poles resembling the north and south poles of a magnet displayed by Earth near the geographic north and south poles

pollen - male reproductive cells produced by plants for fertilization of the female ovum

polyatomic ion - see **ion, polyatomic**

polychaete - any of an order of annelid worms, including marine fan worms, having many (often ornate) bristles

polysaccharide - molecule that is a polymer of simple sugars

population explosion - see **explosion, population**

pore space - air-filled space between particles in soil

Porifera - phylum of the sponges

post-transition element - see **element, post-transition**

potable - fit for drinking

potential energy - see **energy, potential**

precession - secondary motion around a central axis as the wobbling of a top as it spins

predation - process of one organism killing and feeding on another

predator - organism that lives by killing others for food

premolar - tooth resembling a molar but having a somewhat smaller grinding surface

pressure, barometric - pressure occurring at a specific location due to the mass of gases above that body in the atmosphere

prevailing wind - see **wind, prevailing**

primary consumer - see **consumer, primary**

primary producer - see **producer, primary**

prion - a protein, without nucleic acids, capable of transmitting disease

prism - angular glass device used for splitting a beam of light into its component colors

producer, primary - organism at the bottom of the food chain responsible for fixing carbon by removing carbon dioxide from the atmosphere and using it to manufacture organic molecules by photosynthesis; includes all photosynthetic organisms

product - in chemistry, a substance resulting from a chemical reaction

prokaryote - organism (such as a bacterium or archaeon) that lacks a membrane-bound nucleus

protein - highly ordered compound that is a polymer of amino acids

protein, structural - protein that is used in the building of biomass

protochordate - animal having a nerve cord but lacking a spine, considered by evolutionists to be the ancestors of true vertebrates

proton - positively-charged particle having an atomic mass of 1 AMU and occurring in the nuclei of atoms

protoplasm - see **cytoplasm**

protozoan - see **microzoan**

pterophytes - any of a large subphylum of plants which includes all of the vascular plants except the horsetails and club mosses, comprised of ferns, gymnosperms and angiosperms

radial symmetry - see **symmetry, radial**

radiation, electromagnetic - waves of electromagnetic energy consisting of electric and magnetic fields continuously generating each other; also called "light"

radioactive - describing atoms that give off energy and subatomic particles as their unstable nuclei decay (break up)

rain forest, tropical - dense forest land in the tropical regions of the globe where cooling air from above the equator drops its water daily on the Earth

rare earth metal - see **series, lanthanoid**

rate, birth - rate of formation of new life through sexual reproduction measured in births of new organisms per unit of time

rate, death - rate at which a particular organism is eliminated from a population by death, measured in number of deaths per unit time

rate, growth - rate at which a particular organism increases in numbers within a population by reproduction, or the rate at which the biomass associated with a particular organism increases by growth and reproduction of cells within the organism, measured in number or mass per unit of time

react - in chemistry, describing what takes place when substances combine with other substances by the forces of attraction and repulsion that exist between them to take on different forms

reactant - initial chemical involved in a chemical reaction which rearranges with other reactants to form products

reaction, chemical - interaction among chemicals that results in chemical products that consist of different combinations or arrangements of the same atoms

receptor - specialized cells that receive sensory impulses from an organism's environment and translate them into electrical signals which are sent to the brain

rectum - bulb-shaped widening near the end of the large intestine that accumulates waste material until it is eliminated from the body

refinery, petroleum - man-made facility for separating individual fractions of petroleum for various uses

reflect - bounce light as from the surface of a mirror

refract - bend light

refractometer - instrument used to measure the refraction of light

repel - push apart, as two like charges or similar magnetic poles

replication - in biology, the process of DNA being copied to prepare for the making of a new cell

reproduction - process by which organisms give rise to new organisms of the same kind

reptile - any of a class of mainly terrestrial (living

on dry land) vertebrate animals (animals with backbones) having hard bones and scaly skin

resistance - device that converts electrical energy to heat energy by collisions among its atoms and the electrons that flow through it

respiratory system - see **system, respiratory**

reticulum, endoplasmic - folds of membrane found within cells that are high in surface area and partition the cell into functional areas

revolve - in planetary science, description of the motion of the planets in a nearly circular pattern around the sun

rib cage - entire set of ribs in a given animal

ribose nucleic acid - see **acid, ribose nucleic**

ribosome - site of protein manufacture in cells

Richter scale - logarithmic scale used to measure seismic (earthquake) activity

ridge, mid-ocean - band of mountain-like structures on the ocean floor thought to mark joints between tectonic plates upon which the continents ride

Ring of Fire - 32,500 kilometer-long rim around the Pacific Ocean that is the focus of considerable volcanic and seismic activity

rise, continental - short, steep incline at the base of a continent where it meets the ocean floor

RNA - see **acid, ribose nucleic**

rock - large cleft of earthen minerals

rodent - typically small mammal characterized by incisors that grow throughout its lifetime

rotate - in planetary science, description of the turning motion of planets around an imaginary central axis resulting in day/night cycles due to the planet's position in relationship to the sun

saddle joint - see **joint, saddle**

saliva - mucus fluid of the mouth that lubricates and that contains enzymes that begin the digestion of food

salt - product of the ionic bonding of an anion with a cation such as results from the neutralization of an acid with a base

satellite - orbiting body, either natural (called a "moon") or man-made

saturated - condition of completeness or fullness such as a gas that is saturated with a liquid or a liquid solution that is saturated with a solid

scientific method - see **method, scientific**

sediment - that which settles from liquid suspension under gravity

seed - dormant form of a plant resulting from sexual reproduction containing an embryonic plant that germinates when conditions are suitable for growth

seismic wave - see **wave, seismic**

selective breeding - see **breeding, selective**

semiconductor - substance that is neither an excellent nor poor conductor of electricity used in the manufacture of integrated circuits (*e.g.*, computer chips)

semisolid - substance that is neither completely solid nor entirely liquid such as ice cream, agar or gelatin

senescence - the process of aging

sensory endings - see **endings, sensory**

sepal - green leaf which forms the lower support for a petal or petals of a flower and together with other sepals forms a cup-like base called the "calyx"

series, actinoid - series of chemicals that follow (in order of atomic number) actinium and that react similarly

series, lanthanoid - series of chemicals that follow (in order of atomic number) lanthanium and that react similarly; also called the "rare earth metals"

sex - referring to one of two different forms (called male and female) of a particular type of organism that contribute genetic material to a new individual as a way of reproducing

sexual - relating to reproduction involving male and female contributors of genetic material

shelf, continental - shallow area of flat, gently sloping earth surrounding the edge of each continent

shoulder girdle - see **girdle, shoulder**

sirenian - any of an order of large aquatic mammals with hind limbs lacking, having a horizontal tail flipper and front limbs as paddle-like flippers, small eyes, no external ears, few teeth and having bristles around the mouth; includes manatees, dugongs and sea cows

skeletal muscle - see **muscle, skeletal**

skeletal system - see **system, skeletal**

slope, continental - steep slope extending from the ocean floor to the continental shelf

small intestine - see **intestine, small**

smooth muscle - see **muscle, smooth**

soil - granular material at the surface of the Earth's crust thought to have formed by the weathering of "parent" rock beneath or to have been transported from other rock due to erosion by wind or water

solar wind - see **wind, solar**

solenogastre - any of a subclass (Aplacophora) of worm-like, deep-marine mollusks

solid - phase of matter in which matter is rigid (as opposed to fluid) in form due to the dense arrangement of, and the strong forces of attraction among, its particles

solubility - tendency of one substance to dissolve (completely and randomly disperse) in another

soluble - of a particular substance which has a tendency to dissolve in another particular substance

solute - substance which dissolves in another

solution - complete dispersion and random distribution of one substance within another

solvent - substance in which another dissolves or which is intended for use in dissolving another

southern hemisphere - see **hemisphere, southern**

species - group of organisms which mate with others of the same group producing fertile offspring, and which, along with other species, make up a genus; species may be further subdivided into varieties

spectrum - entire range of wavelengths of electromagnetic radiation

sperm - male gamete or sex cell containing half a genome (called "haploid") responsible for fertilization of the female egg cell (the two combine to become "diploid," that is, to contain a complete genome)

spinal cord - see **cord, spinal**

spine - chain of bones surrounding the spinal cord and providing longitudinal (or "lengthwise") support to the body; also called "vertebrae"

spontaneous - occurring naturally without input of energy

spore, asexual - seed-like structure that has the ability to form a separate free-living organism like the one that gave rise to the spore without sexual involvement

sporophyte generation - see **generation, sporophyte**

spring (mechanical) - device typically made of a heavy coiled metal wire that coils under pressure and recoils when that pressure is released

spring (season) - time of year between the spring equinox and summer solstice

stable, kinetically - describing a substance that, although reactive, reacts so slowly as to make the compound non-reactive for practical purposes under a given set of conditions

stable, thermodynamically - describing a substance that is non-reactive under a given set of conditions because it exists at a low level of potential energy

stamen - male reproductive apparatus of a flower consisting of an elongated bulb-like anther on the end of a filament

staminate flower - see **flower, staminate**

starch - polysaccharide of glucose used as an energy reserve in plants

starvation - process of change in an organism that results from a lack of food and that will eventually terminate in death

static - staying the same; opposite of dynamic

steam - water above its boiling point and in its gaseous state

stigma - cap of the female reproductive parts of a plant that receives the pollen

stoma (pl. stomata) - opening in a leaf that allows escape of water through the cuticle, regulated by guard cells

stomach - sac-like organ in animals that collects swallowed food and thoroughly digests it by mixing it with digestive juices then sends the digest to the intestines for absorption of the digested materials

strata - layers; in soil science, layers of soil or sediment presumably laid down in succession in order of occurrence from bottom to top

stratocumulus cloud - see **cloud, stratocumulus**

stratosphere - layer of the atmosphere extending from approximately 12 to 50 kilometers above sea level in which the temperature increases from approximately -60 to 0 °C; contains a few of the highest clouds and is the layer of the atmosphere in which commercial jets usually fly, being above the height of most weather systems

stratus cloud - see **cloud, stratus**

structural protein - see **protein, structural**

style - in the female reproductive parts of a flower, the stalk connecting the stigma to the ovary through which the sperm cell must pass to fertilize an ovum

subjective - that cannot be determined with certainty due to lack of a clear standard for comparison; opposite of objective

subterranean - beneath the surface of the earth

succession - occurring in a progression or sequence

sucrose - sweet disaccharide of fructose and glucose ($C_{12}H_{22}O_{11}$) most often concentrated from sugar cane or sugar beets; "table sugar"

sugar - hydrocarbon typically consisting of a five or six-carbon pyran (oxygen-containing) ring structure

sun - name given to the star at the center of the Earth's solar system

superconductor - substance that makes an excellent medium for acceleration of subatomic particles because it poses little resistance to their flow

suspension - support of bits of one substance by another, as a suspension of solid particles in a liquid, or of dust particles in the air

symbiosis - relationship among organisms upon which the organisms are dependent for their survival

symbol, atomic - internationally recognized symbol for an element used broadly in chemistry to refer to that element

symmetry, bilateral - body plan of higher animals wherein two halves of the organism approximate mirror images of one another

symmetry, radial - body plan of invertebrate animals and other organisms wherein a certain number of body segments radiate from the center of the animal

synergism - relationship among organisms that is beneficial to all of those organisms but unnecessary for their survival

system (biological) - group of organs having a specific function in support of the organism

system (physical) - portion of the universe under study or consideration when isolated from the rest of the universe; an experimental system, for example, may consist of a flask containing the subject under study

system, nervous - system responsible for sensing, interpreting and directing the response to environmental influences including the brain, spinal cord, sensory endings and many other features

system, respiratory - system by which animals obtain oxygen and rid themselves of carbon dioxide

system, skeletal - framework upon which the body is built, composed of bones and cartilage in humans and higher animals, providing support and protection to soft tissues and a physical framework for locomotion

system, urinary - series of organs acting together to remove excess ions and fluid and other soluble wastes from the body; includes the kidneys, ureters and urethra in humans

system, weather - zone of high or low atmospheric pressure associated with certain conditions of temperature, moisture, wind and precipitation

systematics - science of determining the relative importance of characteristics of an organism on its classification in relationship to other organisms

tail (comet) - stream of ionized gases trailing behind the body (coma) of a comet

tardigrade - any of a phylum of small (< 1 mm), cylindric, unsegmented animals having four pairs of stubby, unjointed legs, each having four, single or two, double claws used for clinging; commonly called "water bears," and living in water or moist environments

taxonomy - science of classifying and naming organisms according to their characteristics

tectonic plate - see **plate, tectonic**

temperate - area on the Earth's surface between the

tropics and the arctic areas where notable changes in weather are frequent and where seasonal changes can be dramatic

tendon - stiff cord of connective tissue used to provide firm, flexible support to joints between bones

terrestrial planet - see **planet, terrestrial**

theory - conceptual model that serves as a framework for thinking or solving practical problems; a presumed reality upon which hypotheses may be formed for conducting scientific experiments

theory, big bang - theory accepted by many scientists that the perceived expansion of the universe resulted from an explosion of all matter once highly compacted at the center of expansion

thermal air column - see **column, thermal air**

thermocline - zone in a vertical column of water wherein the temperature changes rapidly with increasing depth from the warm water at the surface to the cool water beneath

thermodynamic - describing the changes in temperature and associated changes in energy that accompany chemical reactions

thermodynamically stable - see **stable, thermodynamically**

thermometer - device for measuring temperature consisting of an expansive liquid (typically mineral spirits or mercury) sealed in a glass vacuum bulb; application of heat to the bulb causes expansion of the liquid, the level of which indicates the temperature

thermosphere - outer layer of the Earth's atmosphere continuously bombarded by the sun's most energetic radiation variously divided into the ionosphere and the exosphere

thorax - middle body section (between the head and the abdomen); chest cavity in humans containing the heart and lungs

thumb, opposable - digit on the human hand that can be brought across (in opposition to the palm), making the hand capable of great manipulation of objects

thunderhead cloud - see **cloud, thunderhead**

tidal wave - see **wave, tidal**

tissue - collection of cells of a particular type and similar function; arrangements of tissues are found in organs of higher animals

tissue, connective - tough and stretchy soft tissue found throughout the bodies of animals and providing flexible support, tenacity and adhesion to organs

tissue fluid - see **fluid, tissue**

tornado - violent, circulating winds resulting from the collision of warm and cold weather fronts and characterized by winds of over 100 miles per hour

trachea - air tube leading from the throat to the bronchi (which take air to the lungs); also commonly called the "wind pipe"

trade wind - see **wind, trade**

transition metal - see **metal, transition**

translucent - passing distorted light such that images may not be clearly seen

transmit - in reference to light, to allow its passage (as through a substance) without absorption or reflection

treatment - describing an experimental subject that is manipulated to potentially bring about an anticipated change relative to a control

treatment group - see **group, treatment**

trench - deep-ocean crack in the earth resulting in greater depth of ocean water at that site

trichina worm - see **worm, trichina**

trichinosis - disease of humans accompanied by cycles of chills and fever caused by a nematode infesting poorly cooked pork

trigonometry - series of mathematical techniques useful for analyzing cyclic patterns such as waves and curves

trilobite - extinct arthropod having three body segments with fossils abundant in Cambrian rock

tropical rain forest - see **forest, tropical rain**

troposphere - portion of the atmosphere touching the Earth and extending to approximately 12 kilometers above sea level at which the temperature is approximately -60°C; encompasses most clouds and weather systems that affect the Earth

tube foot - see **foot, tube**

tungsten filament - see **filament, light bulb**

turbine - device for converting fluid motion to mechanical motion used to turn a shaft

tusk - long, projected tooth

ultimate consumer - see **consumer, ultimate**

ultraviolet - band of the electromagnetic spectrum more energetic than visible violet light

uniformitarianism - doctrine that uniformity of processes over time should be assumed unless there is compelling reason to believe that some non-uniform event has occurred

uniformity, assumption of - assumption that things have always been as they are and processes have always occurred as they do

upper appendage - see **appendage, upper**

upper extremity - see **extremity, upper**

upwelling - nutrient-laden, bottom water in the ocean sweeping toward the ocean surface in a current of ascending water

ureter - tube in higher animals and humans collecting and carrying liquid waste from the kidney to the urinary bladder

urethra - tube in higher animals and humans carrying liquid waste from the urinary bladder outside the body

urinary bladder - see **bladder, urinary**

urinary system - see **system, urinary**

urine - liquid waste produced by mammals composed largely of water, urea and excess ions

uterus - female reproductive organ in humans and higher animals that receives and serves as an incubator for the developing young; also called womb

vascular plant - see **plant, vascular**

vein (circulatory) - blood vessel that collects de-oxygenated blood from capillaries and returns it to the heart

vein (leaf) - tissue in plants that distributes nutrient-laden water from the soil to the leaves and returns food-laden sap to the tubules that will eventually return it to the roots

venule - small vein

vertebra (pl. vertebrae) - spinal bone providing support to the body and protection to the spinal cord

vertebrate - higher animal possessing a true spine

veterinarian - professional specializing in the care and treatment of disease in animals

virus - parasitic particle of protein and nucleic acid that infects and ultimately kills cells of a host by using the DNA of the host organism for its reproduction

viscous - thick, often sticky

volcano - opening in the Earth's surface that ejects lava, rock, steam and gases from within the Earth

volume - measured portion of three-dimensional space, typically expressed in units of cubic meters or other subunits (cubic centimeters or cubic millimeters)

wall, cell - rigid, outer coating of the cells of archaea, bacteria, fungi and plants (each of these groups having its own characteristic cell wall chemical makeup)

water, ground - water that exists beneath the ground surface, filling the spaces between soil particles and rocks

wave, seismic - potentially destructive wave of water resulting from seismic (earthquake) activity beneath the ocean surface

wave, tidal - wave of water resulting from the gravitational pull of the moon on ocean water

wavelength - distance from wave crest to wave crest in a series of waves and indicating the amount of energy generating the series of waves (the shorter wavelengths corresponding to higher levels of energy)

weather - conditions of temperature, pressure, cloud cover, precipitation and humidity affecting the atmosphere in a given location

weather system - see **system, weather**

weathering - changes in the structure of minerals and mineral matter over time through natural processes

weight, molecular - combined masses (weights) of the atoms comprising a molecule; total mass of a molecule, generally measured in atomic mass units

wind - movement of air resulting from expansion and contraction of atmospheric gases and other factors that influence fluid motion on the Earth's surface

wind, prevailing - persistent air currents that are typical of certain areas on the Earth's surface; also called "trade winds" when occurring over the ocean

wind, solar - rush of energetic, charged particles (electrons and protons) constantly emanating from the sun

wind, trade - see **wind, prevailing**

womb - see **uterus**

work - in physics, the application of a force over a distance

worm, trichina - nematode responsible for trichinosis

zoology - study of animals

zooplankton - animal (typically microscopic or slightly larger) that lives suspended in natural water

zygote - single-celled embryo occurring immediately upon fertilization of an egg by a sperm in sexual reproduction

Index

chemical reaction 55, 69, 86, 95, 98, 114, 115, 123, 129, 130, 132, 134, 141, 145, 243
chest 245
chevrotain 225
chimaera 207
chinchilla 225
chinchilla rat 225
chlorate 96
chloride 83, 91, 94, 117, 126
chlorine 43, 83, 84, 86
Chlorophyta 167
cholera 158
chromate 96
cicada 201
civet 231
clam 190, 204
clay 12, 78, 283
climate 279, 290, 291, 293, 297-9
cloud 75, 124, 303-5
club moss 171
coast 273, 279, 280, 290, 302
coccolithophorid 167
codfish 207
collar bone 239
colon 243
community 261, 277, 298
competition 261, 263
computer chip 89, 98
conductor 36, 88, 89, 253
cone (pine) 172
connective tissue 141, 239
consumer 183, 259, 260
copepod 196, 260
Copernicus 186
copper 70, 78, 80, 86, 89
coral 187
cormorant 219
cotinga 219
cowry 190
coyote 231
coypu 225
crab 195, 197
cracking 102
crane 219
crappie 207
crayfish 197

creation 136, 142, 212, 270, 283
Creator 1, 9, 136, 138, 149, 150, 248, 270, 281
creeper 219
cricket 201
crinoid 204
crocodile 212
crows 219
crude oil 101
cuckoos 219
curassow 219
current (air) 272, 295-6, 297-9, 300
current (electric) 33-4, 38, 56
current (water) 279
cuscus 221
cuttlefish 191
cyanate 96
cytosine 188

D

daddy-longlegs 195
dam 25, 277
damselfly 201
dark 61-2, 270, 287
Darwin 149, 155, 156
dead 167, 198, 259, 260, 261, 269, 276, 279, 281
decapod 197
deer 225
deoxyribose 108, 138, 144
desert 197, 220, 225, 278, 297
desert dormice 225
design 1, 21, 53, 109, 113, 136, 142, 144, 166, 192, 220, 245, 270
Designer 122, 124, 192, 216, 220, 239, 251
desman 221
devil 221
dew 71
diatom 167, 168
digest 98, 187, 188, 190, 198, 242-3
digit 212, 239
dinoflagellate 167
dinosaur 212, 308

dipper (bird) 219
disaccharide 111
disease 108, 158, 257, 258, 264
distance 16, 20, 36, 37, 38, 40, 46, 59, 72, 130, 283, 306, 312, 313
diversity 136
DNA 138, 138, 144, 146, 153, 159, 255-6, 257
dog 231
dolphin 220, 229
dormouse 225
double bond 99, 100
dove 219
dragonfly 201
duckbilled platypus 220
ducks 219
dugong 232
dynamic 129, 263-4

E

eagle 219
eardrum 13
earless seal 229
earthquake 13, 273-4, 279
earthworm 192
earwig 201
ecology 189, 257-8, 261, 279
eel 207
egg 89, 172, 177, 248-50
elbow 239, 240
electromagnetism 29-30, 31, 38-40, 46, 56-7, 150
electron 31-2, 35-7, 41, 42, 69, 82-4
elephant 158, 231, 232
elephant shrew 221
emu 216
energy 19-28, 46-8, 51-60, 105-6, 129-35, 145, 147, 154, 164
environment 90, 156, 159, 167, 212, 254, 257, 264, 265, 268, 287, 289
enzyme 109-10, 145, 243
equator 279, 293, 294, 295, 297, 300, 311

human 108, 138, 139, 142, 149, 155, 183, 188, 190, 234, 239, 247, 248, 259
humidity 169, 290
hummingbird 219
hunger 104, 253, 283
hutia 225
hydra 187
hydrobromic acid 127
hydrocarbon 100, 101-2
hydrochloric acid 94-5, 126-7
hydrogen 44, 69-70, 77, 80, 84, 86, 91, 92, 94, 100, 127, 132-3, 272, 306, 310
hydroiodic acid 127
hydrothermal vent 159
hyena 231
hyoid bone 237
hypochlorite 96

I

ibis 219
ice 53, 73, 122, 132, 280, 283, 303, 305, 308
infrared 28, 53, 56, 60, 280, 293
iodate 96
ion 83, 96, 125-8, 287
ionosphere 287
iron 43, 86, 89

J

jaeger 219
jaw 196, 240
jay 219
jellyfish 187
jerboa 225
jet 287, 303, 305
jumping mouse 225
Jupiter 306

K

kangaroo 221
kangaroo rat 225
kingfisher 219
kiwi 216, 219

knee 239
koala 221

L

lamprey 207
lancelet 207
lanthanium 86
lark 219
Law of Moses 283
lead 77, 78, 89
leaf 175, 259
leafhopper 201
leech 192
leg 194-5, 197, 198, 216, 231, 239, 240
lemur 234
lever 15-7
lice 201
lichen 160
life 122, 136-8
life cycle 172
light 24, 56-68, 166, 253, 275, 293
limpkin 219
lion 231
liquid 55, 66, 71-5, 114, 119, 120-3, 134, 247
lithium 77
liverwort 169
lizard 212
llama 225
lobster 196-7
locomotion 55, 194, 198, 204
loon 219
loris 234

M

magnesium 92
magnesium hydroxide 127
magnet 29-30, 38-40, 46, 47, 56, 62, 68, 268
magpie 219
male 138, 172, 177, 237, 248-50
manatee 232
mandible 196
mantle 268

marmoset 234
Mars 306
marsupial 221
mass 1-9, 76-7
mass spectrometer 77
math 1, 13, 14
matter 1, 41-44, 58-60, 71-9, 150-1
mayfly 201
medusa 187
melting 73, 132, 134, 268, 273, 280
Mendel, Gregor 255
meningitis 158
Mercury 306
mercury 70, 89
methane 91, 102, 117, 152, 306
methanol 117
microscope 158, 160, 169
Milky Way 313
Miller, Stanley 152
millipede 197-8
mineral 119, 123-4, 145, 163, 239, 268, 270, 279-84
mirror 58, 188
mockingbird 219
moisture 85, 97, 169, 174, 287, 294, 301
mold 160, 257
mole 221
mole rat 225
molecule 41, 70, 72, 91, 100, 101, 103, 107-13, 139, 144
monkey 234
moon 7, 60, 273, 287, 306, 310
mosquito 201
moss 169
moth 201
motion 1-6, 10-14, 60, 84, 108, 168, 240, 293, 295, 311
mountain 220, 268, 272, 279
mountain beaver 225
mouse 225
mouth 158, 197, 198, 216, 232, 242-3, 244-5, 247, 253
mullet 207
muscle 106, 141, 239, 240-1, 243, 247, 253